D1157076

The

Prestes

Column

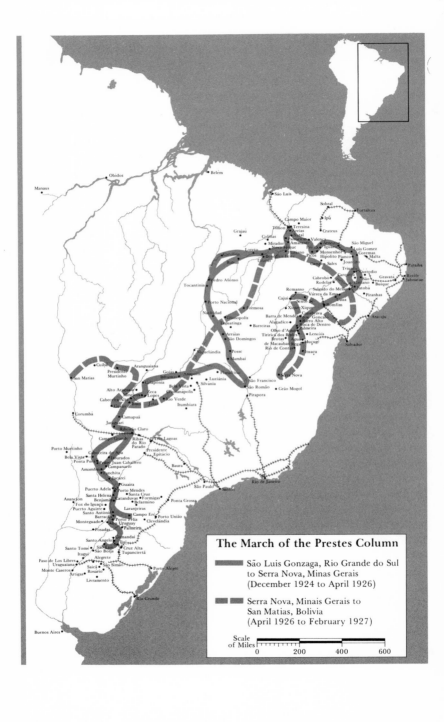

The March of the Prestes Column

▬▬▬ São Luis Gonzaga, Rio Grande do Sul
to Serra Nova, Minas Gerais
(December 1924 to April 1926)

▬ ▬ ▬ Serra Nova, Minais Gerais to
San Matias, Bolivia
(April 1926 to February 1927)

Scale
of Miles
0   200   400   600

Stamford Branch Library
University of Connecticut
Scofieldtown Road
Stamford, Conn. 06903

The Prestes Column

Revolution in Brazil

by Neill Macaulay

New Viewpoints

A DIVISION OF FRANKLIN WATTS, INC. • NEW YORK • 1974

F
2537
M143
1974

Library of Congress Cataloging in Publication Data

Macaulay, Neill.
    The Prestes Column.

      1. Brazil–History–Revolution, 1924–1925.
I. Title.
F2537.M143 1974   981'.05   74-1030
ISBN 0-531-05356-3
ISBN 0-531-05563-9 (pbk.)

Copyright © 1974 by Neill Macaulay
Printed in the United States of America
6 5 4 3 2 1

To my mother and father

9/75

Contents

Foreword

Brazil covers half the continent of South America. Only the Soviet Union, China, and Canada occupy greater contiguous land areas than this giant of the Southern Hemisphere. It is a land incredibly rich in natural resources and inhabited, for the most part, by descendants of European immigrants and African slaves, who have demonstrated a capacity for orderly development markedly superior to that of their neighbors in Latin America. In total agricultural and industrial production Brazil is first in Latin America by a wide margin. It is, in fact, the most heavily industrialized country in the tropical world—a nation to be reckoned with.

A big country, Brazil has big problems. Poverty, illiteracy, and disease have plagued Brazil since its founding as a Portuguese colony in the sixteenth century. Nowhere in the Western Hemisphere has the exploitation of man by man been more blatant than in this land where slavery remained a legal institution as late as 1888. Millions of Brazilians continue to endure economic and social oppression with remarkable forbearance. Brazilian patience springs from hope: No matter how bad things are, they usually seem to be getting better. Since the revolution of 1930 there has been more than a little basis for this optimism.

Before the revolution Brazil was a league of planter-rancher satrapies dominated by coffee exporters. After 1930 the nation was made whole, export agriculture was downplayed, industry was promoted, the economy was expanded, and some social legislation was enacted. This process has continued through the dictatorship of Getúlio Vargas, a lawyer put into power with the help of army officers and removed, fifteen years later, by the military; through a period of democratic government initiated and ended by military coups; and into the era of direct rule by the armed forces that began in 1964.

Thus, modern Brazil has been shaped, to a large extent, by its armed forces. For a generation after 1930 this institution developed unevenly, feeding on an inconsistent mythology derived from the prerevolutionary period. By the 1960's, however, time had resolved the contradictions and the Brazilian military had achieved a sense of identity and purpose that impelled it steadily toward the acquisition and exercise of political power.

No episode looms larger in the mythology of modern Brazil than the march of the Prestes Column. A military, revolutionary movement was defeated in the civilized centers of Brazil in 1924, thus launching fifteen hundred rebel soldiers, like Aeneas' Trojans, across the frontiers of barbarism on a mission to reconstitute the nation. For more than two years they wandered over 25,000 kilometers, from the pampas of southern Brazil, through the forests of the Paraná valley, back and forth across the arid interior of the Northeast and the savannas of central Brazil, through the swamps of Mato Grosso to the borders of Bolivia and Paraguay. Resisted almost everywhere by bandits, hired gunmen, and all the forces the warlords of a benighted land could muster, they were forced by cruel necessity to despoil the already impoverished, to burn villages, and to cut the throat of at least one priest. They were unable to revive the revolution in the backlands, but they learned much about their country.

The effects of the march on those who survived it are not obvious. The nominal commander of the column died an intransigent socialist, while its chief-of-staff, with whom it is popularly identified, became the secretary-general of the Brazilian Communist Party. But other veterans served the Vargas dictatorship in its most fascistic phase. One was almost elected president of

Brazil as a conservative nationalist. Two were still available in 1964 to head ministries, to help the new dictatorship try to identify with the remote, heroic past.

While an analysis of the legend of the Prestes Column, as it has evolved to this day, would be useful to those seeking to understand contemporary Brazil, I have not attempted such a study. I have tried only to tell the true story of the march, based primarily on firsthand reports recorded at the time of the events. Obviously, I consider the story worth telling—and hope that others find it worth reading.

Those who furnished information for this study are cited in the footnotes. Special thanks are due Dr. Hélio Silva, the late Major Wálter Meier, Senator Horácio de Matos Júnior, the late Colonel Arquimedes de Matos, and Senhor Walfrido Moraes, all of Brazil, and General Mark W. Clark and Professor John W. F. Dulles of the United States for making it possible for me to locate and utilize particularly fruitful sources. I am deeply grateful to the Ford Foundation, which awarded the postdoctoral grant under which the project was begun, and to the Foreign Area Fellowship Program, which administered the grant. As always, I am indebted to my wife, Nancy, for her help and encouragement. Charles Macaulay, our son, deserves a word of appreciation for his efficient cartographic assistance.

I should like especially to thank Senhor Luís Carlos Prestes for taking time out from his busy schedule in Moscow to look over the manuscript and verify "that in the general sense it is just." For whatever errors the book may contain, I alone must bear the responsibility.

The terms "militia" and "militiamen" in this work are applied exclusively to the full-time, militarized constabularies of the individual states of Brazil. Part-time soldiers in government service are referred to as "volunteers" or "provisionals."

The

Prestes

Column

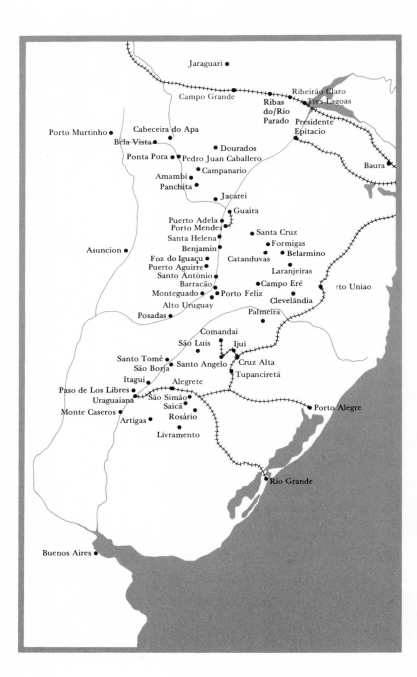

Jaraguari •

Campo Grande •• Ribeirão Claro
Ribas •Três Lagoas
do/Rio
Parado Presidente
Epitacio

Porto Murtinho • Cabeceira do Apa
Bela Vista •
• Dourados Baura •
Ponta Pora •• Pedro Juan Caballero
•Campanario
Amambi •
Panchita • •
• Jacarei
• Guaira
Puerto Adela •
Porto Mendes •
Santa Helena • • Santa Cruz
Benjamin • • Formigas
Asuncion • Foz do Iguaçu • Catanduvas • Belarmino
Puerto Aguirre •
Santo Antônio • • Laranjeiras
Barracão • •Campo Erê rto Uniao
Monteguado • •Porto Feliz
Alto Uruguay • Clevelândia
Posadas • • Palmeira

Comandai
São Luis Ijui
Santo Tomé • Santo Angelo •Cruz Alta
São Borja • Tupanciretã
Itagui • Alegrete
Paso de Los Libres •
Uraguaiana • São Simão •
Saicã • • Porto Alegre
Monte Caseros • Rosário
Artigas • •
Livramento

Rio Grande

Buenos Aires •

Isidoro and the Lieutenants

*M*utinous elements of the federal army and the state militia seized control of the city of São Paulo in July 1924. Such occurrences had become almost routine after 1889, when an army revolt deposed the emperor of Brazil, proclaimed the republic, and ended four decades of internal peace. The first president of the republic assumed dictatorial power in an auto-coup and was subsequently overthrown by the Brazilian navy. The second president survived both a naval revolt and a rising of *gaúchos*, who drove to the borders of São Paulo before being forced to retreat to the pampas of Rio Grande do Sul, Brazil's southernmost state. The third president ended the southern insurrection, launched a bloody but successful campaign against a community of suspected monarchists in the northeastern backlands, and narrowly escaped death at the hands of an assassin, who did manage to kill his minister of war.[1]

The violence had subsided with the dawn of the new century, but in 1904 military academy cadets in Rio de Janeiro, in collaboration with riotous civilians who objected to compulsory vaccinations, rose up against the government; although the revolt was crushed in short order, the authorities nonetheless saw fit to make vaccinations voluntary. Two years later the capital of the frontier state of Mato Grosso was seized by local rebels, who then killed the governor and handed power over to their favorite, the lieutenant governor; the federal government in Rio was much disturbed, but in the end did nothing—after all, the new governor had constitutionally succeeded his deceased predecessor. There was trouble in the navy in 1910 when mutinous seamen took over the nation's two brand-new battleships, fired on Rio, and forced the government to meet their demands for better treatment. The "strong man" of that weak government, Senator Pinheiro Machado, was assassinated in Rio five years later. Elsewhere in the republic, from the state of Santa Catarina in the south to Amazonas in the north, the second decade of the twentieth century was marked by coups and countercoups, revolts and counterrevolts, involving federal troops, state militias, backcountry ruffians, and religious fanatics. Army officers, civilian political bosses, priests, and bandits fanned the regional flames as Brazil, the Portuguese-speaking giant of South America, came ever more closely to resemble its volatile Spanish-American neighbors.

There was an abortive army revolt in Rio in 1922 that culminated in a spectacular fire fight on Copacabana Beach. The next year a rebellion broke out in Rio Grande do Sul against Borges de Medeiros, the ironfisted governor who had kept the peace in the gaúcho state since his first inauguration in 1898. The "treaty" ending that conflict left Borges in office, but his enemies were already plotting another uprising when the São Paulo insurrection erupted in July 1924, a month that also saw barracks revolts in such far-flung cities as Manaus, Belém, and Aracajú.

The revolution of 1924 was launched in São Paulo on July 5, the second anniversary of the abortive military revolt in Rio de Janeiro. A number of young officers who had taken part in the Rio rising, including one of the survivors of the Copacabana Beach shoot-out, were on hand in São Paulo to guide the new effort. The young army rebels—the *Tenentes,* or lieutenants, as they were commonly called—had found a retired senior officer to head their movement, Colonel Isidoro Dias Lopes, whom they promoted to "general." On July 17, while the rebels were in control of the city of São Paulo, General Isidoro formally set forth the rebel demands: the resignation of President Artur Bernardes and the installation of a provisional government that would convoke a convention to write a new constitution for Brazil.[2] Before the end of the month army garrisons in the states of Mato Grosso, Sergipe, Pará, and Amazonas joined the revolution. While the new adherents might stress the need for local reforms in their appeals for popular support,[3] they fully shared Isidoro's first objective: the overthrow of the regime of President Artur Bernardes.

The Tenentes despised Artur Bernardes, the lawyer-politician who, in 1922, had risen from the governorship of Minas Gerais to the presidency of Brazil. Minas Gerais had more people than any other state in the republic, and neighboring São Paulo had the most wealth; when the big agricultural interests that controlled these two states acted in concert, as they did in most national elections, they were able to name the president of Brazil. They backed Bernardes' candidacy in 1922 with the understanding that the choice of the São Paulo oligarchy would receive their support in the next presidential election in 1926. This deal was naturally resented in an officer corps that was drawn mostly from the relatively powerless states, from the Federal District (the city of Rio de Janeiro), and from the city of São Paulo—whose sons were among the most hostile to the coffee planters who dominated their state. While some of the Tenentes doubtlessly shared the aspirations of an incipient urban middle class, all of them were not long out of military school where they had been taught that their duty was to serve the nation, not selfish regional interests. The latter they identified with Bernardes. Their initial antipathy for him was transformed into hatred during the election campaign of 1922.

Brazil's politicized army and navy officers were strong for Nilo Peçanha, the presidential candidate put forward in 1921 by the middle-sized states of Pernambuco, Bahia, Rio de Janeiro, and Rio Grande do Sul. All of the other fourteen state governments, however, climbed aboard the Minas Gerais–São Paulo bandwagon. This meant that Nilo stood no chance of being elected president, since elections in Brazil in those days were rigged in the state capitals, and the Bernardes states had by far

the most voters. Nothing short of a military coup could put Nilo
in the presidential palace. Some months before the election a letter, allegedly written by Bernardes, appeared in the Rio press.
Considered grossly insulting to the army, the letter referred to
the venerated Marshal Hermes da Fonseca as an "overblown
sergeant" (*sargentão*) and a "scoundrel" (*canalha*).[4] Bernardes
claimed the letter was a forgery, but after a long investigation,
the Military Club—the pompous officer fraternity of which Marshal Hermes was president—pronounced the letter genuine. In
the meantime the election was held and Bernardes was declared
the winner. The Military Club joined other partisans of the defeated candidate in demanding a recount. Not only did some
officers swear that they would never recognize the mandate of
Artur Bernardes, but Marshal Hermes suggested that his
comrades disregard certain orders from outgoing President Epitácio Pessoa. This led to the arrest of Marshal Hermes, the abortive military revolt in Rio de Janeiro in July 1922, and an equally
futile putsch in Mato Grosso that same month.

Epitácio Pessoa had enough influence in the armed forces to
overcome the military rebels in July and prevent any further
outbreaks before he turned the presidency over to Artur Bernardes in November 1922. The new president was forty-seven
years old and looked a little like the wartime Charles de Gaulle:
tall, erect, aquiline nose, close-clipped moustache, the restless,
uncertain eyes of a myopic. Fastidious in dress, he carried himself with dignity even under the most trying circumstances—as
in the election campaign when a Rio mob, whipped up by military agitators, screamed epithets and hurled potatoes at him.
Educated in the law and trained in oligarchic politics, he spoke
without emotion and shunned demagoguery. In private conver-
sation he seemed to choose his words as carefully as he did in
public speeches. Courteous and attentive, he smiled readily, but
was never known to laugh. A practicing Catholic and a devoted
family man, his private life was impeccable. He read Goethe and
had a sense of mission. He was brave, energetic, strong-willed,
crafty, cold, stubborn, and vindictive. "His defects and virtues,"
a contemporary noted, "are rare in combination, especially in
Brazil." He would not fail to display them in "the perilous defile

through which the country was forced, in large part because of him." [5]

As president, Bernardes set out to discipline the unruly elements in the armed forces and to reduce the civilian centers of opposition to his rule. On his orders military investigators undertook to identify and bring to trial those responsible for the July 1922 mutiny, prompting a number of officers to desert their units and go into hiding. A "state of siege" (modified martial law) proclaimed at the time of the rising was continued after Bernardes' inauguration for the Federal District and the neighboring state of Rio de Janeiro, where federal intervention brought down a government friendly to the defeated presidential candidate, Nilo Peçanha. The two northeastern states that had backed Nilo, Pernambuco and Bahia, felt the pressure from Rio and chose new governments amenable to Bernardes. In the far south, Governor Borges de Medeiros of Rio Grande do Sul, who had supported Nilo, insisted on staying in office. In January 1923 the gaúcho state was plunged into civil war.

Rio Grande do Sul was the only Brazilian state that permitted the reelection of its governor, and Borges de Medeiros had been elected to that post five times since 1898. Whereas in other states executive power was passed around among the oligarchs, in Rio Grande do Sul it remained in the hands of a single tyrant. Borges hardly looked the part of a gaúcho strong man. His long nose, weak chin, and emaciated appearance made him a perfect target for unfriendly cartoonists who drew him as a *chimango*—a long-legged bird that lives on ticks that it picks off the bellies of cattle. The enemies of the Chimango, divided since the 1890's, finally united as the Liberator Alliance in 1922 and, early the next year, took the field with high hopes for federal intervention on their side. But the government of President Artur Bernardes hung back while the Liberators and Borges' *chimangada* exhausted themselves in indecisive conflict. Finally, toward the end of the year, a federal mediator arranged a truce and imposed a settlement: Borges would serve out his fifth term, but would not run for reelection, and the Liberators would get some seats in the state legislature and in the federal Congress. [6] Borges' control of the state, though weakened, continued; he was granted a temporary lease on power in return for an oath of fealty to Artur Bernardes. The president of the republic was the only victor in Rio Grande do Sul, as the Liberators, now disarmed, soon perceived. Assis Brasil, the political head of the Liberator Alliance, who had expected Bernardes to help him attain the governorship of Rio Grande do Sul, now aligned himself with the president's foes. With the death of Nilo Peçanha on March 31, 1924, Assis became Brazil's most prominent opposition politician. The Tenentes who rose in revolt in 1924 would name him "civilian chief" of their revolution.

Assis Brasil's Rio Grande do Sul was the third state in the union in terms of total agricultural and industrial production, with 11 percent of the national total in 1920, as compared with Minas Gerais' 14 percent and São Paulo's 29 percent.[7] Thus these three southern states accounted for more than half of Brazil's economic output, although they had only 41 percent of the country's people. While the nation's industrial production had increased fivefold since the turn of the century, agriculture and stock raising still predominated—coffee in São Paulo; livestock and grain in Rio Grande do Sul; coffee, livestock, and food crops in Minas Gerais. It was the city of São Paulo that had made the greatest strides in industrialization, manufacturing a wide variety of textiles and other soft goods. The city was also the hub of the vast railroad system that moved the state's export-bound coffee from backland plantations to the port of Santos. As the economy of São Paulo expanded, the city's population grew apace. By 1920 it had 579,033 people, 35 percent of whom were foreign-born.[8] The flow of immigration to Brazil, interrupted during World War I, resumed in the 1920's. Central Europeans and, especially, Italians flocked to the city of São Paulo.

Those who had fled to Brazil hoping to escape the postwar European recession were disappointed by the conditions they found there. Wages and salaries in Brazil remained low, while the cost of living soared; food prices nearly doubled between 1920 and 1923.[9] When world coffee prices plunged after World War I, the Brazilian government bailed out the planters by buying much of their production—and tried to force up world prices by withholding it from the market. To pay for this price-support program the amount of currency in circulation was doubled between 1920 and 1923. During this period the value of the Brazilian currency unit, the *milreis*, fell from twenty U.S. cents to ten cents. British bankers, who held most of the Brazilian government's bonded debt, dispatched to Brazil a financial mission, which lectured President Bernardes about fiscal irresponsibility. In return for refinancing a portion of the debt due in 1927, the British, some feared, would insist on taking over Brazilian customs collection.[10]

As it turned out, this would not be necessary. World coffee prices improved in 1924 and President Bernardes' government began to act effectively against inflation: Money was withdrawn from circulation and burned. The effects of the new fiscal policy and the new coffee prosperity, however, were not felt immediately. By blaming the federal government for "the economic disorders that threaten to devour the future, after having ruined the present," [11] the military rebels in São Paulo could still, in July 1924, hope to rally wage earners and salaried people to their cause.

São Paulo was enveloped in a cold predawn fog on July 5, 1924, as a light infantry battalion from a nearby federal garrison moved into the city and deployed around the barracks of the state militia, near the Luz railroad station, and called upon the local troops to join the revolution. The adherence of the state cavalry regiment to the movement had been prearranged by its executive officer, Major Miguel Costa. The state infantry and artillery troops, in the absence of their senior officers, fell in with Miguel's* men on the side of the federal army rebels. By 5:15 A.M. two thousand six hundred federal and state troops in the city of São Paulo were committed to the revolution.[12]

The federal commanding general of the São Paulo military district had just returned home from a Fourth of July dance given by the American consul when he was informed of the

---

* In Brazil a leader may be known to his followers, and to the public, by one or more of his Christian names. Thus, Miguel Costa, whose full name was Miguel Alberto Crispim da Costa Rodrigues, was often referred to as Miguel or Major Miguel, but rarely as Costa or Major Costa.

unauthorized troop movement. He personally checked out the information, had a warning telephoned to the governor's mansion before five o'clock and then, still in his dress uniform, rushed to the Luz barracks where he persuaded some individual federal soldiers and an entire battalion of state troops to return to the side of legality. Before he could countersubvert any more rebels, the general was seized by mutinous junior officers and put under armed guard.[13]

The hassle with the general delayed the rebel drive on the governor's mansion, in the downtown area, where some fifteen hundred loyal policemen, firemen, and militiamen were now concentrated. At ten o'clock the rebels commenced their attack on the governor's mansion with an artillery bombardment—at precisely the time that a mass was being said at the São Bento monastery for the souls of those killed in the 1922 uprising. The first 105-millimeter projectile exploded over the monastery and spewed shrapnel through the roof of the Sacred Heart of Jesus secondary school, causing extensive material damage and severely wounding one pupil. Subsequent rounds also fell wide of their mark, causing a number of civilian casualties. Apprised of these results, the rebel commander in chief, Colonel Isidoro Dias Lopes, federal army retired, ordered his big guns to cease firing. Deprived of artillery support, the rebel infantry and cavalry did not assault the governor's mansion, which remained in loyalist hands at nightfall, along with much of the downtown area. The rebels, however, held the railroad stations that ringed the city. Some rebel reinforcements from outlying garrisons arrived on July 5, and on the next day the first federal troops sent by President Bernardes to suppress the mutiny arrived on the scene—and many of them promptly went over to the revolution. The newcomers added little to rebel combativeness and no concerted effort was made to dislodge the loyalists from their positions around the governor's mansion, although rebel artillery did resume firing on July 7 with somewhat more accuracy than before.[14]

As the stalemate developed in the city of São Paulo, planters and merchants in the interior of the state raised volunteer battalions, which they placed at the disposal of their governor. One such battalion provided itself with weapons by disarming a federal army garrison considered of doubtful loyalty. But other federal units rallied to the government cause as the loyalist buildup outside the city began to take on formidable proportions. Revolutionary Commander in Chief Isidoro, fearing a double envelopment and disturbed by a mounting rate of desertion in his forces, decided to evacuate the city.[15]

Isidoro Dias Lopes had arrived in São Paulo on July 4, the night before the revolt began, by train from Rio, where he had been living for some years. He was a native of Rio Grande do Sul, where he began his military career by enlisting in the army of Emperor Dom Pedro II. A 26-year-old second lieutenant when the republic was proclaimed in 1889, he served the new regime until 1893, when he joined the gaúcho insurrection of that year. This Revolt of the Maragatos—the name of an Iberian ethnic group derisively applied to the insurgents—was not openly restorationist, but most of its top leaders were monarchists or cryptomonarchists. Isidoro was with the Maragato force that drove to the border of São Paulo in 1894. Facing obviously superior state and federal forces, the Maragato command decided to withdraw, and Isidoro took part in his first retreat—the epic one thousand kilometer march of the gaúcho rebels back to the pampas of Rio Grande do Sul, where their revolt fizzled out the next year. The republic in those days could deal magnanimously with its defeated foes and Isidoro was allowed to rejoin the federal army in 1897. In 1921 he retired in Rio, where he enjoyed watching the girls on the Carioca streets, and where he attended meetings of the Military Club and got to know many dissident young officers.[16]

Isidoro was no revolutionary firebrand. A courtly, soft-spoken gentleman, he was genuinely moved by the idealism of the Tenentes. The young officers, for their part, were impressed by the honesty and disinterested patriotism of this modest retired colonel. Isidoro's conservative temperament commended him to the revolutionaries whose posturings reflected, in part at least, a lack of self-confidence. Mistrusting their own audacity, they sought a wise and experienced leader who would treat

them with the respect they felt they deserved and not use them
to further his own personal ambitions. The slender, silver-
haired Isidoro seemed to fit the bill: His clear blue eyes flashed
with intelligence and energy; though professorily firm, he was
no authoritarian. Articulate, often ironic, he was not, however,
the perfect commander: At times he would be unable to impose
his will on his subordinates. When his polite persuasion failed,
Isidoro could be excessively critical, if not personally abusive, of
those who defied him.[17]

Isidoro's decision to evacuate São Paulo was opposed by the
second-ranking rebel officer, Miguel Costa, a major of the São
Paulo militia and a colonel of the revolution. The Argentine-
born Miguel Costa had lived in São Paulo since childhood and
was a devoted local patriot. Most of the five hundred men of his
cavalry regiment were native or adopted Paulistanos and no less
reluctant to abandon their city. The cavalry commander favored
an all-out attack to crush the loyalist resistance downtown, after
which, he felt, the hitherto indifferent civilian population would
rally to the cause. Miguel clung to the hope that the elimination
of the enemy force within the city and the distribution of arms to
civilian volunteers would enable the revolutionaries to repel the
anticipated attack from without. But Isidoro was unconvinced;
on July 8 he ordered the withdrawal to begin the next morning.[18]

Miguel Costa rejected the order; he and his men would not
join the evacuation. Miguel, at fifty, was twice the age of many
Tenentes, but his impetuosity—and his willingness to endure
prolonged hardship—often exceeded that of the youngest revolutionaries. Although some Tenentes and their enlisted followers cast their lots with Miguel and his regiment, the rebels who
chose to remain were clearly incapable of mounting a successful
attack on the loyalist forces downtown. They began preparing
defensive positions in the Luz barracks, where they would await
the expected government offensive. As dawn approached,
Miguel Costa became increasingly pessimistic: The revolution
was lost—there was no reason to sacrifice his brave comrades.
He wrote a letter to the governor offering to surrender if the
governor would grant amnesty to his men and reinstate them in

the militia, at their revolutionary ranks; Miguel declared that he alone should be held responsible for the mutiny of the state troops. At first light on July 9 the letter was dispatched under a flag of truce to the governor's mansion. It was not delivered; the messenger returned to inform Miguel that the governor's mansion was practically deserted. The governor had fled and the loyalist troops had slipped out of the city during the night.[19]

Isidoro, who in the face of Miguel's intransigence the night before had offered to resign his command, was notified of the dramatic turn of events. The rebel exodus was halted and the Tenentes, flushed with their unexpected victory, reaffirmed their confidence in Isidoro: He would remain their general and the supreme chief of the revolution. His position was not coveted by Colonel Miguel Costa, who was as devoid of personal ambition as the general he had defied. While Isidoro concerned himself with restoring municipal services and regularizing life in the occupied city, Miguel tried to attract the civilian population to the revolutionary cause.

Both officers apparently had a hand in the manifesto of "the chiefs of the revolutionary movement" that appeared in the São Paulo press, now free of government censorship, on July 10. Their movement, the chiefs declared, was not regional, but national; it was patriotic and "of the highest social and political significance." The movement sprang from the "National Army," which "cannot, and cannot ever, accept the government of Dr. Artur Bernardes."* But, the chiefs avowed, their objective was not simply the overthrow of Bernardes, whose government was only the latest in a series of corrupt and incompetent administrations; they were fighting for no less than the regeneration of Brazil. Reflecting, perhaps, Isidoro's philomonarchist past, the manifesto declared that "the Army wants the Fatherland like the Empire left it, with the same principles of moral integrity, patriotic conscience, administrative probity, and lofty political foresight." The chiefs went on to denounce recent governments for "abusing the credit of the country" and the Bernardes administration for allowing the English financial mission to humiliate

---

* Any college degree gave one the right to be addressed as *doutor.*

Brazil publicly.[20] A second manifesto, published a week later, omitted favorable references to the monarchy, mentioned the economic crisis, denounced presidential despotism and the perversion of the judiciary, and declared that "the armed forces" were "defending the rights of the people, taking up arms to reestablish the rule of Law, the decorum of Justice, by limiting the authority of the Executive." [21]

But most Paulistanos were unmoved. Only the foreign elements in the city seemed to respond favorably to the revolution—though they were hardly influenced by the rhetoric of the manifestos. A German company, a Hungarian company, and an Italian company were mustered into the rebel service. In all, about three hundred foreigners, many of them combat veterans of peasant stock who had been lured to São Paulo after World War I by false promises of economic opportunity, signed up, accepting revolutionary promises of fifty hectares of land in the interior along some railroad. The native proletariat, however, did not suffer from land hunger and was not sufficiently destitute to be attracted by the modest pay and end-of-the-war bonuses held out by the revolutionaries—nor was it much interested in the political reforms they promised. Indeed, Isidoro, in his determination to maintain law and order and protect private property in the city, seemed as beholden to the vested interests as the governor who had fled. Nevertheless, the fighting had upset the equilibrium of the city and the new authorities, despite their best efforts, could not prevent the looting of some stores and at least one big warehouse. The revolutionary command itself, to meet operating expenses, "withdrew" 500,000 milreis from the local branch of the Bank of Brazil and requisitioned 1,341,560.46 milreis from the safe at the federal treasury office.[22]

The news of the rebel capture of São Paulo soon spread to all of Brazil. But only in Mato Grosso, in the remote Amazon, and in the small northeastern state of Sergipe were other military conspirators spurred to action by this event. The rebels in São Paulo knew only of the uprising in neighboring Mato Grosso, which was quickly suppressed; for all they knew there had been no response elsewhere in the country to their revolutionary initiative.[23] In fact, other states were sending police and militia units to combat them in São Paulo. The federal army seemed impervious to further subversion, as it moved troops and artillery to the outskirts of São Paulo. Nevertheless, loyalist commanders felt it necessary to conceal from their men the true nature of the situation in São Paulo, which was variously described as a general strike, an uprising of Italians, and as a strike by the state militia for higher pay.[24] Between fourteen thousand and fifteen thousand government troops—including units of civilian volunteers, soon to be federalized and designated Patriotic Battalions—converged on São Paulo. On July 12 the city, defended by three thousand to three thousand five hundred armed insurgents, was brought under heavy loyalist artillery fire.[25]

São Paulo was not completely surrounded. Isidoro had detachments operating along the railroads to the west to keep open these exits from the city. For the civilian population, trains from São Paulo maintained intermittent service, evacuating thousands of refugees seeking safety from the artillery bombardment. The refugees were not a good advertisement for the revolutionary movement, which lacked the resources of the government for communication with the Brazilian people. The powerful government-controlled radio station in Rio de Janeiro beamed nightly broadcasts to São Paulo. Eminent Paulistas (residents of the state) and Paulistanos (residents of the city) spoke over the airwaves from Rio, urging support for "legality." The Italian ambassador, General Pietro Badoglio, made a special radio appeal on behalf of the government to São Paulo's *italiani*.[26]

Since the weak radio station in São Paulo could not carry the revolutionary message to the national capital, the rebels sought to answer the government propaganda barrage by dropping leaflets on Rio from the air. A Nieuport Oriole took off from São Paulo with thirty thousand leaflets and a dynamite bomb for the presidential palace, but the plane developed engine trouble and had to make a crash landing short of Rio. The revolutionaries used their other three aircraft—all unarmed—to greater advantage in reconnoitering loyalist positions. The government had at its disposal two squadrons of Spads, which, on July 22, flew over São Paulo at an altitude of more than one thousand meters and dropped some bombs near the Luz barracks.[27]

In the meantime, even the most sanguine rebels were beginning to realize that the revolution had come to a dead end in São Paulo. On July 17 Isidoro formally stated that his forces would lay down their arms if President Bernardes were replaced by a neutral provisional government pledged to constitutional reforms, including introduction of the secret ballot, abolition of state customs duties, and the overhaul of the federal revenue system to eliminate corruption.[28] Ten days later Isidoro declared that the rebels would yield if the government would proclaim a general amnesty for all those involved in military uprisings since 1922. The government commanding general, who now had one hundred artillery pieces within range of Isidoro's positions, replied that unless the rebels surrendered unconditionally, he would annihilate them with his big guns. Probably of greater concern to the revolutionaries—who thus far had stood up rather well to the bombardment, which killed mainly innocent civilians—was the fact that loyalist troops were now threatening to close their only possible avenue of escape, to the west. By July 27 Isidoro, Miguel Costa, and the Tenentes were all agreed that they had to leave São Paulo immediately, while they still could.[29]

Where would they go? They could follow the Northwest Railroad across the Paraná River into the sparsely settled border state of Mato Grosso. Then they could blow the railroad bridge at Três Lagoas and set up a defense line along the river. Of course, the frontier guard troops stationed in Mato Grosso would have to be dealt with, but revolutionary sentiment was known to be strong among their junior officers: Some had been involved in the abortive barracks revolt earlier in July and others could be expected to join the movement if a strong rebel force invaded the state. In southern Mato Grosso the rebels could try to set up a revolutionary "free state." Should this not work out, they could take the Northwest Railroad to the Bolivian border or swing south to the Paraguayan border and find safety in exile.

The retreat from São Paulo began at ten o'clock on the night of July 27 when the first rebel troop train rolled out of the Luz station. By dawn the evacuation was complete: Thirteen trains had left the city with some three thousand troops and fourteen field guns. The rebels left behind only two of their artillery pieces, which were still firing as the last train pulled out, maintaining the illusion of a continuing defense of the city. With no patrols operating at night and no infantry contact with the insurgents, the artillery-obsessed government command knew nothing of the evacuation until the next morning, when it had been completed. The rebels had clear tracks as far as the town of Bauru, where their westernmost detachment was posted, about halfway between São Paulo and the Mato Grosso border at Três Lagoas.[30]

At Bauru, Isidoro learned that there was an extensive buildup of government forces around Três Lagoas, where the Northwest Railroad trestle spanned the mighty Paraná River. Isidoro decided that to plunge on along the Northwest, where the enemy was expecting them, would be too risky. They should take the spur south to the Sorocabana Railroad and follow this line west to the Paraná River where the Sorocabana ended. There, at Pôrto Presidente Epitácio, which was virtually undefended, there were always plenty of boats. The rebels could either cross into Mato Grosso at Pôrto Presidente Epitácio or they could descend the river and establish a beachhead nearer the Paraguayan border.[31] Isidoro's planning and flawless execution of the São Paulo evacuation had dispelled what doubts the Tenentes might have had about their general. They accepted the change in plans: Instead of driving directly on Três Lagoas, they would detour south to Pôrto Presidente Epitácio.

From Bauru, on July 30, the revolutionaries launched their drive on Pôrto Presidente Epitâcio. Since the government by this time had occupied São Paulo and was beginning to shift troops west on the Sorocabana, there were some head-on clashes as the rebels switched to that rail line. The loyalist advance elements were forced back, in the first significant infantry actions of the revolt, as Isidoro's trains rolled onto the Sorocabana tracks. In the towns and in the countryside people gathered along the railroad to enjoy the spectacle of the passing troops, whom they cheered with gusto. On August 6 the rebel vanguard reached Pôrto Presidente Epitácio and received the surrender of its defenders, a medical officer and a handful of enlisted men. The town would remain under revolutionary control for thirty-seven days as Miguel Costa, commanding the rebel rearguard, held off a sluggish loyalist advance.[32]

In the meantime, other rebel units crossed the river in commandeered boats and probed the Mato Grosso side. One fifteen-man patrol was virtually annihilated by loyalist volunteers under the command of a local landowner, and a rebel force of one hundred twenty men fled in panic when its commander was shot down in an ambush.[33] Men who had hardly flinched as enemy artillery battered down their civilized surroundings in São Paulo—who had shown fine spirit as their troop trains rolled through Paulista towns, villages, and coffee plantations—were terrified by the strange new war in the desolate forests and glades of the Paraná valley. Their officers were disheartened by the falling troop morale and by the absence of the expected defections from government forces in Mato Grosso. A bold stroke was called for to lift the spirits of the troops and rouse to action the revolution's sympathizers among the loyalists. The rebels would strike in force against the government concentration at Três Lagoas. The attack would be led by Juarez Távora.

One month past his twenty-fifth birthday, the tall, muscular, square-jawed Juarez Távora was an imposing figure. Born into the literate elite of the impoverished northeastern state of Ceará (a relative, Franklin Távora, had achieved national fame as a novelist), Juarez had a way with words. Men were impressed by his "elegance of style," spellbound by the "enchanting raptures of his eloquence," and stirred by his "magical power" to convert souls to "the new ideas and awaken enthusiasm for the victorious struggles of democracy." [34]

In his military and revolutionary career, Juarez followed in the footsteps of his older brother, Joaquim Távora. Joaquim, a federal army captain in 1922, was one of the instigators of the mutiny that year in Mato Grosso, where he was stationed. Juarez, then a lieutenant on the staff of the Realengo Military Academy near Rio, was one of the officers who led more than six hundred cadets in a march on a nearby garrison in what was supposed to be a general military uprising on the morning of

July 5, 1922. The garrison troops unexpectedly fired on them, killing one, after which the cadets and their officers retreated to the academy, where they meekly surrendered that afternoon to the first loyalist force to appear on the scene.[35] In December 1923, facing prison sentences of unforeseen severity, the Távora brothers and four other young officers, then on provisional liberty pending disposition of their case, deserted the army.[36]

For the next six months the Távoras traveled secretly through southern Brazil, laying the foundations for new revolts. It was Joaquim Távora, the head and heart of the Tenente movement, who was chiefly responsible for launching the São Paulo uprising. But he and his brother, Juarez, were put out of action early on the morning of July 5, 1924, when they walked unsuspectingly into the headquarters of a state militia battalion that had just switched back from the rebel to the government side. They remained there as prisoners until the loyalist withdrawal from São Paulo on July 8, when they were released. Joaquim died eleven days later of wounds received in the artillery bombardment, the only revolutionary officer killed in São Paulo.[37] Misfortune would continue to stalk his brother, Juarez, now a major in the revolutionary army.

At Pôrto Presidente Epitácio, which the rebels renamed "Pôrto Joaquim Távora," Juarez Távora's 570-man-reinforced battalion—including the German and Italian companies, which accounted for about half of its strength—embarked on two steamboats for the vicinity of Três Lagoas. They landed some twenty-five kilometers downstream from that town, on the morning of August 17, and began their overland march, swinging wide to the left in order to fall upon the loyalists from the southwest. The battalion traveled light and on foot; there was no supply element. Major Távora ensured that each man had his blanket roll and plenty of ammunition, but no food was issued to the soldiers and few carried more than one canteen of water. Having spent so many days along the great river, nobody, perhaps, could imagine a shortage of water. But it was the middle of the dry season; beyond the banks of the river the land was parched—most of its streams had run dry.[38]

Távora's men were in no condition to make the long forced march. For more than a week they had done little more than loll on the cool banks of the river. Nor had many exerted themselves physically in the previous weeks, either in the defense of São Paulo or during the railroad movement to the river. The foreigners of the battalion were especially unprepared for the change from the climate of upland São Paulo to that of the low-lying Paraná valley, where even in midwinter the subtropical sun frequently reached a scorching intensity that was seldom experienced in a European summer. The battalion spent August 17 crossing a sandy plain that was devoid of water or any vegetation other than a spotty covering of brown grass and some scrawny shrubs scattered here and there. The soldiers plodded on under the merciless sun in silence, hardly a whisper escaping from their parched throats until, late in the day, an enemy cavalry patrol was sighted. Orders were shouted, the battalion deployed, some shots were fired, and after the loyalists rode out of sight, the march was resumed—but only for a short distance, for the rebel vanguard had reached the banks of a stream in which there was still a trickle of water.[39]

There beside the stream the weary soldiers collapsed for the night. The cold air that suddenly descended at dusk was almost as welcome as the water that slaked their thirst, but there was no food. In the worst days of the war in Europe they could at least fill their stomachs with hardtack; here there was nothing. At dawn the next morning, their hunger pangs more acute now that their bodies were rested, Távora's men moved out to attack Três Lagoas. As they neared the town the sand underfoot gave way to hard clay, which made walking easier, and the grass grew thicker and taller. Soon the battalion was swallowed up in the high, dry grass.[40]

When enemy automatic weapons opened up on the battalion's vanguard, the main body quickly deployed in a skirmish line. With their officers shouting, in various languages, such commands as "Forward, boys!" they began a steady, relentless advance. They overran one line of enemy trenches, then another. But it was not easy to tell where the enemy was, out there in the tall grass. A loyalist company was bypassed on the right flank, a fact that became evident as the rebels began receiving fire from the right rear. This development, together with the capture of a loyalist field kitchen, stopped the battalion short of the last government positions before Três Lagoas. Famished rebel soldiers broke ranks and crowded around the kitchen, where they made splendid targets. The battalion already had suffered heavy casualties in reaching this point, tantalizingly close to its objective. Távora's men could hear locomotives clanging and chugging on the Northwest Railroad as the loyalist fire slackened. Were the government troops withdrawing, the rebels wondered, loading onto the trains to escape across the river? [41]

Whiffs of smoke drifted toward the insurgents, for the wind was blowing their way. Then flames began to leap up in front of them. The grass was on fire. Although the initial panic that swept their ranks was soon controlled, the rebels saw no choice but retreat. Enemy gunners opened up now with everything they had as Távora's men withdrew, abandoning their dead and many of their wounded to be consumed by the flames. The encounter at Três Lagoas left a third of the battalion killed, wounded, captured, or missing.[42] Juarez Távora had lost the bloodiest battle of the revolution of 1924. Perhaps it was also the decisive battle of the revolution.[43]

The return of the steamboats with Major Távora and the forlorn survivors of the Três Lagoas expedition dissipated all hopes at rebel headquarters for establishing a "free state" in Mato Grosso. It was decided that the revolutionary forces would move downstream into the Brazilian state of Paraná, across the river from the Republic of Paraguay. The thrust south would be headed by Colonel João Francisco Pereira de Sousa, who had long advocated such a move.

João Francisco was a singular figure in the revolution of 1924. He was a native of Rio Grande do Sul and a veteran of the 1893–1895 civil war, in which, unlike Isidoro, he fought for the republic. He had been one of those radical republicans who called themselves "Jacobins" and liked to see "royalist" heads roll. In the 1890's João Francisco and his gaúchos were notorious for cutting the throats of their Maragato prisoners. Colonel João Francisco was schooled in the irregular warfare of the pampas. His commanding general in 1924, the ex-Maragato Isidoro, was familiar with this mode of fighting but had been trained as a regular and had spent most of his life as a professional soldier. Serious differences were bound to arise between Isidoro and João Francisco, whose military career, in the state militia of Rio Grande do Sul, had ended around the turn of the century when he broke with Governor Borges de Medeiros and went back to his prewar occupation of cattle ranching—and, some say, horse stealing.[44] He sat out the 1923 revolt against Borges but arrived in São Paulo the next year to join his son-in-law, a lieutenant of the São Paulo militia, in the new revolution. Isidoro found João Francisco's peculiar skills hardly relevant to the defense of the city, but when the time came to withdraw to the river, he put him in command of the cavalry that scouted ahead of the troop trains. João Francisco performed this task well, and when it was decided to move south he was the unavoidable choice to lead the vanguard. Miguel Costa, whose men were holding off the loyalist advance from São Paulo, could not be spared as commander of the rearguard.

On August 23 João Francisco, now a general commanding three hundred to five hundred revolutionaries—including Juarez Távora and some veterans of his ill-fated battalion—began his descent of the Paraná River in a steamboat, towing two barges loaded with cavalrymen and their horses. Slowly and methodically he reduced a succession of government outposts along the river, sending his cavalry ahead by land, whenever possible, to scout the enemy positions. On September 14 João Francisco's men overcame the defenders of Guaíra, about eighty men, and occupied that strategic river town four hundred kilometers south of Pôrto Presidente Epitácio.[45]

The town of Guaíra was owned and operated by the Laranjeira Mate Company. The company dealt in *erva mate,* or Paraguayan tea, the favorite beverage of the gauchos of Argentina, Uruguay, and southern Brazil. At Guaíra bags of mate leaves from the Brazilian states of Paraná and Mato Grosso and from adjacent Paraguay were collected for shipment to the Argentine town of Posadas, five hundred kilometers down the

Paraná River. Although some Brazilian capital was invested in the company, Laranjeira Mate was largely an Argentine enterprise. The company's foreign character was evident in its town of Guaíra, where the Portuguese language of Brazil was seldom heard and Brazilian money did not circulate. Business was transacted in the Spanish of Argentina or the Guarani of Paraguay and payments were made in Argentine *pesos.* Guaíra was a forgotten corner of Brazil.[46]

The mate shrub, a kind of holly, was found scattered throughout the forest that extended in all directions from Guaíra. The collection of mate leaves was strictly a forest gathering operation: It was generally believed in Guaíra that the shrub could not be cultivated. Some said that mate shrubs were propagated exclusively by seeds that had passed through the intestines of certain birds that inhabited the Paraná woods, a principle that was perceived as early as colonial times by the Jesuit fathers who founded missions in this area. The Jesuits had succeeded in planting some mate orchards and, old hands in the mate trade insisted, in substituting Indians for birds: They fed mate berries to their indigenous charges and had them defecate on designated spots. But the Jesuits were expelled from South America in the eighteenth century and their horticultural science was forgotten or ignored. In the first quarter of the twentieth century Guarani Indians in the pay of the Laranjeira Mate Company followed the pre-Columbian practice of stripping leaves from shrubs growing wild in the deep woods.[47]

Guaíra was on the east bank of a placid lagoon, five kilometers wide, at the head of the Seven Falls of the Paraná River. Below Guaíra the river roared through a red sandstone gorge less than one hundred meters wide, dropping one hundred meters in the course of a few kilometers, swirling over seven major cataracts in the stupendous display that gave the river its name: Paraná, "Boiling River" in the Guarani tongue. The falls were skirted by the mate company's narrow-gauge railroad, which ran from Guaíra sixty kilometers through the forest on the Brazilian side of the Paraná to Pôrto Mendes, where the river current, though still strong, no longer impeded navigation. The mate that was shipped by rail from Guaíra was lowered one hundred meters from the top of the canyon to the water's edge by means of a rail and cable system at Pôrto Mendes; there it was loaded onto the steamboats that would carry it to the Argentine railhead at Posadas. Across from Pôrto Mendes there was a similar setup at Puerto Adela to load mate gathered in the adjacent Paraguayan forest. Other settlements and forest clearings, strung out along the river both above and below the falls, served as collection points for mate or for wood to fuel steamboats or the locomotives of the Guaíra-Pôrto Mendes railroad.

João Francisco's rebels followed up their capture of Guaíra on September 14 by taking possession of the railroad to Pôrto Mendes that same day. While João Francisco and most of his troops remained in the Guaíra-Pôrto Mendes area awaiting the arrival of Isidoro and the rebel main body, an advance party under Juarez Távora continued down the river. On September 24 Távora's men occupied the town of Foz do Iguaçu, which they found unguarded and practically deserted, its population having fled across the Iguaçu River to the Argentine town of Puerto Aguirre. In the meantime, the rebel main body was having trouble descending the river to Guaíra. Loyalist volunteers from Mato Grosso managed to cut the river south of Pôrto Presidente Epitácio and trap in a narrow channel a steamboat and two barges carrying a revolutionary battalion; the rebel craft were disabled and beached on an island, where the two hundred twenty stranded rebels, all professionals from the São Paulo state militia, surrendered as a unit to the one hundred eighty backland provisionals on September 24. The loyalists, however, were unable to hold their positions in the face of a coordinated attack by the bulk of Isidoro's forces. After three days of fighting and maneuvering, the passage was cleared and Isidoro and his men resumed their voyage to Guaíra, which they reached on October 15.[48]

Isidoro's arrival in Guaíra was preceded by that of another famous revolutionary, Antônio de Siqueira Campos, the hero of the fight on Copacabana Beach. Siqueira, who had been living in exile in Argentina and Uruguay since 1923, appeared in Guaíra on October 6, 1924, accompanied by a representative of gaúcho político Assis Brasil. Siqueira was anxious to get the revolution going in Rio Grande do Sul, and after discussing the matter with João Francisco, he left for Foz do Iguaçú, without waiting any longer for Isidoro, to see Juarez Távora, an old friend from Rio days. Siqueira, with João Francisco's consent, proposed to Távora that they go immediately to the gaúcho state, where the situation was now ripe: The followers of Assis Brasil were ready to join with revolutionaries in the federal army in an armed movement against Governor Borges de Medeiros and his newfound friend in Rio, President Artur Bernardes.[49]

Siqueira Campos was a native of the state of São Paulo, the son of a coffee-plantation manager. He had wanted to study engineering at a civilian institution, but the best his family could do was send him to the Realengo Military Academy, from which he graduated as an artillery officer. Commissioned in 1920, he was stationed at Fort Copacabana during the acrimonious presidential election campaign of 1922. Siqueira fell in naturally with the military plotters who were determined to prevent Artur Bernardes from taking office as president. He was a passionate revolutionary, but his fire burned within. Small, dark, fine featured, Siqueira thought more and talked less than his comrade Juarez Távora. When he did speak his words were likely to be laden with irony. Usually calm, often smiling, Siqueira was never serene: His eyes, deep set beneath their thick, gloomy brows, betrayed an abiding melancholy.[50]

A general military uprising in Rio was planned for the predawn hours of July 5, 1922. Troops from various garrisons around the city were supposed to converge on the presidential palace, arrest outgoing President Epitácio Pessoa, and proclaim Marshal Hermes da Fonseca provisional chief executive of the nation. The marshal then, presumably, would order a recount of the recent election, certify Nilo Peçanha as president-elect, and pave the way for the November 15 inauguration of that gentleman, instead of the hated Artur Bernardes. At 1:15 A.M. on July 5, 1922, Fort Copacabana fired the cannon shot that was to signal the beginning of the uprising. There was no response, except from the Realengo Military Academy—but even the cadets abandoned the revolution within a few hours, after one of their

comrades was killed in a clash with loyal troops. Fort Copacabana stood alone, its long-range coast artillery firing in vengeance against garrisons that had forsaken the revolution.[51]

Siqueira Campos was one of twenty-nine revolutionaries who
remained in the fort after it came under government bombardment—after it was obvious that the revolt had failed. When their
commander was taken prisoner, outside the fort while attempting to negotiate surrender terms, leadership of the holdouts
passed to the next ranking officer, First Lieutenant Siqueira
Campos. By telephone the army high command demanded the
unconditional surrender of the mutineers. Soon their water and
electricity would be shut off. In the meantime, four thousand
government troops were on their way to bar the only exit from
the fort, which squatted on a rocky promontory, at the intersection of the crescents of Copacabana and Ipanema beaches. But
Lieutenant Siqueira Campos and his men refused to surrender.
After considering and rejecting a proposal to put a torch to the
powder magazine and blow up the fort—and themselves with
it—they decided to march out onto Copacabana Beach and con-
front the enemy. They would walk straight down beachfront
Atlantica Avenue in the direction of the presidential palace, nine
kilometers away. They would not shoot first, in hopes that the
government soldiers, instead of attacking them, would be so
inspired by their example as to join the march on the palace.

Early on the afternoon of July 6, 1922, the fort's Brazilian
flag was lowered and cut into twenty-nine pieces, one for each of
the four officers and twenty-four men present and one for their
captured commander, which would be carried by Siqueira.
Everyone, including the officers, was issued a shoulder arm
and at least two hundred rounds of ammunition—and a drink
of cognac, to make it easier to "endure the sun." In his final
instructions, Lieutenant Siqueira Campos cautioned his men
to hold their fire unless shot at; in that case they could return
the fire without waiting for orders to do so. Shortly before
2 P.M. Siqueira gave the signal to move out and the twenty-eight
rebels jumped over the barricade they had erected at the entrance to the fort.

There were no government troops to be seen on the street,

only some curious civilians, who scattered as the revolutionaries came bounding out. As the rebels stepped off down the mosaic sidewalk along Atlantica Avenue, some of the bolder spectators ran after them to ask them questions. Four of Siqueira's men took this opportunity to desert, disappearing among the civilians. It was a bright, sunny afternoon, but few bathers were on the beach—perhaps because of the revolution or maybe just because it was midwinter, when the surf was too cold for all but the hardiest Cariocas. The revolutionaries were sweating profusely as they walked briskly along, in loose formation, about half on the sidewalk, half in the street, their officers in the front rank. As they passed the Mére Louise Bar, some girls called out, "Good-bye, fools!" Other civilians walked alongside them, trying to convince them of their folly. In some cases they succeeded: The desertions continued. From the dwindling band came cheers, in unison and on command, of "Long live the army! *Viva* Marshal Hermes! Long live the defenders of Fort Copacabana!" There was some applause from the bystanders, and occasionally vivas were shouted back from second-story windows across the avenue.

After walking more than ten blocks down Atlantica Avenue and seeing nothing of the enemy, Siqueira gave the order to halt at the Londres Hotel. There they rested for ten minutes, consumed nearly twenty liters of water, and talked with the people. When the time came to resume the march, several of Siqueira's men had disappeared into the hotel. The desertions were partially offset by the appearance of a civilian, a friend of Siqueira's, who insisted on joining the rebels. One of the officers gave the civilian his rifle (keeping a pistol for himself) and Siqueira presented his friend with a piece of the flag from Fort Copacabana. Including the civilian, the revolutionaries numbered sixteen when they finally ran into government troops near the corner of Atlantica Avenue and Barroso Street, which is today Siqueira Campos Street.

Two government platoons were taking up positions on the inland side of the avenue as the rebels began to pass in front of them. The platoon officers crossed into the middle of the avenue to talk with the rebels, to try to persuade them to give up.

There was scuffling, some angry words were exchanged, and the revolutionaries kept on walking. The loyalist officers returned to their side of the avenue, a shot was fired, and a rebel soldier fell dead on the asphalt. The other revolutionaries scurried for the beach and threw themselves down behind the mosaic sidewalk, in the sand that sloped away toward the water. Within seconds there was heavy firing on both sides of the avenue.

On the beach, near the spot where the fighting began, a storm drain was being constructed and there were some large pipes lying about. Four rebel soldiers broke away from their comrades and sought refuge inside the bulletproof pipes. One of the deserters attached a white cloth to the end of his rifle and waved it so that it could be seen across the avenue, giving some of the loyalists the impression that the rebel band was surrendering. The eleven revolutionaries behind the sidewalk, however, continued to fire, cutting down at least half a dozen soldiers in what, to the loyalists, seemed to be an act of treachery. Government reinforcements appeared on the scene and the firing intensified, but no attempt was made to rush the rebel position.

After an hour and a quarter, when the rebels had exhausted all their ammunition except for a few pistol rounds, Siqueira Campos, who was shot through the left hand and weak from loss of blood, gave the order to disband, but only two enlisted men were physically able to make a run for safety. One dashed across the avenue, bounded over a wall, and was not captured until the next day; the other leaped into the ocean and swam to safety. Now that all signs of rebel resistance had ended, a loyalist officer ordered a bayonet charge. Dozens of government troops, remembering the supposed treachery of the hour before, swarmed across the avenue and fell upon the nine revolutionaries, all of whom were already dead or wounded. Siqueira mustered what strength he had left to raise his pistol and shoot a loyalist sergeant through the mouth. The sergeant, in his death agony, still managed to plunge his bayonet into the lieutenant's liver.

But Siqueira Campos survived the final action on the sand, along with one other officer and one enlisted man. Seven rebels were killed that afternoon or died later of their wounds. Thirty-five government soldiers were either killed or wounded in the fight on Copacabana Beach. As Siqueira lay recuperating in the Army Central Hospital, he was idolized by the political opposition and celebrated by romantics of every stripe. Even President Epitácio Pessoa visited his bedside. At the age of twenty-four Siqueira Campos was passing into legend as the immortal leader of the "Eighteen of the Fort." [52]

By December 1922 Siqueira was judged sufficiently recovered to be transferred from the hospital to the barracks of the Command and General Staff School, where he was held under an indictment handed down by a military and police board of inquiry. Siqueira's detention at the school lasted only three weeks: He and twenty-one other indicted rebels were released on a writ of habeas corpus issued by the Supreme Court on January 10, 1923. The court action infuriated the new president, Artur Bernardes, and heartened the rebels, who resumed their military duties pending trial—which most expected to be only for defying legally constituted authority, punishable by sixteen months in jail. But President Bernardes applied pressure to the judicial process and, in December 1923, the rebel officers were formally charged with attempting to change the constitutional system of Brazil by use of force, which could put them in prison for years. It was then that Juarez Távora and five other indicted officers deserted the army and went into hiding. Siqueira Campos, less optimistic than his comrades, had made his move much earlier; he deserted in February 1923 and fled to Uruguay. [53]

In exile Siqueira became a partner in a small export-import firm and devoted himself to business. Marshal Hermes, for whom he had shouted vivas on the beach at Copacabana, died in September 1923, but Siqueira did not seem to care; he was thoroughly disillusioned with military politics. The death of Nilo Peçanha a few months later did not move him—to Siqueira, "nilo" had become one of those "revolutionaries of the mouth" whose names he insisted on writing in the lower case. While residing in Uruguay, Siqueira apparently did have some dealings with Assis Brasil's Liberators across the border in Rio Grande do Sul, but these were probably for business purposes. In April 1924 Siqueira wrote his father that he would even send a tele-

gram of support to Artur Bernardes if the president would
throw a little business his way. By this time Siqueira's firm had
moved to Buenos Aires and the ex-lieutenant was absorbed in
plans to import Brazilian coffee into Argentina.[54] But the revolt
in São Paulo in July took his mind off business.

When the revolt erupted in São Paulo, Assis Brasil ran for
Uruguay; later he went to Argentina. Other veterans of the
1923 Liberator struggle in Rio Grande do Sul crossed into the
neighboring republics, where they discussed the possibility of a
new uprising in alliance with certain units of the federal army—
some of whose officers had been friendly to their cause in 1923.
Inevitably, Siqueira Campos was drawn into the discussions. The
name of one of Siqueira's comrades from the Realengo Military
Academy, Luís Carlos Prestes, was frequently mentioned. Prestes, probably the only cadet Siqueira had looked up to, was now
a federal army captain stationed at Santo Ângelo, Rio Grande do
Sul, and was secretly committed to the revolution. By August
1924 federal and state authorities had gotten wind of the military conspiracy in Rio Grande do Sul and arrested several of its
members. Prestes and those who thus far had escaped detection
were anxious to begin the revolt. By early October hundreds of
civilian veterans of the Liberator campaign were armed and
organized for the new movement. Before launching it, however,
the civilian and military conspirators wanted to know the situation of Isidoro's forces on the Paraná River—and what support
could be expected from that quarter. Siqueira agreed to go to
Isidoro's headquarters and bring back the information.[55]

Siqueira and two Liberators took a steamboat from Posadas,
Argentina, to Foz do Iguaçú. One of the Liberators remained
there while the other continued on with Siqueira to Pôrto Mendes. From there they went to Guaíra via the Laranjeira Mate
railroad. Isidoro was still upriver when Siqueira arrived in
Guaíra on October 6; it would be nine days before the rebel general in chief reached Guaíra. Siqueira could not wait. After conferring with João Francisco, he returned to Foz do Iguaçú and
picked up Juarez Távora. On October 9 Siqueira and Távora,
traveling under assumed names, were in Posadas, where they
took a train for the Uruguayan town of Artigas, on the border of

Rio Grande do Sul, where the top Liberator "general" was assembling his troops.[56]

In Artigas, on October 12, Távora penned a letter to "My dear Prestes," briefing the captain at Santo Angelo on the desires and capabilities of the men on the Paraná River, who for "three months have been fighting, alone, against the rest of Brazil." Isidoro's forces, Távora maintained, were spread over the rest of the state of Paraná, from the São Paulo border in the north to Foz do Iguaçú in the south, and as far east as the town of Catanduvas. They numbered, he claimed, about three thousand brave men, well armed and supplied with a superabundance of ammunition. They had some twenty pieces of artillery—from pack howitzers to heavy field guns—forty or fifty automatic weapons, about six million rounds of ammunition, and close to two thousand extra Mauser rifles, available for arming recruits. A linking of these forces with the revolutionaries of Rio Grande do Sul was entirely possible, but it would be unjust to require troops on the Paraná to march two hundred leagues (Távora's statistics were as inflated as his rhetoric) south to close the gap. The revolutionaries of Rio Grande do Sul had to realize that these men had covered much ground since leaving São Paulo "without knowing rest." Távora felt that the two revolutionary contingents could reasonably expect to join forces somewhere in the vicinity of Ponta Grossa, Paraná. The movement north, he emphasized, had to begin as soon as possible; should the revolutionaries from the south be much delayed in reaching Paraná, the rebels from São Paulo, by themselves, would have to defeat everything President Bernardes was still able to throw against the revolution. In that case the projected revolt in the gaúcho state would be irrelevant. Prestes was urged to explain these facts to his military colleagues in Rio Grande do Sul.[57]

Távora had already conferred with Liberator General Honório Lemes in Artigas and was leaving that day, October 12, for Argentina to see Assis Brasil. They would agree on a date for launching the rebellion and inform Prestes by coded telegram. Prestes would be told how to decipher the telegram by the messenger bearing Távora's letter.[58] The time that was eventually set for the new uprising was the night of October 28, 1924.

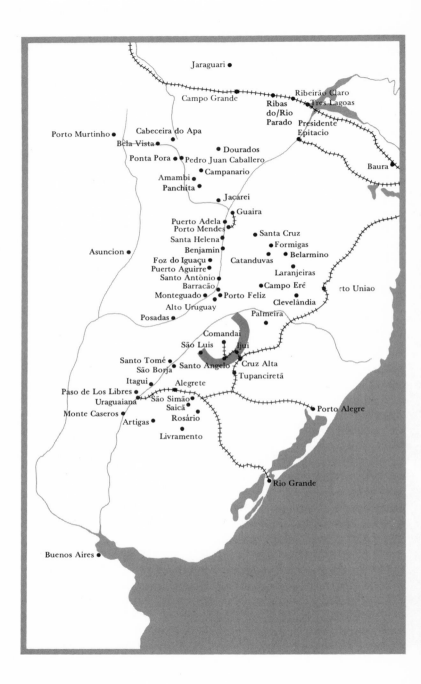

Prestes and the Gaúchos

LL Luís Carlos Prestes was born into the bourgeoisie of Pôrto Alegre, the capital city of Rio Grande do Sul, where one of his grandfathers had been a judge and the other a well-to-do merchant. But the merchant, the maternal grandfather, had lost his fortune before the birth of his grandson and the judge had died years earlier, while Luís Carlos' father was still a child, leaving only a modest estate. Luís Carlos' father was a federal army officer stationed in Pôrto Alegre when his son was born on January 3, 1898. As a cadet at the Military Academy in Rio, his father had taken part in the coup that overthrew the monarchy in 1889; he was a fervent republican and a devotee of the positivism of the French philosopher Auguste Comte. Luís Carlos' mother was a French teacher and an avid reader of the novels of Émile Zola.[1]

Luís Carlos Prestes' father spent most of his military career in his native Rio Grande do Sul, which was not unusual, since much of the federal army was concentrated in that strategic border state. His last post, however, was in Rio de Janeiro, where he died in 1908, at the age of thirty-nine, after an extended illness. He died a captain, leaving his widow, Dona Leocádia, a pension that was insufficient to support her and their five children: the ten-year-old Luís Carlos and four daughters. Nevertheless, his army service gave his son a chance for an education; at the age of eleven, Luís Carlos was admitted to the Military Preparatory School in Rio, one of three such institutions in Brazil that were operated by the War Ministry and provided scholarships to qualified and needy sons of officers. With her son boarded at the military school, Dona Leocádia was able to make ends meet by giving lessons in music and French and occasionally by working at home as a seamstress. She and the four girls lived in a small house on an unpaved street in a working-class suburb of Rio.[2]

Upon graduating with honors from preparatory school, Prestes was admitted to the Realengo Military Academy. When his father had been a cadet, the academy was located on Vermelha Beach, at the foot of Sugarloaf mountain, not far from downtown Rio. His father's classmates had helped overthrow Brazil's last emperor, and other cadets, six years later, had rioted against the country's first civilian president. The rioters were expelled, but the mutinous tradition remained. In 1904 the cadet corps rose in arms against the federal government in the vaccination rebellion. The positivist doctrines that Prestes' father had ingested at the academy in the 1880's were still taught there in 1904, including Auguste Comte's prejudice against Dr. Edward Jenner's smallpox vaccine. After suppressing the 1904 uprising, the federal government moved the troublesome academy to a site more distant from the seat of government—to the suburb of Realengo, twenty-five kilometers from downtown Rio —and apparently tried to forget about it. When Prestes matriculated at Realengo in 1916, little had been done to update or professionalize the curriculum. Comte's elitist dogma and a sullen spirit of rebellion continued to haunt the academy.[3]

While philosophy and politics were major concerns at the Military Academy, other professional schools were involved in equally extraneous matters. At the medical school in Rio, Professor Aloísio de Castro composed effeminate sonnets and gave lectures in the purest and most affected European Portuguese. Medical students in Bahia "discussed grammar under the baton of professors more preoccupied with classical Portuguese than with microbes," while at the law school in Rio, Professor Ronald de Carvalho did research in poetic meter.[4] But the professional schools accounted for virtually all the higher education in Brazil at a time when there were no universities offering graduate or undergraduate training in liberal arts. Brazilian students went directly from secondary schools into the professional schools.

At every level, from primary to professional school, education was almost exclusively for the elite. When Luís Carlos Prestes graduated from the Military Academy in December 1919, no more than 25 percent of his countrymen could read and write. This appalling situation had political as well as social implications, since literacy was a qualification for voting in Brazil. Even if elections had been honest, if the secret ballot had been used, the government would still have been able to ignore the needs of a vast majority of the Brazilian people. Though excluded from the political process, Brazil's urban masses had begun to stir during Prestes' academy days, when workers in Rio and São Paulo struck for higher wages and better working conditions—occasionally with success.[5]

But the rumblings from the proletariat were lost in the clamor over Brazil's entry into World War I. The vocal elite was deliriously in favor of going to the aid of France; the army was excited; a draft law was put into effect; and the navy was readied for combat. A Brazilian task force sailed for the Mediterranean in October 1918 and joined the allied fleet there a few days before the armistice. The sailors came home sprinkled with glory and bearing the terrible influenza virus that would kill thousands of Brazilians before running its course.

Involvement with Europe continued after the armistice, with Brazil's participation in the Versailles Peace Conference and the League of Nations. A French Military Mission was contracted to train the federal army. The state of São Paulo had been paying French officers to instruct its state militia since 1906. The coffee barons of São Paulo did not limit themselves to supporting modernization only in the military art: They financed the celebration of Modern Art Week in February 1922, which launched the "modernist" movement in Brazilian literature. The modernists deprecated literary Portuguese and insisted that writers use the language as it was spoken in Brazil. Modernism was "the complete revolution of form, preserving the most reactionary contents." [6] Nevertheless, it had nationalistic implications that indicated a countercurrent to the prevailing mania for things European. The dichotomy was evident in the federal army, which welcomed the French officers in 1919, yet put the Realengo Military Academy off limits to the foreign mission. [7] Not until long after Prestes' graduation would the Military Academy be brought under the influence of the French Military Mission.

Short, slender, slightly stooped, Cadet Prestes was a cerebral and serious young man who quickly earned the admiration and affection of his classmates. He seemed always able and willing to help those who had difficulties with their studies. His unselfishness was as celebrated as his intellect. When not tutoring other cadets, he spent his free time working mathematical puzzles or visiting his mother and sisters. He did not run around with girls or carouse with academy chums. Graduating first in his class, he was commissioned a second lieutenant in the army engineers. He was glad to be stationed in the Rio area, where he could be near his mother and sisters; his familial devotion and his austere habits were not changed when he became an officer. [8]

There was a new minister of war when Prestes began his career as a commissioned officer. João Pandiá Calógeras, a cultivated gentleman of Greek descent, was the first civilian to head the War Ministry since the days of the monarchy. A sensitive and sensible man, Calógeras went out of his way to avoid provoking his uniformed subordinates, many of whom, he realized, deeply resented his appointment over them. He bought them presents—guns, airplanes, even tanks—from the surplus stocks of Europe. Calógeras continued the "professionalization" program of his predecessor, who had contracted the French Military Mission. While French instructors were barred from the Military

Academy, Brazilian officers who had served with the troops and demonstrated a preference for soldiering over politics were sent to Realengo to train the cadets, who referred to them as the "indigenous mission." But some talented and seemingly professional-minded recent graduates also were employed as instructors at the academy, including Luís Carlos Prestes, who during his cadet days had showed little interest in politics and seldom even read the newspapers. Prestes taught engineering at the academy and became notorious in administration circles for his constant complaints about a shortage of instructional materials. Calógeras' War Ministry assured the lieutenant that he would receive the materials, but they never came. Early in 1922 Prestes, at his own request, was transferred to a railroad construction unit of the engineer corps.[9]

The First Engineer Company, to which Prestes was assigned, was stationed in the Rio suburb of Deodoro, on the Central of Brazil Railroad, between Realengo and the closer-in suburb of Meier, where Dona Leocádia and her daughters lived. Between Deodoro and Realengo was the largest army installation in the Federal District, at Vila Militar. Thus, Prestes' company was strategically situated on the main line of communication between the government center in downtown Rio and the all-important Realengo–Vila Militar military complex. Inevitably, Prestes was drawn into the conspiracy of 1922.

At first, when he was still on the faculty at Realengo, Prestes steered clear of military politics. He was a member of the Military Club, but for a long time he did not show up at its meetings. He did attend the special session called to consider the insulting letter allegedly written by presidential candidate Artur Bernardes. At that meeting he voted against setting up an investigating committee to determine if Bernardes had actually written the letter: Since the candidate had already denied writing it, and had disavowed its sentiments, Prestes saw no reason to pursue the matter. The majority of the members of the club felt otherwise, and after the vote, Prestes let it be known that he would stand with his comrades in whatever action they might decide upon—as long as it was carefully considered and well planned. Early in 1922 he was invited to join some coup planners, but soon left the group disillusioned by the conspirators' lack of organization and direction. Later, when the conspiracy came under new leadership, Prestes was persuaded to rejoin it.[10]

Prestes was second-in-command of the First Engineer Company when he committed himself to the revolution. The company commander, a captain, was studying medicine and appeared at the barracks in Deodoro only when necessary to sign papers. The junior lieutenants of the company professed to be ardent revolutionaries and looked to Prestes for leadership in the coming insurrection; the captain was not brought into the conspiracy. The plan called for Marshal Hermes da Fonseca, president of the Military Club and ex-president of the republic, to take command of the troops at Vila Militar before dawn on the appointed day. While the cadets at Realengo marched to join the marshal at Vila Militar, Prestes' company was to cut the telephone and telegraph lines into the city of Rio.[11]

Lieutenant Prestes came down with typhoid fever on June 13, 1922. He was still very sick, in bed at his mother's house, on the night of July 4, when a fellow officer informed him that the revolution was to begin within a few hours. Prestes told his mother to prepare his uniform and he dragged himself out of bed. But he barely managed to get dressed before he passed out. The revolt was launched without him, and it went badly. Marshal Hermes never appeared at Vila Militar and the troops there fired on the Realengo cadets when they arrived. The First Engineer Company did not cut the telephone and telegraph lines. The Military Academy surrendered on July 5 and the garrison of Fort Copacabana, the only other unit to honor its commitment to the revolution, was overcome by government forces the next day.[12]

The military and police board of inquiry did not link Prestes to the mutiny of July 1922. While twenty-two of his officer colleagues were being indicted in Rio for seditious activity, Prestes was promoted to captain. Nevertheless, with the investigation going on in Rio, which remained under a state of siege, Prestes found conditions in the federal capital intolerable. When he was sufficiently recovered from his illness, he requested a furlough and a transfer to Rio Grande do Sul, both of which were granted. The atmosphere was no less tense in the gaúcho state, where the Liberators of Assis Brasil and the Chimangos of Governor Borges de Medeiros were soon engaged in open warfare. But the federal army was officially neutral in this struggle, in which both sides tried to ingratiate themselves with the government of President Bernardes, and Captain Prestes went about his business of supervising the construction of army barracks, apparently little concerned with the local civil war. His revolutionary interests were revived after the gaúcho war ended, when a fugitive Tenente, Juarez Távora, visited him in January 1924. Prestes told Távora that he could count on him in any serious revolutionary undertaking.[13]

At the beginning of 1924 Prestes was no longer supervising the construction of army barracks. He had filed a number of reports citing collusion between corrupt government officials and profiteering contractors. The War Ministry, instead of taking action against the grafters, gave Prestes another assignment. When Juarez Távora found him in January, he was stationed in Santo Angelo, Rio Grande do Sul, with a railroad battalion that was laying tracks to the nearby town of Comandaí. Juarez Távora hoped that an uprising in Rio Grande do Sul could be coordinated with the military revolt that his brother, Joaquim, was planning to set off in São Paulo. But the situation in the gaúcho state required time to mature: The Liberators, still licking their wounds from the civil war, were only beginning to become disillusioned with the settlement that President Bernardes had imposed upon them. Given ample time, Prestes and the military conspirators in Rio Grande do Sul could persuade the Liberators to combine forces with them in a joint revolutionary effort that would be much more effective than the unassisted revolt of a few federal garrisons in the state. But Joaquim Távora insisted that the revolution begin in São Paulo on July 5, the second anniversary of the Rio rising. Revolutionary elements in Rio Grande do Sul, and in other states, could join the movement when they felt the time was ripe for them to do so.[14]

The conspirators in Rio Grande do Sul were not ready on July 5 and did not respond to the rising in São Paulo, which did, however, spark barracks revolts in Mato Grosso, Sergipe, Pará, and Amazonas. The Mato Grosso rebels were quickly overpowered by loyalists in their midst, but the suppression of the revolts in the north required a longer and more complex operation. As government soldiers closed in on São Paulo, a navy-army task force was sailing north toward Aracajú, the capital of Sergipe, which had been in rebel hands since July 13.[15]

By August 2 the Sergipe mutiny was crushed and loyalist troops were boarding their transports for the voyage to the Amazon. Belém, at the mouth of the great river, the capital of Pará, had not fallen to the federal troops who mutinied there on July 26. Unable to take Belém, the rebels fled upriver on July 28 and joined other revolutionaries at the fort at Óbidos, where the river was only three kilometers wide. Thus the rebels controlled the approach to Manaus, the capital of Amazonas, which had been under revolutionary rule since July 23. Toward the end of August one cruiser and two destroyers, escorting five troop transports, weighed anchor at Belém and steamed up the muddy waters of the Amazon toward Óbidos. The ships' guns did not have to open first on the fort; the rebels surrendered after two seaplanes flew over and dropped bombs on them. The fall of the fort at Óbidos on August 25 was followed three days later by the unresisted occupation of Manaus and the arrest of the Tenentes who, according to the U.S. vice-consul, had given the state of Amazonas the first honest administration in its history.[16]

What news Prestes and the conspirators in Rio Grande do Sul received from the north in August could not have been very encouraging. Censorship was in effect in all the states where revolts had occurred and also in the Federal District. President

Bernardes had retained the state of siege stemming from the July 1922 uprising until shortly after Congress enacted a new press law in December 1923, which provided severe penalties for libeling government officials.[17] In July 1924 Bernardes reimposed the state of siege, with full censorship, in the Rio area, the center of Brazilian news gathering and dissemination. The censorship would remain in effect, with the consent of a rubber-stamp Congress, for the remainder of Bernardes' presidential term. But in September 1924 when the São Paulo rebels reached Foz do Iguaçu, they were able to feed information to the Argentine news media. Argentine and Uruguayan newspapers and radio broadcasts carried news of the rebellion to much of southern Brazil.[18] Excitement mounted in the army barracks of Rio Grande do Sul and among the civilian followers of Assis Brasil. The long-projected uprising in the gaúcho state would not be much longer in coming.

Government suspicions of revolutionary plotting by young army officers in Rio Grande do Sul were confirmed by August 1924. Not long after the São Paulo revolt a lieutenant from the federal cavalry regiment at Uruguaiana arrived in Pôrto Alegre to fetch his unit's payroll—and to deliver a letter from a conspirator in his garrison to another federal officer in the state capital. The lieutenant first picked up the payroll and then went to the Caçadores Club to try his luck at roulette. He lost the entire sum entrusted to him and, in order to replace it, sold the incriminating letter to the state government. Shortly thereafter numerous arrests were made by state and federal authorities in Pôrto Alegre and in Uruguaiana.[19] The letter did not implicate Luís Carlos Prestes at Santo Angelo, in the northwest of the state, more than three hundred kilometers from both Pôrto Alegre and Uruguaiana.

The secrets of the revolution were relatively safe with Captain Prestes, who was free of such potentially compromising vices as gambling, whoring, and heavy drinking. For some time after committing himself to the revolution in January 1924,

Captain Prestes had given his superiors little reason to suspect him of sedition. Although Prestes had made no secret of his disgust with the corruption he encountered as a supervisor of barracks construction, he appeared willing—for a while, anyway—to work within the military system to correct such abuses. Indeed, his great integrity would seem to preclude his betraying the solemn oath he, as an army officer, had taken to defend the government of Brazil. Furthermore, he had little time for revolutionary plotting—at least while he was with the railroad battalion during the early months of 1924.

Prestes and his crew of some three hundred soldiers worked up to twelve hours a day laying tracks across the rolling prairie between Santo Angelo and Comandaí. They were extending a spur that began at Cruz Alta, on the meter-gauge São Paulo–Pôrto Alegre trunk line, and was planned to traverse the northernmost range of the Brazilian pampas: the *coxilhas,* or grassy hillocks, that descended in gentle waves from Rio Grande do Sul's central plateau to the Uruguay River. At regular intervals along the roadbed, stands of fast-growing eucalyptus trees were planted to provide wood to fuel future locomotives, because Brazil, for all its natural wealth, was short of both coal and petroleum. Some coal was dug out of the ground in northeastern Rio Grande do Sul and neighboring Santa Catarina, but it was of poor quality, high in ash content. The Brazilian government went to considerable expense to adapt the engines of its warships to this inferior fuel, but most of the country's trains, like its riverboats, would be propelled for years to come by steam generated over wood fires.[20]

The Australian eucalyptus would thrive on the Brazilian coxilhas, providing welcome shade as well as fuel. But there were only a few native trees—mostly *umbus,* the "lighthouses" that marked otherwise empty horizons—to provide temporary relief from the summer sun as Prestes' men used pick and shovel to cut through the pale green sod and shift the red-brown dirt to form the railroad bed between Santo Angelo and Comandaí. This was cattle country, where there was strong prejudice

against work that could not be performed from the back of a
spirited horse by a gaúcho attired in a flowing poncho and ex-
pansively draped breeches. Gaúchos fished from horseback;
they drew water from wells while mounted. To mix mortar, a
gaúcho would ride his horse back and forth through the sludge.
Captain Prestes, however, did not have the gaúcho's contempt
for pedestrian labor; he spent more time than any other officer
of the battalion in the roadbed on foot with the men—not just
giving orders, but explaining things to them, helping them,
earning their respect and affection. After working hours he devoted much of his time to teaching the illiterates among them
how to read and write. His close association with the battalion's
enlisted men facilitated the coordination of a military-civilian
uprising in Santo Angelo, since among the recent recruits were
veterans of the Liberator forces who sought refuge in the federal army from the reprisals of partisans of Governor Borges
de Medeiros.[21]

Prestes' revolutionary involvement eventually led him to try
to resign from the federal army. Perhaps he felt he needed more
time and freedom for plotting, or maybe, as a biographer
suggests, his conscience compelled him to seek release from his
oath to defend the government that he was working to overthrow. (Apparently he had experienced no such qualms in
1922.) At any rate, sometime before the São Paulo uprising,
Prestes was granted an indefinite furlough pending action by
the War Ministry on his resignation. He remained in Santo
Angelo, where he maintained contact with the troops of the
railroad battalion and was employed as an engineer by a civilian
company that was bringing electric power to the town. In
October, when he received notice of the date set for the statewide revolt, his resignation from the army still had not been
accepted.[22]

A little after dark on October 28 some civilians appeared at
the Santo Angelo home of the major who commanded the
railroad battalion. The major was persuaded to join the civilians
for an automobile ride on the pampas. At about ten o'clock the

executive officer of the battalion, a lieutenant, received a telegram, purportedly from the commanding general of the district,
ordering him to locate Captain Prestes and turn over to him
command of the railroad battalion. The executive officer found
the captain at his residence and escorted him to headquarters,
where Prestes assumed command of the battalion, declared that
there was no change in standing orders, and began conferring
with some sergeants. It was an hour and a half later before the
executive officer and another lieutenant realized that they had
been tricked. By that time Prestes had command of the battalion
in fact as well as in name, and the two loyalist lieutenants were
immediately put under arrest when they moved to counter the
subversion. A third lieutenant and virtually all of the battalion's
three hundred and fifty enlisted men followed Prestes into the
revolution.[23]

Before dawn on October 29 soldiers and civilians wearing
red ribbons on their hats were patrolling the streets of Santo
Angelo. The town hall, police arsenal, railroad station, and telegraph office were all occupied without resistance. Forty soldiers
and some civilians were dispatched by rail under the command
of an army sergeant to the town of Ijuí, some fifty kilometers to
the east. But this expedition was fired upon by Chimangos—
civilians loyal to Governor Borges—when it tried to take over the
Ijuí town hall as day was breaking. The sergeant was killed and
his men beat a hasty retreat to Santo Angelo. Certainly disappointed that his forces had failed their first combat test, Prestes
was cheered by the arrival at 10 A.M. of some soldiers from the
garrison at São Luís, sent by automobile to establish liaison with
the rebels of Santo Angelo. Federal troops at São Luís, São
Borja, and Uruguaiana had revolted as planned. Before noon
copies of a bulletin signed by Prestes were being distributed in
Santo Angelo.[24]

The hour had come, Prestes' bulletin proclaimed, for the
people of Santo Angelo to contribute to "the great national
cause" that the "heroes from São Paulo" had been upholding for
the last four months. The cause was that of the people of

Brazil—"a sublime mixture of Brazilians and foreigners"—who demanded the secret ballot, honest elections, punishment for politicians who stole from the government, and freedom for the army officers imprisoned for sedition in 1922. The people of Rio Grande do Sul were entering the struggle now, in time to help "reestablish the financial situation of Brazil, to recover the money that our bad governments have robbed from us, and thus be able to prevent the English government from coming in 1927 to take control of our customs houses and rich new agricultural developments to collect Brazil's debt." The general uprising in Rio Grande do Sul was ordered for that day, October 29, by General Isidoro Dias Lopes. Taking part in the armed movement, the bulletin claimed, were ten federal army garrisons, various concentrations of gaúcho revolutionaries in the interior of the state and along the entire southern border, and the exile forces of the two principal generals of the Liberator campaign, who had invaded the state that morning. A communion had been forged—of Paulistas and gaúchos, of the army and the people, of natives and foreigners—that would conclude the struggle in Brazil quickly, with honor, and for "the glory of our ideals and our rights as a civilized and proud people." [25]

Thus the purpose of the revolution, as Prestes defined it, remained about the same as had been declared in São Paulo in July. Where the objectives Prestes announced went beyond punishing the federal government for wounding the pride of the military (and, now, for its ill-treatment of the gaúcho Liberators as well), they were political and essentially conservative. Adoption of the secret ballot, one of the rebels' few specific proposals, would have been an innovation but hardly a radical one. Neither Prestes nor the São Paulo rebels advocated suffrage for the illiterates who comprised the overwhelming majority of the Brazilian people. There was no denunciation of "imperialism," only a condemnation of Brazilian governments that, because of ineptitude and corruption, had failed to meet the payments due foreign creditors.

Besides informing the people of Santo Angelo of the objec-

tives of the national revolution, Prestes' bulletin of October 29
purported to give a true picture of the military situation on the
Paraná River. Despite press and telegraph censorship and the
government's lies, the Brazilian people, Prestes maintained, had
not been fooled: Everyone knew that the São Paulo rebels had
not been defeated. "Everyone knows that they withdrew [from
São Paulo] to give the troops a rest." Multiplying the already
inflated estimates of Juarez Távora, Prestes declared that all the
artillery of the city of São Paulo was still in revolutionary hands,
that the rebels along the Paraná River had twenty million rounds
of ammunition and "five thousand new rifles that had not yet
gone into action," and that they were the masters of southern
Mato Grosso, the richest part of that state, and of much of
Paraná.

Prestes' public estimate of the revolutionary situation in Rio
Grande do Sul was equally inaccurate: Only four of the ten army
garrisons he mentioned in his bulletin were actually under rebel
control. Having thus misinformed the people of Santo Angelo,
Prestes' bulletin ordered the town's reservists to report for duty
and called for civilian volunteers to join the regulars, who would
be marching soon to fight for the revolution. Furthermore, all
automobiles, horses, and wagons in town were to be handed
over immediately to the soldiers of the railroad battalion. Signed
receipts would be given for all requisitions—which would be
charged to the War Ministry. Three days later Prestes' forces
evacuated Santo Angelo—after destroying the railroad bridges
between that town and Ijuí, where the Chimangos were concentrating—and proceeded to São Luís. There the Third Cavalry
Regiment of the federal army was placed under his command by
the lieutenants who had seized control of it on October 29. As he
established his general headquarters at São Luís, Prestes'
strength reached twelve hundred men, about half of whom were
armed civilians.[26]

Two other federal cavalry regiments, the Second and the
Fifth, both of which were stationed on the Uruguay River—at
São Borja and Uruguaiana, respectively—had gone over to the

revolution on October 29. At São Borja the rebel leaders included an outsider, a man who, wearing a cape and a wide gaúcho hat pulled down over his eyes, was escorted into the barracks on the night of October 28 by two lieutenants and introduced to some assembled troops as their new commander, the Hero of Copacabana, Antônio de Siqueira Campos. Now a captain of the revolution, Siqueira was accepted with enthusiasm by the cavalrymen. Once firmly in control of the garrison, he and the other rebel officers sent patrols to arrest the senior officers of the regiment at their homes in São Borja and to occupy the town. At daybreak the rebels began distributing copies of a manifesto, signed by Isidoro and eight other revolutionary "generals," including João Francisco and Liberator Commander Honório Lemes.[27]

This manifesto of the revolutionary high command that was distributed in São Borja on October 29 stated revolutionary aims more explicitly than did the bulletin signed by Prestes and issued that same morning in Santo Angelo. The "maximum principle" of the revolution, according to the manifesto, was "to save the Constitution, modifying it in some secondary points so that professional politicians may not corrupt and demoralize it in its fundamentals." Specifically, the manifesto called for limitations on the power of the president to intervene in the states; reorganization of the judiciary, to free it from the influence of federal and state administrations; the creation of national, unified systems of education, elections, and taxation; compulsory schooling for all children and the encouragement of professional education; making voting compulsory, by secret ballot, for all qualified electors; eliminating wasteful government spending; punishment of grafters; and the energetic and impartial enforcement of the laws of the land. Thus, the generals called for federal control of education, voting, and taxation and at the same time sought to reduce the power of the national executive. Unlike Prestes' bulletin, the manifesto issued at São Borja did not deal with the military situation.[28]

At Uruguaiana, one hundred and seventy kilometers down

the Uruguay River from São Borja, Juarez Távora took command of the Fifth Cavalry Regiment at about two o'clock on the morning of October 29. Like São Borja, Uruguaiana was occupied without resistance by troops from the local garrison in the name of the revolution. Once in control of Uruguaiana, Major Távora dispatched a force of one hundred and fifty men by rail toward Alegrete, one hundred and forty kilometers to the east on the Uruguaiana-Pôrto Alegre line. The federal garrison at Alegrete, a field artillery battalion, was supposed to throw in with the revolution upon the arrival of the rebel troops from Uruguaiana. But the revolutionaries from Uruguaiana did not appear as planned on the morning of October 29. They stopped at the station of Inhanduí, near the trestle over the river of that name, where they received the false information that hordes of armed Chimangos were already pouring into Alegrete. The rebel officer in charge decided that they could not proceed to Alegrete with only one hundred and fifty men, so he and his troops settled into a eucalyptus grove near the trestle, thirty kilometers short of his objective, while a messenger returned to Uruguaiana to ask Távora for reinforcements. Since the rebels themselves had cut the telegraph lines out of Uruguaiana, there was no other way for the detachment to communicate with its base of operations.[29]

While the rebels from Uruguaiana dallied at the trestle and the military conspirators inside Alegrete fretted, the Chimangos there girded themselves for action. The gaúcho "provisionals"— mostly civilian employees of the state government and their retainers, who had served Governor Borges well in the civil war of 1923—were called to arms in Alegrete, to keep an eye on the federals and hold the town pending the arrival of units of the regular state militia, the Brigada Militar. At ten o'clock on the morning of October 29 a federal lieutenant and a provisional lieutenant were sent by rail with twenty men apiece, each contingent occupying a separate car on the same train, to blow the trestle over the Inhanduí River. When they reached the eucalyptus grove, the federals from Alegrete threw in with their comrades from Uruguaiana and together they overpowered and disarmed the provisionals on the train.[30]

The rebel lieutenant from Alegrete, João Alberto Lins de Barros, urged his colleague from Uruguaiana to move immediately on Alegrete. The latter, however, insisted on waiting for the reinforcements he had requested, which arrived late in the afternoon under the personal command of Major Juarez Távora. Shortly thereafter the rebels, with Távora in charge, set out for Alegrete. About dusk a gun carriage and some horsemen came bounding across the pampas toward them: Fifty men from João Alberto's battery had slipped out of town with a 75-millimeter cannon and had come to join the revolution. The rest of the federal troops in Alegrete, faced with the vacillation of the rebels from Uruguaiana, had decided to remain loyal to the government. Including the newly arrived artillerymen, Távora had three hundred rebels outside Alegrete, facing more than five hundred armed men who had declared themselves loyal to the government. He decided to attack anyway, at dawn on October 30.[31]

The loyalists were well dug in on the edge of town, the rising sun at their backs, and had an observation post in the steeple of the Methodist Church, which afforded an excellent view of the rebel positions on the plains to the west. The loyalist observation post, however, was knocked out early in the fighting by a 75-millimeter round personally aimed by Lieutenant João Alberto, whose wife and nine-day-old son were at home not far from the church. But the rebels were unable to overrun the enemy trenches. By nine o'clock, after about four hours of combat, the revolutionaries were running low on ammunition and were beginning to break and run, abandoning automatic weapons and other cumbersome equipment. Their commander, Major Juarez Távora, disappeared in the direction of Uruguaiana. João Alberto's artillery position, which also served as a collection point for rebel wounded, was left virtually defenseless. The lieutenant turned back the first counterattack by firing his cannon at point-blank range into the approaching Chimango cavalry. He decided to withdraw while the enemy was regrouping but could not drive the gun carriage away because one of the horses hitched to it had been killed. He and his gun crew fled on foot. The wounded were left behind, and the Chimangos, following the gaúcho custom, cut their throats.

While the enemy was occupied with the rebel wounded, João Alberto and his men made good their escape down the motor road toward Uruguaiana. They finally stopped to rest at Capivari creek, when they realized that they were no longer being pursued. It was not long before they spotted a cloud of dust approaching from the direction of Alegrete. As it turned out, the dust was raised by the automobile of João Alberto's parish priest. It was rumored in the town that the lieutenant had been killed, and his family had sent the padre to recover the body. The priest, delighted to find his parishioner alive, informed him that his wife and child were safe and congratulated him on his fine marksmanship in knocking down the steeple of the Methodist Church. From the priest João Alberto learned that the Chimangos did not realize the full extent of their victory. They expected the rebels to mount another attack on Alegrete at any minute. The lieutenant concealed from the padre the fact that his comrades were in disorganized retreat. João Alberto told the cleric that he was in charge of an outpost of the rebel main body, which was encamped to his rear, awaiting reinforcements from Uruguaiana and preparing to renew the assault on Alegrete.

When the priest left for Alegrete with this false information, João Alberto began the task of rounding up the survivors of the three-hundred-man force that had been abandoned by Juarez Távora. He found most of the demoralized and leaderless rebels on the railroad near the trestle over the Ibirocaí River. By early evening João Alberto had regrouped into platoons some two hundred rebels, whom he posted along the river, where they set about brewing mate tea and roasting fresh-killed beef. With the troops thus reorganized and occupied, their spirits lifted immensely by the traditional gaúcho fare, João Alberto and six soldiers set out on foot along the railroad to the west in search of transportation to take the men to Uruguaiana. They had to walk fifty kilometers before finding a locomotive, standing at a water tank just outside Uruguaiana. João Alberto went no farther; with this engine he returned immediately to the Ibirocaí trestle. Designating one platoon to guard the bridge, he ordered the other men—all one hundred and fifty of them—to climb aboard the engine or pile into the wood car. At noon on October 31 they rolled into Uruguaiana like conquering heroes. It was indeed a victory for the gallant João Alberto.

Later that day the rebels in Uruguaiana were treated to another stirring sight: the arrival of General Honório Lemes and eight hundred high-spirited gaúcho warriors. Wearing wide-brimmed hats, baggy pants, and red bandanas, laughing and gesticulating as they swayed gracefully in sheepskin-covered saddles, the Liberators rode into Uruguaiana, flourishing a variety of picturesque weapons, including lances, and driving hundreds of spare horses along with them. General Honório and his men had come up from the valley of the Quaraí River, which separates southwestern Rio Grande do Sul from the Republic of Uruguay. In Uruguaiana the gaúcho general assumed command of all revolutionary forces in southern Rio Grande do Sul.[32]

By November 3 the rebels in Rio Grande do Sul were concentrated in three places, all near the Argentine border. In the south, at Uruguaiana, Honório Lemes was in charge of a force that was growing rapidly toward two thousand men, as gaúcho volunteers flocked to the standard of that illustrious chieftain; in the north Luís Carlos Prestes commanded some twelve hundred soldiers and armed civilians based at São Luís; and, in the center, the area around São Borja was held by several hundred revolutionaries under various leaders, including Antônio de Siqueira Campos. Prestes at São Luís was in touch with the rebels at São Borja, but direct contact between the São Borja and Uruguaiana forces was blocked by a loyalist concentration on the Uruguay River at Itaqui. Beyond the three rebel enclaves the loyalists controlled the state. The revolutionaries, however, had reason to believe that, by striking out from their bases, they could rally to their cause several federal army garrisons and vast numbers of civilians. In the second week of November the rebels would launch another round of attacks.

General Honório Lemes was about sixty years old in 1924, although he looked much younger. He had fought in the 1893 revolution as a Maragato and in the 1923 civil war as a Liberator. Between wars he was a cattle drover; he knew every trail, every fold in the pampas, every river crossing in southwestern Rio Grande do Sul and adjacent Uruguay. A man of medium height and build, with skin browned by the sun, he spoke little but was considerate and cordial to all. The general entered Uruguaiana, like the troops he led, wearing gaúcho clothes: *bombachas,* loose-fitting trousers of gray wool; black boots that reached halfway to his knees, with accordianlike folds above the ankles; a checkered cotton shirt; and a high-peaked, wide-brimmed, gray hat. His insignia of rank was a sword that hung from his wide gaúcho belt, along with two revolvers. He wore the red ribbon of the Maragatos and the Liberators—and all gaúcho rebels—around his hatband, the ends falling like streamers from the brim onto his shoulders. Embroidered on the ribbon in white were "suggestive phrases." Honório Lemes was illiterate.[33]

To gaúcho tacticians like Honório, movement was the first principle of warfare. Horses were considered far more important than firepower. As they moved across the land, Honório's men stripped it of horses—to ensure plenty of remounts for themselves and to deprive the enemy. Battles were quick, usually on a small scale, and seldom decisive. Bands of reds (revolutionaries) and whites (loyalists) would charge at each other screaming a war cry borrowed from the Indians who once ruled the pampas, firing carbines and pistols, swinging swords, and aiming lances. Contact would not last long after the collision; one band would gallop away toward its *cavalhada,* or remount pool, change to fresh horses, and ride off to fight another day. Rather than pursue the foe, the gaúchos in possession of the field more likely would busy themselves looting enemy bodies and slitting the throats of those who still stirred. Wars were won by wearing the enemy down in innumerable such clashes over a long period of time. But it was hard to break the spirit of the gaúcho: The pampas armies demonstrated extraordinary powers of recuperation. As long as each man had two or three good horses, a pair of wire cutters, and some kind of weapon, a gaúcho outfit could operate in style and comfort in the rich grazing country of southernmost Brazil.

General Honório was devoted to the comfort and welfare of his troops, who feasted on *churrasco,* spit-roasted beef, as they awaited his orders in Uruguaiana early in November 1924. Churrasco took little time to prepare. An experienced gaúcho could kill a steer with one knife stroke across the jugulars and, in a matter of minutes, skin the animal and peel off the choicest slabs of meat; these were skewered on wooden stakes, sprinkled with salt water, and turned once over an open fire. Moments later the churrasco was done, and the stakes were taken from the fire and, with the meat still attached, driven upright into the ground. Two or three gaúchos would squat around each stake, cutting off large strips of beef with the long knives they all carried in their belts. With one end of the meat in his hand and the other in his teeth, the gaúcho would use the knife in his free hand to slice off a bite-sized portion near his lips. No utensil other than the ubiquitous knife was required for preparing or eating the churrasco.

João Alberto and Juarez Távora, both of whom were from northeastern Brazil, generally enjoyed the churrasco prepared by their gaúcho allies, but they found the cold leftovers hard to stomach at breakfast. Furthermore, they were anxious to get on with the revolution. Honório, however, would not be pushed into hasty action by the Tenentes who had produced the Alegrete disaster. Major Távora was still the nominal commander of the regular contingent at Uruguaiana and General Honório had little respect for him, although he treated him courteously. The general was hardly impressed by a two-day railroad excursion that Távora and 200 men made in the direction of Itaqui; they returned to Uruguaiana on November 4, having been unable to find the rebel force from São Borja that they were supposed to link up with. Honório was perhaps more displeased by Távora's poor horsemanship than by his inept leadership. Hunched over the saddle, his long legs kicking and spurring a mystified horse, this engineer officer from the Northeast was the antithesis of the gaúcho *cavaleiro*.

After nearly a week in Uruguaiana, Honório led the combined revolutionary forces to the banks of the Ibirocaí River, where they camped, about three thousand men and five thousand horses. João Alberto noted that only about one thousand of the men were well-armed; the rest carried revolvers, Winchester rifles, lances, and other weapons that belonged in museums. The regular contingent, some two hundred men under Major Távora, was armed with Mauser rifles and fairly well-trained in marksmanship. The gaúchos were notoriously poor shots. After nearly three days on the river, they made a night march to the high plains of Guaçu Boi, the watershed between the Ibirocaí and Inhanduí rivers. They made camp there at about 3 A.M. on November 9 and were attacked at dawn.

The assault was led by Chimango "General" José Antônio Flores da Cunha, Honório's nemesis in the 1923 war. The Chimangos had tracked the revolutionary column through the night before, which was not hard to do. Honório's men had given no thought to security as they rode along, accompanied by automobiles with headlights burning and followed by creaking wagons loaded with everything from spare lances to mate kettles to drums, trumpets, and accordians. The rebels were caught completely by surprise at Guaçu Boi, but they reacted quickly: Some of the regulars set up firing positions while Honório jumped onto his horse and galloped back and forth, indifferent to the bullets flying about him, shouting "Form a line! Form a line!" But most of the gaúchos who were able to mount up rode off in other directions. João Alberto tried to stop some of the fleeing irregulars and force them into the line, but soon realized his folly: There was nothing he or anyone else could do to prevent the disintegration of Honório's forces. It was not long before the general himself took flight, along with the army regulars. Most, including Honório and Távora, fled south, toward the Uruguayan border, while João Alberto collected several dozen men around him, including a number of wounded, and set out for Uruguaiana, picking up stragglers along the way.

João Alberto and his dejected crew from Guaçu Boi reached Uruguaiana the following day, November 10, just ahead of a loyalist force sent to occupy the town. As soon as they had deposited the wounded at the local hospital, João Alberto and the others crossed the river to Paso de los Libres, Argentina. From there the lieutenant took the first train to Santo Tomé, opposite São Borja. After only one day in Argentina, João Alberto was back in Brazil, at São Borja, where Prestes had arrived from São Luís to help in the campaign to capture Itaqui.[34]

The federal field artillery battalion at the river town of Itaqui was supposed to have revolted on October 29, but its officers vacillated. In the meantime, Oswaldo Aranha, a tough Chimango lawyer and politician, called out the provisionals and made sure that the town would not be handed over to the revolutionaries without a fight. As rebel forces approached from São Borja, Aranha took charge of the defense of Itaqui, ordering trenches dug and barbed wire entanglements erected at the entrances to the town. Aranha's men spread the rumor that they had electrified the barbed wire. On October 30 Siqueira Campos, with about seventy revolutionaries, occupied a position east of Itaqui, while another rebel force from São Borja established itself to the northeast of Itaqui. There they waited in vain for the federal officers in Itaqui to honor their commitment to the revolution. Once convinced that the federal garrison was firmly on the loyalist side, Siqueira requested reinforcements from São Luís so that he could attack Itaqui.[35]

Prestes ordered two companies to proceed from São Luís to Siqueira's position six kilometers east of Itaqui. The first company left immediately by automobile for São Borja, where it embarked on a train for its final destination. Prestes followed the second company as far as São Borja to get a closer look at the situation. When informed of the electrified wire around Itaqui, the cerebral Prestes, it was said, devised a plan to stampede a herd of

cattle against the wire, shorting it out and clearing a path for the
attackers. If Prestes actually conceived such a plan, he never had
a chance to put it into effect. A Chimango column from the east
cut the railroad south of São Borja and routed the force guarding Siqueira's right flank. The second company Prestes sent to
aid Siqueira was unable to get through to him and returned to
São Borja. The Chimangos then concentrated their forces
against Siqueira, who fell back toward the south, having already
sent an urgent plea to Uruguaiana for reinforcements. But it
was now November 12: The rebels to the south had been
trounced at Guaçu Boi and Uruguaiana had been occupied by
the Chimangos, who were beginning to move north on the
railroad to Itaqui.[36]

Siqueira received the bad news from the south on the morning of November 13. Realizing the hopelessness of the situation,
he disbanded his two-hundred-man force. Horses and unit
funds were distributed—each man got 100 milreis—and the
men were told that they were now on their own. Fifty-four of
them, however, insisted on remaining with Siqueira and another
officer who planned to cross the Uruguay River to Argentina.
But when this group reached the riverbank, there were no boats.
Siqueira entered the water with an inflated inner tube around
his chest and swam to the other side, where he found a raft. Several raft crossings were required to bring all fifty-six rebels to the
Argentine side. Siqueira did not remain long in Argentina:
Within a few days he was back in São Borja, on his way to Prestes' headquarters in São Luís.[37]

After the disasters around Itaqui, Prestes put João Alberto in
command of the armed civilians at São Borja and ordered him
to bring them to São Luís, where the captain was concentrating
his forces. Prestes and João Alberto were convinced that nothing
more could be expected of Honório Lemes and the other rebels
in the southern part of the state. But it was too early to write off
General Honório. After the debacle at Guaçu Boi, Honório re-
formed his band in the Caverá hills—the badlands just north of
the Uruguayan border, where his warriors had often gone to
catch their breath in the 1923 war—and was soon riding out

again across the pampas, with Juarez Távora at his side. Eventually, Honório's forces were joined by some federal army engineers, who had marched south from Cachoeira, in the center of the state, where they had revolted on November 9, the day of the battle at Guaçu Boi.[38]

Another belated uprising took place in Rio de Janeiro on November 4, when revolutionary elements in the Brazilian navy seized control of the battleship *São Paulo*. Mutinies on the dreadnaught-class *São Paulo* and her sistership, the *Minas Gerais*, were supposed to have occurred in Rio harbor two weeks earlier, in conjunction with an army revolt in the Federal District. But the army-navy conspiracy was discovered before October 20, most of its leaders were arrested, and the rebels aboard the *São Paulo* had only the fleeting support of the crew of one other warship, a destroyer, when they finally made their move on November 4. On the other hand, the *Minas Gerais* and the other loyal ships in the harbor made no serious effort to engage the *São Paulo* in decisive combat. The *São Paulo,* responding to the commands of mutineers for the second time since her commissioning in 1910, steamed out into the Atlantic Ocean and turned south, toward the coast of Rio Grande do Sul. But there was little that the big ship could do to support the rebels in that state, who were operating more than two hundred kilometers from the coast. The *São Paulo* continued on to Montevideo, where she was turned over to the Uruguayan government on November 12. Some of the rebel sailors managed to make their way from Montevideo to Rio Grande do Sul and join the forces of Honório Lemes. About a dozen of the sailors, however, were caught along the border by Chimangos, who cut their throats.[39]

It had not taken Honório long to bounce back from his defeat at Guaçu Boi. Within a week he and Juarez Távora and eight hundred men were on their way from the Cavera hills to an objective that no gaúcho warrior could resist: the federal cavalry's stud farm at Saicã. One federal lieutenant and a few enlisted men went over to the rebels when they appeared at Saicã before dawn on November 16, but the rest of the stud farm garrison remained loyal to the government. The outnumbered federals, knowing that a contingent of the state militia was on its way to relieve them, parleyed with the rebels, stalling for time. But Honório, suspecting a trick, mounted an assault and forced the surrender of the holdouts, one of whom informed his captors of the impending arrival of the militia force. Honório's men immediately rode out of Saicã, fell upon the 300-man Brigada Column, and sent the Chimangos fleeing back to Rosário. Having disposed of that threat, the revolutionaries returned to the stud farm and rounded up some of the best horses in Brazil. From Saicã the jubilant gaúchos and regulars rode off to São Simão, where they seized another federal army horse farm and added many more fine animals to their cavalhada.[40]

Honório's column was constantly on the move, changing directions frequently, cutting telegraph lines and tearing up railroads, always collecting horses, and sowing fear and confusion in loyalist ranks. Then, on November 23, Honório fought a bloody but indecisive battle with the Second Cavalry Regiment of the state militia north of Livramento. By this time, however, Juarez Távora had had his fill of gaúcho warfare. He and some of the other former federal soldiers pulled out of Honório's column before the fight on November 23 and crossed the border into Uruguay. Most of the ex-federals remained there in exile, but Tavora wandered off to other lands, and after three months on foreign soil, he returned to Foz do Iguaçú by steamboat on the Paraná River. Prestes and the forces he was concentrating at São Luís, what was left of the army rebels in Rio Grande do Sul, would march overland to Foz do Iguaçú. Honório Lemes, deserted by his military allies, would carry on in the extreme south for a few more weeks and then cross the border to exile in Uruguay.[41]

In the meantime, the old Jacobin gaúcho General João Francisco had gone to survey the situation in his native state. He and his personal staff left Foz do Iguaçú soon after learning of the October 29 risings in Rio Grande do Sul from Argentine radio broadcasts; but authorities in Argentina caused them some delay as they crossed the territory of that republic by automobile and rail, and it was not until after the Chimango reoccupation of

Uruguaiana that they reached Paso de los Libres, opposite that Brazilian town. There João Francisco listened to firsthand reports of Honório Lemes' rout at Guaçu Boi and decided that the old Maragato and his men were no longer a factor in the revolutionary struggle. The only significant rebel forces in Rio Grande do Sul, João Francisco concluded, were those concentrated in São Luís under the command of young Captain Prestes. João Francisco promoted Prestes to colonel on November 15 and then returned to Foz do Iguaçú, via Monte Caseros, Argentina.[42]

By November 18 Colonel Prestes' forces to the north and east of São Luís had fallen back to positions along the Ijuí and Ijuizinho rivers, giving up Santo Angelo. South of São Luís the rebels had their main line of defense along the Piratini River, although they retained an outpost at São Borja and tenuous control of the motor road to that river town. This area was held by some three thousand men, a revolutionary force equal, in numbers at least, to that on the Paraná River. For more than a month after receiving his colonel's commission from the high command on the Paraná, Prestes made no move to link up with the rebels in the north. His position was relatively secure in São Luís, which became the unofficial revolutionary capital of Rio Grande do Sul. Seven issues of a revolutionary weekly, *O Libertador,* were published there under the editorship of Dr. José Damião Pinheiro Machado. It was during this period that the number-one Liberator, Dr. Assis Brasil, finally accepted Isidoro's invitation to become Civilian Chief of the revolution.[43] But instead of going to Isidoro's headquarters on the Paraná or to Prestes' stronghold at São Luís to set up a revolutionary government on Brazilian soil, the prudent Dr. Assis remained in exile in Uruguay.

From São Luís Prestes wrote to various Liberator chieftains who were lying low in west-central Rio Grande do Sul, urging them to take an active part in the revolution. With help from the Liberators, the young colonel hoped to cut the São Paulo–Pôrto Alegre railroad east of São Luís. He led the bulk of his forces in this direction early in December, after a detachment of three hundred men had occupied Santiago and secured his southern flank. On December 3 Prestes attacked the railroad town of Tupanciretã, which was defended by several units of gaúcho provisionals and two federal infantry battalions. Prestes hoped that the federal troops would defect to the revolution upon the arrival of his forces. The federals remained loyal, however, keeping the opposing forces fairly evenly matched at more than two thousand men each, although the loyalists had the advantage of prepared defense positions. At five o'clock in the morning, João Alberto's men, with gaúcho irregulars in the van, initiated the action with an assault on the loyalist line. The rebel vanguard overran the enemy positions and pushed into the town of Tupanciretã, but was soon ejected by a vigorous loyalist counterattack. Not long afterward, when a rebel attempt to turn the loyalist right flank failed, the battle lines were stabilized along a four-kilometer front. Small-arms fire was exchanged for eleven hours, until Prestes' forces withdrew toward São Luís, leaving fifteen dead and some wounded on the field. The loyalists, although they had lost only two dead and seventeen wounded, did not pursue.[44]

Prestes' retreat to São Luís was orderly. The eleven-hour fight at Tupanciretã was unusual in an area where combat traditionally lasted only a few minutes, followed by the disbanding of the disadvantaged force. Although Prestes had managed to keep his troops together, his position was precarious after his defeat at Tupanciretã. When the colonel returned to São Luís, he was greeted by an emissary from Isidoro's headquarters who suggested that the time had come for Prestes to leave Rio Grande do Sul and march north across the state of Santa Catarina to link up with the rebels in Paraná. On December 8 Prestes wrote Isidoro that he would soon be crossing into Santa Catarina.[45] It would be nearly three more weeks, however, before the march actually got under way.

The gaúcho Liberators among Prestes' troops were not happy with the colonel's decision to abandon their state. Rather than follow him onto the unfamiliar grounds of Santa Catarina and Paraná, to fight a war that no longer seemed to be theirs, many gaúchos deserted Prestes. No more than two thousand men were left to form the column that the colonel finally led out of São Luís on December 27, 1924. The column skirted Santo Angelo, skirmishing with loyalist forces to the south and east of that town, and on New Year's Day 1925, forced a crossing of the railroad bridge over the Ijuí River. Continuing on a northeasterly course, the revolutionaries ran into a large loyalist force near Palmeiras early on January 3; the column lost about forty men killed and one hundred wounded, some to artillery fire, in the all-day engagement that followed. Late in the afternoon the rebels withdrew to the northwest, into the forests of northwestern Rio Grande do Sul and western Santa Catarina. On January 25 the Prestes Column entered the state of Santa Catarina.[46]

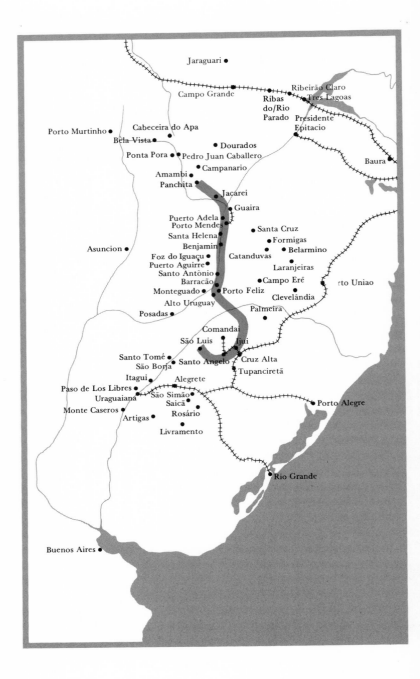

The Revolution versus Rondon

III General Cândido Mariano da Silva Rondon was named commander in chief of all loyalist forces operating in Santa Catarina and Paraná on September 25, 1924. For the first time in his military career, which began with his enlistment in the Imperial Army in 1881, Rondon, who enjoyed an international reputation as a peacemaker, was going to war. The general was a native of Mato Grosso and a descendant of some of South America's fiercest warriors: the *bandeirantes* of seventeenth-century São Paulo, who scoured the Brazilian hinterland in search of gold and Indian slaves, and the Guaicuru Indians, who rode out of the Paraguayan Chaco toward the end of the eighteenth century to plunder convoys along the trade route that the bandeirantes established between São Paulo and the mines of Mato Grosso. As the gold and diamonds played out, the bandeirantes in Mato Grosso turned to cattle ranching and the Guaicurus became somewhat less truculent, eventually settling down on lands granted them by the Brazilian government. The bandeirantes intermarried freely with the Indians in Mato Grosso, as they had done in São Paulo, and General Rondon's Indian ancestors included not only freebooters from the Chaco but also red men indigenous to the region of his birth.[1]

Rondon was born on a ranch on the edge of the Pantanal, the vast floodplain south of Cuiabá, the capital of Mato Grosso. The future general's family had little money, although they owned thousands of hectares of land, which was cheap in Mato Grosso. Cândido, an orphan at the age of two, went to live with relatives in Cuiabá, where he could attend school. Upon graduation from Normal School at the age of sixteen, he enlisted in the army, hoping to win an in-service appointment to the Military Academy in Rio. The appointment was delayed, because of his inferior secondary education, and it was not until 1883 that he entered the academy, where he showed himself to be a bright but headstrong youth, whose Indian stoicism was sometimes compromised by a flood of uncontrollable tears. His body was weak and he lost an entire year at the academy because of an intestinal illness; he was so sick that his classmates despaired of his recovery and took up a collection to pay for his funeral. But Rondon survived and, adhering to a rigorous self-imposed regime that proscribed alcohol and included strenuous exercise, went on to achieve an extraordinary level of physical strength and endurance.[2]

It was at the Military Academy that Rondon came under the influence of Major Benjamin Constant Botelho de Magalhães, a mathematics professor and fervent exponent of the positivism of Auguste Comte. Benjamin Constant, like the master, was devoted to "order and progress." Progress—the material and spiritual betterment of all people, "Humanity"—was impossible without order; by serving order, by obeying the scientific laws of society, one served Humanity. The laws of society were constantly at work, improving the condition of Humanity, raising man's consciousness through theological and rationalist phases to the final scientific, or positivist, state—broadening his areas of concern to encompass family, tribe, nation, and, finally, the whole human race. Men's lives were shaped by the societies in which they lived, not by God or by bloodlines. The most backward societies were those in which the positions of individuals were dictated by revealed religion, heredity, or race. Such discrimination could not be eliminated by force—by revolution—but would disappear as men voluntarily accepted the laws of "sociology" (a science devised by Comte) and adopted attitudes in harmony with them. No desirable and permanent social improvement was possible without an appropriate prior moral transformation.

If ever a nation violated social laws, Professor Benjamin Constant preached to the cadets in the 1880's, it was Brazil, with its hereditary monarchy, established Roman Catholic Church, and legalized black slavery. The last institution was by far the most abominable, and the professor and his students, including the *mestizo* Rondon, devoted themselves to antislavery agitation and helped make abolitionism a great popular crusade. Brazilian city dwellers offered refuge to runaway slaves, the army refused to enforce fugitive slave laws, and black men began abandoning the plantations en masse. At the height of the crisis, the emperor departed for a visit to Europe, leaving his daughter, the princess regent, to sanction the Emancipation Act of 1888, which recognized a *fait accompli*. This event proved, to the positivists, that the Brazilian people had experienced a great moral awakening; the monarchy could not long stand in defiance of the evolving social order. Benjamin Constant and his military colleagues, after some soul-searching, gave it a slight shove to hasten its fall.[3] They were vindicated when the whole rickety structure collapsed, in a matter of hours, on November 15, 1889, without loss of life or property. A republic (the only form of government compatible with sociological truth) was proclaimed; separation of church and state was decreed; and a new national flag was adopted, emblazoned with the positivist motto, "Order and Progress."

But the new republic fell far short of the positivist ideal. Comte envisioned a *sociocracy*, a republic governed by a hierarchy of virtuous men who had demonstrated superior skill in the management of industry. Democracy, considered a perversion of the science of mathematics, had no place in the Comtian system. In a sociocracy, the government, devoted through moral conviction to social order and the welfare of Humanity, would intervene in the economy whenever necessary to protect the weak, to maintain an integrated society, and to ensure the participation of the workers in the benefits of industrial development.

Education was to be free and compulsory for all children and was to promote social order—create a "regime of opinion" that would make compulsion unnecessary in adult life. But Comte's sociocracy could not be imposed by revolutionary force; it would evolve gradually as the ruling classes accepted the precepts of the Religion of Humanity. Recognizing that the religious impulse would not disappear with the collapse of supernatural religion, Comte created his own church to harness this impulse for the advancement of Humanity and social order. The philosopher organized his church along the lines of Roman Catholicism, which, though he rejected its unscientific doctrine, he admired: Its universalism and its hierarchical principles, which absolutely excluded heredity, approached the positivist ideal. An Apostolate of the Religion of Humanity—with its hierarchy, sacraments, and saints (Julius Caesar, Shakespeare, Descartes, *et al.*)—was organized in Brazil in the 1880's, and Cândido Rondon became one of its most devout communicants.

Lieutenant Rondon was with the army engineers in Mato Grosso, constructing a telegraph line, when his mentor, Benjamin Constant, "The Founder of the Republic," died in Rio in 1891. During most of the period from 1890 to 1919 Rondon labored in the wilderness, far from the scenes of the naval mutinies, the Maragato revolt, and the uprisings of "positivist" Military Academy cadets—who, fired by Comte's elitist and authoritarian precepts, ignored the master's injunction against revolution. Rondon remained an "orthodox" positivist, convinced that physical force could produce no social good. In fact, this mestizo officer so cherished the humanitarian and integrationist teachings of his religion that he was prepared to accept martyrdom rather than violate them. In dealing with the Indians who occupied the areas across which he was ordered to build telegraph lines, from eastern Mato Grosso to western Amazonas, Rondon's faith was put to some severe tests.[4]

Rondon's engineers would begin no construction without first winning the friendship and voluntary cooperation of the local Indians. "We will die, if necessary," Rondon told his men, "but never kill." Nor were they to overstep any bounds set for them by the indigenous inhabitants of the areas into which the engineers ventured. Rondon's standing orders were to "retreat, flee, if that is what the Indians want, for to flee from them is not cowardice." [5] Eventually Rondon's persistent kindness and patience would win over the savages, who sometimes could be persuaded to settle in permanent villages along the telegraph line to guard it. Once he had "pacified" the Indians, Rondon did what he could to prepare them for eventual integration into Brazilian society. Realizing that this would take time, and fully aware of the greed and duplicity of the white man, the mestizo officer urged the federal government to protect his converts during the period of tutelage. He was gratified when President Nilo Peçanha, himself a man of Negro blood, set up the Indian Protection Service in 1910 with Rondon as director. [6]

In 1914 Rondon, now a colonel, was called away from his pacification work to command a joint Brazilian–United States scientific expedition to western Brazil. The objectives of the expedition included mapping part of the watershed between the Paraguay and Amazon river systems and collecting geological and zoological specimens. The head of the American contingent, Colonel Theodore Roosevelt, was, like Rondon, a firm believer in order and progress. The two became fast friends and mutual admirers during their four months together in the Brazilian wilderness. Roosevelt was deeply impressed by the courage and competence that Rondon demonstrated on this expedition, and by his accounts of previous treks into the wilds when he was out of touch with civilization for as long as a year at a time, enduring hunger, sickness, and all kinds of hardship, including the bite of a piranha, which took off one of his toes. While Roosevelt was acquiring a healthy respect for the virile mestizo peoples of Mato Grosso and Paraguay, Rondon was impressed by the American statesman's great intellectual range and his lack of prejudice. He was pleased to learn that his friend was the one American president who had dined with a black man at the White House. [7]

After the expedition with Roosevelt, Rondon resumed his pacification and telegraph construction work. He was finally recalled from the backlands in 1919, when he was named chief of army engineers, with the rank of brigadier general. His dog,

Caí, a faithful companion on many perilous journeys, died, filling him with sadness, shortly before he left the wilderness for his new post in Rio. Nevertheless, he found happiness in the city, as he strengthened his ties with his family, a wife and seven children, who had seen little of him over the years, but to whom he was deeply devoted, as his religion required. But, as chief of engineers, he still traveled, inspecting barracks construction sites in various parts of the country and touring the Northeast to check on the many drought-control projects undertaken in that region by the federal government under President Epitácio Pessoa. Rondon became a favorite of Epitácio's war minister, João Pandiá Calógeras, whose efforts to modernize and professionalize the army the general ardently supported. Rondon—who spoke some French, the language in which he and Roosevelt communicated—was highly regarded also by General Maurice Gustave Gamelin, head of the French Military Mission, who selected him to command the troops in the Brazilian army's first field maneuvers in Rio Grande do Sul early in 1922.[8]

By this time the election controversy was raging and General Rondon could not avoid being touched by it. His friendship for Nilo Peçanha, who had fought for the creation of the Indian Protection Service, was well known. Yet the Bernardes camp had enough faith in his fair-mindedness to suggest him as judge in the case of the "insulting letter" allegedly written by their candidate. The general declined any role in the matter, citing his positivist convictions, which compelled him to remain aloof "from all matters and all questions that exist and flourish solely because of the electoral processes . . . of democratic politics." [9] Not long after stating this position Rondon left for the maneuvers in Rio Grande do Sul.

Rondon's disdain for democratic politics was shared by the Comtian governor of Rio Grande do Sul, Borges de Medeiros—whose participation in the electoral process, perfunctory as it was, barred him from membership in the Positivist Church. After his candidate, Nilo Peçanha, had been defeated in the presidential election of 1922, Borges had to decide whether or not to join an armed movement to prevent the inauguration of Artur Bernardes. Borges seemed inclined to support a revolution—if Rondon would lead it. When the general was in Pôrto Alegre he was summoned to Borges' office where, as it turned out, the governor was meeting with several other Nilo supporters. When a revolutionary scheme was put forward, Rondon spoke out, addressing himself to the governor:

"Your Excellency knows, for the very reason that we both are inspired by the same doctrine, that we are not permitted to take part in subversive movements." Rondon was inflexible.

"You see clearly, gentlemen," Borges remarked to the others, "that the revolution has no chief." [10]

Neither Borges nor Rondon supported the Tenente revolt of July 5, 1922, and the Chimango was quick to condemn the revolutionary effort in public after it failed, making a positivistic appeal for social order. Rondon's attitude, known to many in the army, was given public recognition by a resolution of thanks passed by the federal congress, which displeased the general considerably. Prior to the revolt he had admonished a rebellion-bent young captain, a member of the Positivist Church, asking, "Have they not taught us that the most retrograde government is preferable to the most progressive revolution?" [11]

Rondon's position on social order was similar to that of Jackson de Figueiredo, a brilliant young polemicist who had been converted to Catholicism from rationalism. "The worst legality," Figueiredo maintained, "is still better than the best revolution." The revolt in São Paulo in July 1924 brought Figueiredo out into a public square in Rio to proclaim a "new creed" that would redeem Brazil: "We believe in the works of the spirit; we believe in discipline; in the reformation of consciences; in the reorientation toward patience and work. Death to the Revolution!" [12]

General Rondon, chief of army engineers, did not escape the polemicist's notice. In an article published on September 20, 1924, Figueiredo praised the general for resisting the entreaties of rabble-rousers, who never ceased trying to exploit his great prestige for their despicable purposes. Rondon was even to be commended for his fealty to the "serious and grave" doctrine of Auguste Comte, which so many of his coreligionists perversely cited as justification for their rebellious behavior. Comte, despite his errors, fully realized the necessity of "safeguarding the spirit of order, which the Catholic Church represents in all the Western World." [13] In the week following the appearance of Figueiredo's article, President Artur Bernardes, a devout Catholic and admirer of the thirty-three-year-old polemicist, approved the appointment of Major General Rondon, positivist and friend of the late Nilo Peçanha, as commander of all forces in operations against the rebels in Paraná and Santa Catarina. [14]

The thought of going to war, especially to fight other Brazilians, greatly disturbed Rondon, but he could not ignore his duty to defend the constituted authority. Reluctantly he accepted the appointment on September 25, 1924, deciding that he would go into combat as a peacemaker, to save his country from revolutionary chaos. [15] Rondon no doubt realized that the ineptitude of those previously in charge of the military campaign against the rebels had contributed significantly to the state of agitation and disorder that had spread over much of Brazil. General Eduardo Sócrates' prolonged and artless siege of São Paulo had caused unjustifiably heavy losses of noncombatant lives and property. While General Sócrates' federal troops included many rebel sympathizers, as did the contingents of the São Paulo state militia under his command, and could not be relied upon to engage the enemy in close combat, this was no excuse for the long-range artillery pounding of São Paulo, which turned many prominent Paulistanos against the government and did not force the revolutionaries to surrender. The rebels evacuated the city when General Azevedo Costa's column, composed mainly of volunteer units raised in the São Paulo countryside, threatened to cut off their avenue of retreat to the west. But Azevedo Costa's volunteers, mustered into federal service as Patriotic Battalions, performed miserably in their "pursuit" of the enemy to the Paraná River. Not until the rebels attempted to cross the river into Rondon's state of Mato Grosso did they face determined opposition. It was a unit of one hundred and eighty Mato Grosso volunteers that on September 24 inflicted on the rebels their greatest loss to that date, capturing two hundred and twenty of them.

From the campaign thus far Rondon could conclude that his federal troops were unsuited for close combat with the enemy but were capable of providing artillery and logistical support.

The São Paulo Patriotic Battalions were worthless: If they would not fight on their home ground, nothing could be expected of them in the forests of Paraná and Santa Catarina. The Mato Grosso volunteers were excellent, but they were few—theirs was a vast but underpopulated state—and needed at home, to keep watch on the state's federal garrisons, to which unruly elements of the army were traditionally assigned as a form of punishment. Furthermore, even the best volunteer units lacked the training and discipline necessary for the kind of large-scale military operations Rondon was about to undertake. Rondon preferred to draw his frontline troops from state militias, like that of his friend Borges de Medeiros, the governor of Rio Grande do Sul.[16]

Early in October 1924, while Rondon was setting up his general headquarters at Ponta Grossa, in the uplands of Paraná, the rebels, driving eastward from the Paraná River, seized a foothold on the western end of the same plateau, in the piney woods around Catanduvas. During the first half of October the rebels pushed on to the Medeiros hills, some fifty kilometers east of Catanduvas, where they were finally halted by a Patriotic Battalion, which had been posted in the area in September. The volunteers were dug in along a line facing the hamlet of Belarmino, where the rebels had paused to gather strength before resuming their offensive. In the meantime, Rondon committed his operational force to action in two main columns: one to move directly west from Ponta Grossa to fix the enemy at Belarmino, while the other swept up from the Santa Catarina border in the south to roll up the enemy's exposed right flank. A smaller detachment was sent to probe the rebel left flank, along the formidable Piquiri River. Rondon had up to twelve thousand men under his command, while rebel forces in Paraná in October hardly numbered three thousand.[17] The uprisings in Rio Grande do Sul at the end of the month produced several thousand more armed revolutionaries, but it would be nearly three months before any of them entered General Rondon's Paraná–Santa Catarina theater of operations.

It was not until November 15 that the rebels at Belarmino launched their long-anticipated assault on the loyalist line in the

Medeiros hills. By this time the loyalist volunteers had been reinforced by advance units of Rondon's column from Ponta Grossa,
and after a day and a night of fighting, the rebels were thrown
back to Belarmino. On November 23 the loyalists began a series
of attacks against the five hundred revolutionaries at Belarmino.
An airfield was constructed at Laranjeiras, fifty kilometers to the
east, and a Spad and a Breguet took off on December 6 to bomb
and drop leaflets on the rebels. The leaflets, signed by General
Rondon, urged the rebel soldiers to give up their "inglorious
struggle"; the general realized that they had been misled by
their chiefs and pledged that enemy soldiers who surrendered
would "not only be guaranteed their lives, but also treated as
brothers."[18] He did not promise that they would escape punishment; President Bernardes was dead-set against amnesty and his
minister of war had ordered that all common soldiers who took
part in the revolution were to be discharged from the army "for
moral incapacity" and turned over to the civil authorities to be
judged as criminals.[19] Nevertheless, forty-two rebel soldiers presented themselves at the loyalist lines to surrender, as their
comrades, now threatened by Rondon's column from Santa Catarina, withdrew toward Catanduvas on December 26.[20]

In the meantime, Rondon had moved his general headquarters to Laranjeiras, where the airfield was. The planes, however, were no longer flying: The Spad had smashed its landing
gear on the improvised runway, and after only one mission, the
air war was suspended. The rainy season had set in and the
runway, like the roads of upland Paraná, was turning into a
morass of red mud. Although movement was difficult, Rondon
was able to maintain communications with most of his units by
field telephone. Nevertheless, as his two columns closed in on
the rebels at Catanduvas, he decided to move his headquarters
closer to the action, to Formigas. The best house in that village
of pine cabins was prepared for the general, who was expected
to move in on January 20, 1925.[21]

In the meantime, Miguel Costa, now a revolutionary general,
had left his headquarters at Santa Cruz to meet with the other
principal rebel officers in his sector in a council of war at Catanduvas. There it was decided to strike at Rondon's supply lines by

infiltrating raiders through the forests along the Piquirí River. The raiding party would consist of two hundred and eighty men, including some Paraguayan recruits, under the command of the macabre João Cabanas, a former lieutenant from Miguel's São Paulo state cavalry regiment. Cabanas' "Column of Death" successfully infiltrated to the loyalist rear and learned, from interrogation of local residents, of Rondon's impending arrival at Formigas. The raiders entered that village, walking past sleeping sentries, just before dawn on January 21. The rebels quickly seized control of the loyalist base, including the commanding general's residence. They were disappointed to find that Rondon was not there: His arrival in Formigas had been delayed when his automobile broke down the day before on the muddy road from Laranjeiras.[22]

Cabanas' men held Formigas all day on January 21, causing the loyalists to pull troops out of the line at Catanduvas to deal with the threat to their rear. When the rebels at Catanduvas learned of this movement, they launched an attack on the weakened loyalist line, pushing the government forces back about four kilometers before the front was stabilized late in the day. Cabanas made good his escape from Formigas that night, but the next day he found a company of the Santa Catarina state militia blocking the forest trail he intended to take back to Miguel Costa's base at Santa Cruz. After suffering heavy casualties in a futile attempt to dislodge the militiamen, Cabanas' Column of Death veered off into the forest and spent the next ten days hacking out a new trail to Santa Cruz.[23]

Cabanas' raid on Formigas and the rebel attack at Catanduvas, both on January 21, 1925, were the last revolutionary offensive efforts in that area to achieve any success. While the rebels made some ineffective sallies against the enemy in February, their main concern was to defend Catanduvas, on the high ground between the Iguaçu and Piquiri rivers, the key to their base area on the Paraná River. Their actions on January 21 had won them time—persuaded Rondon to suspend his offensive while he strengthened his frontline positions and improved his rear-area security. But the rebels in Paraná would not be able to hold out long after Rondon resumed his attacks unless they received reinforcements. The only possible reinforcements were the rebels from Rio Grande do Sul, the Prestes Column, who, by the end of January, were moving north across the panhandle of western Santa Catarina.

On January 9, 1925, the Prestes Column arrived at the Uruguay River, which forms the boundary between the Brazilian states of Rio Grande do Sul and Santa Catarina before turning south to divide Brazil from Argentina. The government force that blocked the rebels' way near Palmeiras on January 3 had deflected the column to the west, so that Prestes reached the river at Alto Uruguai, across from Monteagudo, Argentina, rather than at some point on the Santa Catarina border. The column was now deep in one of South America's thickest forests, a locale entirely uncongenial to the gaúchos who had followed Prestes from São Luís. The narrow forest trails—soaked by the torrential rains of the season and cut to ribbons of mud by the hooves of some four thousand rebel horses—were depressingly confining. There was little pasture for the horses, and cattle were few and wild. The meager results of cow hunts in the dense woods were reflected in the gaúcho churrascos: Whereas thirty men would feast on one cow on the pampas, in the forests of the Uruguay one hundred and twenty had to share a single animal. When the column reached the Uruguay River at Alto Uruguai, nearly half of its two thousand officers and men gave up the struggle and crossed on the ferry to the Argentine side, taking their arms and ammunition with them.[24]

Powerless to halt this mass desertion, Prestes marched what was left of his column eastward along the river, away from the temptation of the international border, in search of a place to cross into Santa Catarina. For two weeks the rebels struggled along the left bank of the Uruguay, crossing its tributaries in canoes, swimming some of their exhausted horses, abandoning others. The Chimango troops of Colonel Claudino Nunes Pereira, who had fought the rebels on January 3, took up the pursuit of the column from Alto Uruguai, skirmishing with its rearguard on several occasions after January 13. Prestes decided to cross the Uruguay near the mouth of the Rio das Antas, on the opposite side, where there was a settlement of German immigrants. At the German colony, Pôrto Feliz, there were a number of canoes, a motor launch, and a boat large enough for carrying horses. The last was essential, for the Uruguay was far too wide—more than half a kilometer—for the animals to swim. João Alberto, commanding the column's vanguard, detached fifty men to slip across the river in canoes and fall upon Pôrto Feliz before its inhabitants could flee upriver in their boats.[25]

The Germans of Pôrto Feliz, however, were aware of the approach of the column and had no intention of leaving and inviting the rebels to pillage their homes and the farms they had carved out of the wilderness. A delegation from the colony crossed the river to parley with the commander of the advancing rebels. They were delighted to find João Alberto, a regular officer, whom they felt they could trust to obey the rules of war and treat their settlement as an open city. In halting Portuguese the Germans told João Alberto that they would not resist his occupation of their village and that they would peaceably give up the supplies and equipment he needed. As an officer and a gentleman, he would, of course, be reasonable in his requisitions and keep a close watch on his troops to prevent looting. João Alberto was invited to stay in the home of the delegation's spokesman, and on January 24 the column's vanguard occupied Pôrto Feliz.[26]

In the meantime, Colonel Claudino's Chimango militia battalion was increasing its pressure on the column's rear. On the day that Prestes' vanguard occupied Pôrto Feliz, the loyalists surprised the rebel rearguard and killed its commander, Mário Portela Fagundes, and about a dozen of his officers and men. The death of the rearguard commander was a severe personal blow to Prestes, who had served with him in the railroad battalion at Santo Angelo. Lieutenant Portela had been Captain Prestes' principal accomplice in subverting the battalion and his right hand in the military operations beginning with the Santo Angelo uprising. Portela and the others were killed on January 24 on the west bank of the Pardo River. They were drinking mate when they were attacked—the last contingent of the column rearguard, waiting for canoes to return from the east bank to take them across. Their fierce resistance won valuable time for the column by making Claudino's Chimangos more wary of their quarry, thus slowing down their pursuit. The loyalists buried Portela under a tree, on the trunk of which they carved: "Here lies Major Portela: He died like a hero, although in the service of an unworthy cause." [27]

The rebels needed more time than they had expected to cross to Pôrto Feliz, because the only boat they found that was capable of transporting horses was in bad condition and could take only three animals per trip. A raft, constructed by Prestes' soldiers, was soon put into service ferrying horses; nevertheless, the crossing still took an entire week to complete. By January 31 they were all on the Santa Catarina side: about one thousand men, perhaps an equal number of horses, and no more than fifty women. Colonel Prestes had ordered that the camp followers be left on the south side of the river, but this order was disobeyed.[28] Prestes, recognizing the limits of his authority, made no further effort to expel the women who, for their part, tried to stay out of the ascetic colonel's sight.

While the main body of the column was crossing to Pôrto Feliz, Claudino's Chimangos were closing in on Prestes' outposts south of the river. A rebel patrol sent along the north bank of the river made contact with another loyalist force east of Pôrto Feliz.[29] There was no sign of enemy activity to the north, along a seldom-used trail that cut through the wilderness of western Santa Catarina to the village of Barracão, in the southwestern corner of Paraná.

Barracão was at the western extremity of a settled area along the Paraná–Santa Catarina border known as the "Contestado," the Disputed Zone. The area had been claimed by both Argentina and Brazil until 1895 when the arbiter of the dispute, President Grover Cleveland of the United States, awarded it to Brazil. The publicity given to the Contestado at the time of the arbitration, and the Brazilian government's desire to secure the area against any future Argentine claim, led to the founding of the town of Clevelândia and the agricultural development of its environs. Prestes decided to approach the Contestado from the west, to march up the wilderness trail from Pôrto Feliz to Barracão, a distance of about one hundred and thirty kilometers. He sent his lead elements along the trail to Barracão before the rest of the column had completed the river crossing. For most of the way the trail ran parallel to the unsettled Argentine border, twenty to thirty kilometers to the west.

The march to Barracão was an arduous one, rations were short, and there was much grumbling among the troops. The column was divided into three more or less equal "detachments," which rotated in the positions of vanguard, center, and rearguard. The vanguard had to contend with the numerous branches and trees that had fallen across the trail, removing them or hacking out detours around them, while the rearguard had to pass through the mire created by all those who had gone before. Prestes, as commander, was permanently attached to the center, but he was constantly circulating back and forth through the column. The men saw a lot of him, but they were not always favorably impressed. This engineer officer seemed grotesquely small, swallowed up in his military saddle with its clutter of saddlebags stuffed with maps. A full, dark beard that he had begun growing in São Luís made him look older—without it he had appeared to be about twenty-one—but the whiskers could not modulate his "metallic voice."[30] There were those who would not follow this strange prophet much longer. Talk of quitting was heard most often in the Third Detachment, composed primarily of federal cavalrymen from São Borja, commanded by João Pedro Gay.

The trail improved as it ascended from the dense lowland forests of the Uruguay River valley into the Serra do Capanema, the Hills of Barren Woods. The hills were misnamed, because there was no lack of game in the area—although some early Guarani-speaking explorer might well have had less luck hunting here than in the Serra da Fartura, the Hills of Plenty, immediately to the east. The men of the Prestes Column, however, were little inclined to pursue the deer, tapirs, and peccaries of the upland woods. After less than a week on the trail from Pôrto Feliz, most of the rebels were on foot, their horses worn out. Occasionally they would chop down a mammoth araucarian pine to get at its cones and pluck the seeds that they roasted and ate with relish.[31] But otherwise they saved their energy for the march, dreaming of what lay just a few days ahead: the rich farms and ranches of the Contestado or, perhaps, Argentina, where a rifle could usually be traded for a few good meals.

Prestes could not allow his men to enter the border town of Barracão in this state of mind. He halted his vanguard about a day's march short of the intersection of the trail from Pôrto Feliz and the Barracão-Clevelândia road. As the column closed up and the three detachments came together, near Flores creek, the colonel set about to restore order and discipline. The situation in the Third Detachment seemed hopeless. Major João Pedro Gay, formerly a lieutenant of the federal garrison at São Borja, was intent on deserting to Argentina and taking his men with him. On February 3 Prestes tried to salvage the Third Detachment by naming Antônio de Siqueira Campos as its commander, replacing Gay. Despite the great prestige of the Hero of Copacabana, who had served intermittently with the São Borja troops since October 29, fewer than half the men of the detachment would accept his leadership. The other two detachments, however, were fairly well under the control of leaders loyal to Prestes: João Alberto in the Second and Oswaldo Cordeiro de Farias, who replaced the deceased Mário Portela Fagundes, in the First. Prestes, Siqueira, João Alberto, and Cordeiro could not prevent Gay and most of his men from quitting, but at least they were able to disarm them and save their weapons and ammunition for the revolution. The desertion of Gay and his followers reduced the strength of the Prestes Column to about eight hundred men.[32]

Brazilian military tradition was no help to Prestes in disciplining his troops. There were no institutions to sustain his authority over men whom he himself had incited to mutiny. This was true throughout the revolutionary "army": Command did not exist. Leadership was exerted through personal example, persuasive argument, or appeals to friendship. This principle was clearly perceived by Isidoro who, after the first week of the São Paulo revolt, practically stopped giving orders. He suggested to his principal "subordinates" the courses of action he thought most appropriate; it was up to them, collectively or individually, to decide whether or not to accept his recommendations. Isidoro did not order Prestes to march north; he simply suggested that it might be a good idea for him to do so.[33] And Prestes could not effectively order his men to march; to move them he had to depend on a network of personal relationships.

It was not until February 1925 that Prestes succeeded in establishing some effective lines of control, and by that time four-fifths of the troops he had "commanded" at São Luís had slipped away from him. João Alberto was completely loyal to Prestes and firmly in charge of the Second Detachment, the nucleus of which he had led since November.[34] Siqueira Campos, who had admired Prestes since their days at the Military Academy, was accepted by the remnants of the Second Detachment in February. The First Detachment was composed primarily of men from Prestes' old railroad battalion, who were devoted to the column commander and had little trouble in accepting the man he appointed to lead them: Oswaldo Cordeiro de Farias. At twenty-three Cordeiro was the youngest of the detachment leaders; like the other two, he was an artillery officer. In October 1924 he was stationed with the federal garrison in Santa Maria, Rio Grande do Sul, but managed to be on hand in Uruguaiana when the revolution broke out. He took part in the operations in the southern part of the state and then, in December, made his way to Prestes' headquarters in São Luís. On February 2, 1925, he assumed command of the First Detachment.[35] Cordeiro, like Siqueira and João Alberto, recognized Prestes as his leader, but, also like the others, expected to be consulted on all important decisions. Prestes realized that his authority depended on the consent of the detachment heads. The leadership of the Prestes Column was, in fact, collective.

While Prestes was revamping the leadership structure of his column, another revolutionary force approached Barracão from the north; it passed through that village on February 5, taking the road to Clevelândia. At the intersection with the Pôrto Feliz trail, just outside Barracão, the rebel chief, Fidêncio de Melo, sent a patrol south while he continued on to the east with the rest of his men, who numbered somewhat more than one hundred. At Flores creek Fidêncio's scouts encountered their fellow

revolutionaries from Rio Grande do Sul. The Prestes Column
then resumed the march to the north and, on February 7,
reached the Barracão-Clevelândia road. The column halted
there while Prestes and an aide rode off in the direction of Clevelândia to see Fidêncio, whom they overtook at Campo Erê,
about sixty kilometers down the road.[36]

"Colonel" Fidêncio de Melo was a civilian politician from Rio
Grande do Sul who had connections in the Contestado. He was
on his way, at the urging of Isidoro, to make a demonstration of
rebel force in the Clevelândia area, which had been left virtually
defenseless since December, when most loyalist forces had left
the Contestado with Rondon's Santa Catarina column as it drove
north on the rebel positions at Belarmino. This threat from the
south helped persuade the revolutionaries to fall back to Catanduvas, where their right flank was more secure. In January the
rebel chiefs in Paraná agreed to try to hold Catanduvas against
Rondon's two columns, while simultaneously striking at the loyalist supply lines—through the Piquiri forest in the north and the
Contestado in the south.

The northern operation was entrusted to João Cabanas, the
southern to Fidêncio de Melo. As there was no direct route then
in use between the rebel-held area of western Paraná and the
Contestado, the revolutionaries decided to reopen an over-
grown logging trail that ran from the village of Benjamin Constant, a rebel outpost linked to Foz do Iguaçu by road and telephone, south through about ninety kilometers of lowland forest
to Santo Antônio at the foot of the Capanema hills. João Cabanas sent one of his officers to join Fidêncio and supervise the
clearing job. Work on the trail was rushed after February 2,
when Isidoro's chief of staff sent Fidêncio a message informing
him that heavy fighting had erupted to the north. While the revolutionaries were advancing on the Catanduvas front, Isidoro's
headquarters explained, João Cabanas was engaged behind
enemy lines; it was urgent that Fidêncio make a demonstration
in the direction of Clevelândia to support Cabanas.[37] Fidêncio
lost no time in emerging from the forest; by February 5 he had
chased a few loyalist volunteers out of the border villages of
Santo Antônio and Barracão and was driving east toward Cleve-

lândia. At Campo Erê he met with Luís Carlos Prestes and they agreed on a joint plan of action: Fidêncio and two hundred and fifty men from the Prestes Column would attack Clevelândia, while two hundred of Prestes' men would march north toward Laranjeiras, on Rondon's main supply route.[38]

Prestes had some more extensive operations in mind, but, as he explained in his report to Isidoro, he lacked the resources necessary to undertake them. His column had been reduced to only eight hundred men, and fewer than five hundred of these were armed; they had a total of about ten thousand rounds of ammunition for all their weapons, including ten automatic rifles. Prestes urged Isidoro to send him four hundred rifles and one hundred thousand cartridges. "With my column armed and supplied with ammunition," the young colonel boasted, "I will be able to march north and, within little time, cross Paraná and São Paulo, directing myself toward Rio de Janeiro." [39] During most of the months of February and March 1925, however, Prestes' forces were confined to the Contestado.

João Alberto's detachment went immediately to join Fidêncio in his march on Clevelândia, and Siqueira's men soon were sent to back them up. Apparently, Prestes decided to await developments around Clevelândia before making a move toward Laranjeiras. Cordeiro's detachment was assigned to guard Barracão, where Prestes established his headquarters, and the trail from Pôrto Feliz. There were good horses to be requisitioned around Barracão and supplies were soon flowing into that village over the trail from Benjamin Constant. João Alberto and Siqueira were delighted to find so many fat cattle in the open country along the road to Clevelândia. Now that there were horses and churrasco for the troops, morale improved, although the rate of desertion remained high, especially in Cordeiro's outfit, camped near the Argentine border. The column's first contact with the enemy in the Contestado was made on February 18, when João Alberto's detachment ran into the advance elements of a force of gaúcho provisionals about thirty-five kilometers short of Clevelândia.[40]

General Rondon was not ignorant of the Prestes Column's threat to his rear. As Prestes' men crossed the Uruguay River into Santa Catarina, Colonel Ferminio Paim Filho's provisional "brigade" was on its way by rail from Rio Grande do Sul to join Rondon's forces in Paraná. Learning of Prestes' move to the north, Rondon ordered Paim to detrain his troops at Pôrto União, Santa Catarina, and march westward through the Contestado.[41] In the meantime, Claudino Nunes Pereira's battalion of the Rio Grande do Sul state militia was assigned to Rondon's theater of operations. Claudino was ordered to cross into Santa Catarina and advance up the trail from Pôrto Feliz to Barracão. Prestes and Fidêncio would be pushed out of the Contestado by a double-pronged maneuver like the one that forced the rebels back from Belarmino.

After skirmishing with Paim's patrols on February 18, Fidêncio and João Alberto were attacked by three hundred to four hundred Chimangos the next morning. The rebels held their positions all day and then withdrew under cover of darkness, having lost two men killed and eight wounded. João Alberto, although he was running dangerously low on ammunition, took up new defense positions seven kilometers to the rear.[42] The Prestes Column with eight hundred men, and Fidêncio, now with perhaps four hundred civilian volunteers,[43] seemed capable of at least holding the line against Paim—if they got the war matériel they requested from Isidoro.

Prestes received some ammunition, but not the one hundred thousand rounds he asked for, because, Isidoro explained, there were only three hundred thousand rifle cartridges left at Foz do Iguaçu to supply all the revolutionary forces. Furthermore, according to a letter Isidoro wrote to Prestes on February 22, there was little money left in the revolutionary treasury to buy war matériel—only 20,000 milreis. Nevertheless, the rebel generalissimo said that things were looking up on the political front. A congressman from Rio Grande do Sul—a member of the Liberator delegation elected under the peace agreement of 1923—had come to Iguaçu and assured Isidoro that opponents of President Bernardes were forming a powerful political movement "from the north to the south of Brazil," drawing strength from the determined stand of the revolutionary armed forces. Everyone in Brazil who had prestige and moral authority, the congressman said, was making common cause with the revolution. The campaign against Bernardes was being carried on both openly and clandestinely: There was a "large secret revolutionary committee" in Rio de Janeiro. In Brazil, according to the Liberator congressman, one name overshadowed all others—that of Assis Brasil, the Civilian Chief of the revolution.[44]

The opposition congressman's claims of government weakness seemed to be confirmed by the peace feelers that Isidoro was receiving at Foz do Iguaçu. A loyalist army captain had arrived under a flag of truce to arrange a meeting between Isidoro and a Chimango congressman, to discuss the prospects for ending hostilities. Isidoro had agreed to the meeting, which would be held before March 3. In the meantime, the rebel chief had consulted his officers on the Paraná front and they had agreed on one precondition for negotiations: the resignation of President Artur Bernardes. Once that demand had been met, the revolutionaries would discuss terms for laying down their arms with "Bernardes' legal successor." These developments indicated, Isidoro told Prestes, that, in order to triumph, they needed only "to survive one or two more months."[45]

The Prestes Column held out in the Contestado for as long as it could. João Alberto and Siqueira Campos slowly fell back toward Barracão under pressure from Paim Filho, while Cordeiro's men dug in south of that village to await the expected attack from Claudino. Cordeiro's outposts were first attacked by Claudino's men on March 22; two days later hundreds of Chimangos assaulted Cordeiro's trenches that blocked the Pôrto Feliz trail, just south of its intersection with the Barracão-Clevelândia road. Two of the seventy rebels manning these positions were killed and the others, after exhausting their ammunition, withdrew to the crossroads and proceeded from there to Barracão. The last of the rebel forces on the Clevelândia road passed the intersection that same day, en route to Barracão, where the column was being assembled. At four o'clock in the afternoon, as the rebels were preparing to begin the march to Benjamin Constant the forces of Claudino and Paim collided at the crossroads. Each mistaking the other for the enemy, the Chimangos fought until nearly ten o'clock that night, as the

Prestes Column, including Fidêncio's group, began the descent from the Capanema hills into the forest of the Iguaçu. The sardonic Siqueira Campos, it was said, left reluctantly: He wanted to wait and see who was going to win the battle.[46]

Nothing came of the peace feelers. Isidoro met with the Chimango congressman—João Simplício, who happened to be a personal friend—in Posadas, Argentina, on March 2; Assis Brasil, who was living in Monte Caseros, Argentina, was brought into the discussions later in the week. João Simplício explained that his peace mission was unofficial, undertaken on his own initiative, though with the consent of President Bernardes. During the talks, however, he received a confidential telegram from the president, who apparently authorized him to propose certain terms to the rebels. The terms, stripped of the congressman's soothing rhetoric, amounted to unconditional surrender: The rebels would give themselves up to the constituted authorities, to be placed under house arrest while Congress decided what to do with them. This proposal, made on March 6, was indignantly rejected by Isidoro, who clung to the belief that public opinion in Brazil was on the side of the revolution.[47]

The revolution's many alleged friends were reluctant to contribute to the cause anything more than words, if that. The rebel military situation deteriorated steadily in March 1925. Although the number of revolutionaries under arms dropped below four thousand there was no end to their overblown talk about brigades, divisions, generals, and even a marshal. That exalted rank had been conferred on Isidoro early in November, after the revolt in Rio Grande do Sul had given his forces a second "division." The commanding general of the Rio Grande Division was supposed to be João Francisco, but the old Jacobin, after a brief reconnaissance along the borders of the gaúcho state, returned to Foz do Iguaçu at the end of November. Marshal Isidoro was incensed by General João Francisco's inexplicable behavior and suggested that the general had misappropriated some revolutionary funds. João Francisco withdrew to Argentina in January, ostensibly for reasons of health, and did not return to the fighting. After the collapse of the Paraná front he denounced Isidoro as a coward, a traitor, and a monarchist.[48]

When Prestes, by default, emerged as commander of the Rio Grande Division, he would seem to have been in line for promotion to general. By this time Isidoro must have realized that the revolution was ridiculously top-heavy with generals. The São Paulo Division was commanded by Major General Bernardo de Araújo Padilha, a former lieutenant colonel of the federal army who had taken part in the revolt in São Paulo city. The division was composed of two "brigades": one, commanded by Brigadier General Miguel Costa, formerly a major of the São Paulo state militia, and the other by Lieutenant Colonel Newton Estilac Leal, an ex-captain of the federal army. It was Estilac Leal's brigade that was responsible for the defense of Catanduvas.

On March 26 General Rondon launched a series of attacks aimed at encircling Catanduvas. Spearheaded by militia units from Rio Grande do Sul and Bahia, the attacks were successful; by March 29 the rebel stronghold was isolated. Surrounded by four thousand government soldiers and battered by 105-mm. howitzers, the four hundred and seven rebels at Catanduvas had little choice but to give up. Colonel Estilac and two other officers, however, managed to slip through the government lines on the night of March 29; the rest of the brigade, fearing an all-out attack on March 30, surrendered before dawn. They turned over to the government a 105-mm. howitzer, two 75-mm. guns, 50 artillery rounds, 398 rifles and machine guns, and more than 10,000 cartridges. Government losses for the entire Belarmino-Catanduvas campaign were 179 dead, 301 wounded, and 60 missing—the highest military casualty toll for any operation during the revolution.[49] But the battles were fought in a sparsely populated area, where noncombatant losses could be kept to a minimum. Some property was destroyed, but General Rondon came through the campaign with his principles intact: His men had not sacrificed innocents on the altar of social order.

The fall of Catanduvas made untenable the position of Miguel Costa's brigade, to the northwest of that village. On March 31 Miguel's men began withdrawing westward along the

road that ran from Catanduvas through Benjamin Constant to
Foz do Iguaçú. The movement was orderly, undisturbed by the
loyalists, who were savoring their victory at Catanduvas and
would not resume offensive operations until April 4. In the
meantime, the Prestes Column had reached the same road, at
Benjamin Constant. There the Rio Grande Division halted to
await the remnants of the São Paulo Division. While his men
moved slowly and deliberately down the road, Miguel rushed
ahead to see Prestes. The meeting between Luís Carlos Prestes
and Miguel Costa occurred at Benjamin Constant do Paraná on
April 3, 1925.[50]

Widely divergent personalities did not prevent the intense
young Prestes and the avuncular Miguel Costa from agreeing on
a course of action. They would not lead their men down the
road to Foz do Iguaçu and surrender or exile; instead, they
would combine their forces and head for Guaíra, there to cross
the Paraná River and invade the state of Mato Grosso. The
quickest route to Guaíra was via the Pôrto Santa Helena trail,
which intersected the Foz do Iguaçu-Catanduvas road about
halfway between Benjamin Constant and the encampment of
Miguel's main body of men. Miguel and Prestes wanted to get
their men onto that trail as soon as possible; without consulting
Marshal Isidoro, they returned to their units and explained the
plan to their officers, who consented to it. With their troops on
the way to Pôrto Santa Helena, where they were to halt for
reorganization before moving on to Guaíra, Miguel and Prestes
proceeded to Foz do Iguaçu to confer with their "commander in
chief." [51]

Marshal Isidoro had just returned from another meeting
with Congressman João Simplício at Posadas, Argentina, when
Miguel and Prestes arrived in Foz do Iguaçu. The marshal was
gloomy; amnesty was out of the question and, he told an assembly of his officers on April 12, "Nothing more can be done in the
military field." There was no choice but to cross the river into
exile. Most of them agreed, but not Prestes.

"I'm not emigrating unless I'm cut down by a bullet!" ex-
claimed the young colonel.[52]

And Miguel Costa, middle-aged playboy turned revolutionary, who had endured as much for the cause as anyone present, surprisingly stood with the upstart from Rio Grande do Sul. Ex-major of São Paulo's elite state cavalry, eminent sportsman and member of the Paulista Racing Association ("refuge of snobs and millionaires"), a man of culture and refinement, divorced from his wife—Miguel Costa wanted to continue fighting. But Marshal Isidoro had had enough, and so had General Padilha, commander of the São Paulo Division, and even young Colonel Estilac Leal, who had slipped through the encirclement at Catanduvas. Prestes and Miguel wanted all the revolutionary forces to move to Guaíra and cross from there to Mato Grosso. But Guaíra was no longer in revolutionary hands: The town had been precipitously abandoned after the fall of Catanduvas. Loyalist forces from up the Paraná River had already moved into Guaíra and the rebels would probably have to fight for it— with Rondon pressing in on their rear. Miguel and Prestes were undismayed; if their path was blocked at Guaíra, they could cross the river south of the town and reach Mato Grosso by marching across the northeast corner of the Republic of Paraguay.[53]

The Miguel Costa–Prestes plan was considered madness by most of the officers assembled at Foz do Iguaçu. But it would do no good for them to reject it, since Miguel and Prestes seemed to have control of their troops and would try to execute the plan anyway. So Isidoro and his staff agreed to the invasion of Mato Grosso. Isidoro, however, would not accompany the troops: He and the Civilian Chief of the revolution, Dr. Assis Brasil, would exercise their supreme leadership from exile. Padilha, Estilac Leal, and the other officers who did not care to accompany Miguel and Prestes to the north were honorably discharged, some for reasons of health, and authorized to emigrate. Only a few of the multitude of revolutionary officers at Foz do Iguaçu chose to go to Pôrto Santa Helena and report for duty with the First Revolutionary Division, commanded by General Miguel Costa.[54]

The First Revolutionary Division was made up of two brigades: the São Paulo Brigade and the Rio Grande Brigade. The Rio Grande contingent, commanded by Prestes, was the smaller, probably consisting of fewer than seven hundred officers and men when the division was formally organized on April 14, 1925; a number of its members had quit early in April, including Fidêncio de Melo. Those who remained were, with few exceptions, grimly determined to go on. The São Paulo Brigade, on the other hand, was initially about twice as large as Prestes', but half its men and almost all of its officers were waiting for an opportunity to desert. With Miguel Costa as division commander, João Cabanas would seem to have been the best choice for brigade commander. But Cabanas was complaining about his health and apparently not interested in the job. Command of the São Paulo Brigade was given to Lieutenant Colonel Juarez Távora.[55]

Juarez Távora had returned to Brazil from exile just in time to take part in the retreat from the Catanduvas line. Having deserted Honório Lemes' rebel forces in Rio Grande do Sul late in November, he had gone into exile in Uruguay. There he remained for a while, disregarding Isidoro's orders that he rejoin Honório. Then he went to Argentina and, finally, to Paraguay. After three months of privation on foreign soil, during which he was reduced to selling his clothes in order to eat, Juarez Távora returned to the front in Paraná.[56] He knew what it was like in exile; he preferred life in the field with the troops.

The first phase of the new campaign was to be the movement of the division from Pôrto Santa Helena up the Paraná River to Pôrto Mendes, with the rebel vanguard continuing north along the Laranjeira Mate Company railroad to test the defenses of Guaíra. The movement from Pôrto Santa Helena took nearly a week, because the troops had to go by land, hacking out trails along the banks of the river. There was only one steamboat available to the division; the other rebel vessels capable of making time against the Paraná current had been commandeered by deserters who took them to Paraguay or Argentina where they were impounded. The division headquarters took the steamboat, the *Assis Brasil,* to Pôrto Mendes on April 20, as the troops began to march along the bank. By April 26, when the division rear reached Pôrto Mendes, one enemy column had occupied Foz do Iguaçu, a second was in Pôrto Santa Helena, and a third had advanced from the west to within a few kilometers of Pôrto Mendes.

It was against this last loyalist force that the São Paulo Brigade, assigned to the defense of Pôrto Mendes, won an incomplete victory on April 24. Attacked on the flank by João Cabanas and one hundred infantrymen, the loyalists fled to the rear, abandoning three automatic weapons and fifty thousand rounds of ammunition. After waiting an hour for the brigade cavalry to execute its role in the attack plan and pursue the retreating enemy, Cabanas went personally to Colonel Távora's command post, where he found the cavalry commander, Captain Ary Salgado Freire, "stretched out in sweet tranquility." At Cabanas' urging, Freire mounted a horse and rode off at the head of a "squadron" of eight cavalrymen in pursuit of the loyalists. The captain "ventured some three kilometers, returning in the afternoon with the news that the enemy was entrenched farther ahead." [57]

With the enemy concentrating on the rebel right flank and rear, and with the loyalists to the front apparently determined to defend Guaíra, or at least to remove from the rebels' grasp the boats that were anchored there—as a reconnaissance in that direction by Siqueira Campos had indicated—the division adopted the Miguel Costa–Prestes contingency plan, to march to Mato Grosso by way of Paraguay. The invasion of the neighboring republic began at five o'clock in the morning of April 27 with the landing of one hundred and fifty troops from the *Assis Brasil* at Puerto Adela. The commander of the tiny Paraguayan garrison there could do no more than verbally resist the landing; he was given written assurances by the Brazilian rebels that they had no hostile intentions toward his country. They did, however, commandeer a Paraguayan steamboat to speed up the crossing from Pôrto Mendes. The river crossing was completed on April 29, and the next day the vanguard of the First Revolutionary Division, led by Colonel João Alberto, reentered Brazil, invading the state of Mato Grosso.[58]

The movement of Miguel Costa's division into Paraguay left General Rondon's Paraná–Santa Catarina theater of operations free of rebel forces. With the evacuation of Paraná the revolution gave up its last military base on Brazilian soil. General Rondon did not consider the remaining armed rebels, deprived of the usual military support facilities, to be much of a danger to the government. In any case, he had accomplished his mission and, as he told his biographer, "felt happy with the conviction that much blood and many tears had been saved." [59]

President Artur Bernardes had refused to compromise with the Tenentes and his government had emerged from its severest test stronger than ever. The federal army, though still no pillar of the regime, no longer posed a serious threat to the government. General Rondon's campaign had shown that state troops, especially those of Rio Grande do Sul, were far more valuable than federal soldiers to the administration in Rio. Having assured himself of the loyalty of all the state governments, Bernardes was not likely to object if they increased the strength of their militia forces—at least not while there was a military threat to his regime. Between 1924 and 1925 the total of all state militia and police forces in Brazil rose from 31,988 to 34,651. The latter figure exceeded that of the federal army in 1925; because of the mutinies, the strength of the federal army fell to 34,244, from 39,764 in 1924. [60]

But the federal army would be rebuilt. It was Brazil's principal national institution—now that the monarchy was gone—a necessary bulwark against the regionalism that periodically threatened to dissolve Portuguese America into a welter of petty republics. The army was composed of men from every region of Brazil, thanks to a conscription law, on the books since 1908 but not implemented until 1916, that assigned draft quotas to each state based on its population. After 1916, enlistment and reenlistment were generally discouraged in order to maintain the large turnover produced by the draft, considered the best means for exposing a large number of Brazilians from diverse backgrounds to military instruction. The modest material rewards of army life were so attractive to many hard-pressed northeasterners that they welcomed the prospect of two years military service, even knowing that it probably would have to be performed far from their homes, since very few army units were stationed in the Northeast. Elsewhere, resistance to the draft was widespread, except in Rio Grande do Sul, where about a third of the army was stationed, making it possible for most gaúcho draftees to be assigned close to home. The northeastern conscripts, 80 percent of them illiterate, were transported the greatest distances, to the federal capital or to the border states, to be mixed with draftees from the more affluent areas and placed under command of officers from every part of the country.[61]

The federal soldiers were strongly attached to their company officers: They followed them into rebellion in São Paulo and Rio Grande do Sul and shared their prorevolutionary sentiments in the loyalist line at Catanduvas, firing into the air rather than at the "enemy." It would take a long time to eradicate Tenentismo from the federal army. In the meantime, the government had little reason to expect good results from federal troops stationed in areas menaced by a roving band of their ex-comrades. The rebel column that escaped from Paraná was commanded by Miguel Costa, formerly of the São Paulo state militia, but federal officers associated it with their illustrious colleague, the pride of the Realengo Military Academy, Luís Carlos Prestes. The attitude of most of the federal army toward Prestes was "let him pass." [62]

But the rebel column would have plenty of state and local forces to contend with. And in Mato Grosso the revolutionaries would even run into one federal officer, of German descent and training, who so loved the profession of arms that he was quite willing to practice it on his friends.

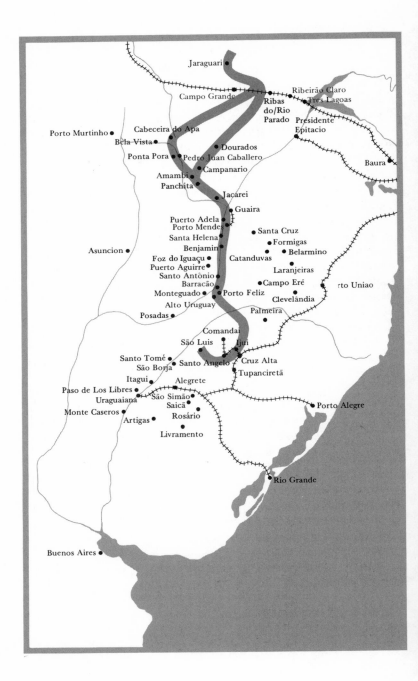

Prestes Takes Command

W No more than fifteen hundred rebels crossed from Pôrto Mendes to Puerto Adela with the First Revolutionary Division. But these men were well-armed and supplied with ammunition from Isidoro's remaining stockpiles and from the matériel that João Cabanas had recently captured. They crossed the turbulent Paraná River in two steamboats between April 26 and 29, taking with them six hundred horses and mules and a battery of three 75-mm. field guns. The artillery was assigned to the São Paulo Brigade, while most of the cavalry mounts went to the Rio Grande Brigade, which furnished the vanguard for the division's march across one hundred kilometers of sparsely settled Paraguayan territory. The number of men under Luís Carlos Prestes had risen to nearly eight hundred, with the incorporation into his Rio Grande Brigade of several dozen volunteers from Isidoro's headquarters and from various other extinguished units. The strength of the São Paulo Brigade, on the other hand, had been lowered by desertions to about seven hundred men—and more would quit in Paraguay, including João Cabanas.[1]

The morale of the fourteen to fifteen hundred rebels who remained with the division as it emerged from the Paraguayan forests, beginning on April 30, was fairly high. It was far superior to that of the federal troops stationed in southern Mato Grosso, who had little reason to respect the government they were supposed to defend. Their commanding general had noted that his officers could be divided into three categories: those who were actively working for the revolution, those who openly sympathized with the revolutionaries, and those who had no enthusiasm for the loyalist cause. Barracks revolts had been breaking out intermittently in Mato Grosso since July 1924; the latest, aborted like the others, occurred in March 1925 at Corumbá. There were plans for more uprisings, made in exile by deserters from these garrisons in collaboration with a few Matogrossense civilians and revolutionaries from Rio Grande do Sul and from the battleship *São Paulo*. Some of the plotters entered Mato Grosso with the revolutionary division at Jacarei ranch, while others approached the border farther to the north, planning to infiltrate the Brazilian town of Bela Vista, the scene of an earlier federal army mutiny.[2]

The officers of the revolutionary division had no reason to believe that the federal army in Mato Grosso would offer them much resistance. Under a little military pressure the federal units would dissolve, the rebels hoped, and many of their officers and men would join the revolution. Furthermore, the revolutionaries had received assurances of some civilian support in Mato Grosso. These, however, were misleading: Few Matogrossenses wanted to break the peace that their state had been enjoying in recent years. In 1921 three decades of fierce political struggle—which periodically erupted into armed conflict—had ended with the formation of the "Fusion," a merging of the state's two rival factions. Public offices and other political favors were shared by the stalwarts of the two parties, who were generally pleased with the Fusion when the rebels from Paraná intruded into their state at the end of April 1925. Mato Grosso, unlike Rio Grande do Sul in 1924, could not provide the revolution with an extensive cadre of alienated local leaders. Only in the remote diamond mining camps on the state's eastern border did local chiefs quarrel with the Fusion.[3]

Nevertheless, the military situation seemed to favor the revolutionaries as they suddenly appeared in southern Mato Grosso,

Prestes Takes Command   • 95

an upland region covered by an eye-pleasing patchwork of
woods and prairies. In the woods Indians from Paraguay gathered mate leaves, while on the prairies cowboys, most of them
descendants of immigrants from Rio Grande do Sul, tended fat
cattle. General Miguel Costa was eager to close with the enemy
in Mato Grosso and deal him a decisive blow. In the ten months
since the revolution began in São Paulo, the rebels had conducted some spectacular retreats and made some determined,
though ultimately futile, defensive stands. But they had never
won a clear-cut victory. General Miguel believed such a victory
was now in his grasp, as his division vanguard, João Alberto's
detachment from the Rio Grande Brigade, pushed rapidly
northward, the Paraguayan border on his left flank, toward
Ponta Porã, headquarters of the federal Eleventh Cavalry Regiment and the southern Mato Grosso command.

The advance of the division as a whole, however, was held up
by its artillery battery, which was still struggling along the trail in
Paraguay long after the rest of the troops had crossed into Brazil. At times the guns were totally submerged as artillerymen on
the banks of rivers tugged on ropes to pull them across. Finally,
on May 10, Miguel ordered the cannons abandoned, but then
changed his mind when some of the artillerymen, after all their
work, objected to leaving the guns on foreign soil. So the three
Krupp 75's were dragged across the border to Mato Grosso
where they were disabled and hidden. Then the battery commander and most of the members of his gun crews deserted and
returned to Paraguay to seek political asylum. In the meantime,
the São Paulo Brigade had reached Campanário, the Mato
Grosso headquarters of the Laranjeira Mate Company.[4]

In their three-hundred-kilometer march from Pôrto Mendes,
Paraná, through Puerto Adela, Paraguay, to Campanário, Mato
Grosso, the rebels had not left the domain of the Laranjeira
Mate Company. The company had grown rich and powerful
providing a product that was indispensable to the people of
Argentina, Uruguay, and southernmost Brazil. Not only
gaúchos out on the range, but their cousins in the towns and
cities of the pampas were accustomed to drinking hot mate tea,
or *chimarrão*, upon awakening each morning and on numerous

other occasions during the day. The arrival of guests or business associates inevitably brought out the host's hot-water kettle, *cuia,* or drinking gourd, and *bomba*—a reed or metal sucking tube with a strainer on the end. The pulverized mate leaves would be placed in the cuia and hot water poured over them; the host would drink the first containerful, considered not as smooth as subsequent ones, after which he would refill the cuia with hot water—without adding more leaves, since one helping was sufficient for several drinks of equal strength—and pass it and the bomba to a guest. Each guest in turn would suck the cuia dry, using the host's bomba. Mate was sometimes prepared and drunk cold, as *tereré,* but whatever its temperature, no true gaúcho would add sugar to it.

In the last years of the nineteenth century Brazilian businessmen moved to exploit the markets for mate in the republics to the south. Tomás Laranjeira got the idea of exploiting the mate that grew wild in the southern Mato Grosso woods and went to the Bank of Rio and Mato Grosso for financing. The president of the bank, Joaquim Murtinho, liked the idea and the Companhia Mate Laranjeira was formed, with the Rio and Mato Grosso bank holding 14,500 of its 15,000 shares of common stock. In 1894, before beginning operations, the company signed a contract with the state of Mato Grosso, the governor of which happened to be Joaquim Murtinho's brother Manuel, to monopolize the collection of mate for twenty-two years on a vast tract of public land, which amounted to virtually all of the state south of the twenty-second parallel. Joaquim Murtinho, one of Mato Grosso's most illustrious sons, was a "cold, skeptical businessman, a Darwinist by instinct and education," who believed that Brazil should devote itself to the only economic activity for which it was fit: to supply world markets with agricultural and forest products.[5] The mate collected in southern Mato Grosso was to be hauled to a port on the Paraguay River, Pôrto Murtinho, and shipped from there to Argentina.

Joaquim Murtinho became federal minister of finance in 1898 and launched a drastic anti-inflation campaign that ruined practically every bank in Brazil, including his own Bank of Rio and Mato Grosso. The liquidation of the bank led to the reorganization of the Laranjeira Mate Company in 1902 and the infusion of a great deal of foreign capital, much of it Argentine. The government of Mato Grosso did not object to the reorganization of the company nor to the rerouting of its exports through the Paraná River port of Guaíra, instead of Pôrto Murtinho.[6] Laranjeira Mate, by this time, was expanding into the forests of western Paraná and eastern Paraguay and the shift was a logical one, agreed to by the Murtinho family, which retained a substantial financial interest in the company.

In the meantime, the company's Mato Grosso domain was invaded by settlers from Rio Grande do Sul. Some Maragatos, finding conditions in their home state disagreeable after they lost the civil war of 1893–1895, emigrated to southern Mato Grosso, where there were grassy plains, interspersed among the woodlands, well suited for cattle raising. The Laranjeira Mate Company became quite disturbed as the original squatters were followed by waves of friends and relatives. In 1907 Laranjeira Mate tried to renegotiate its contract with the state government to give the company outright ownership of more than a million hectares of "unsettled" lands. The company proposed to merge with an English firm, which would manage and police their lands, in the belief that the gaúchos would hesitate to trespass on property held by these powerful foreigners. But Governor Generoso Ponce—an old half-breed war-horse, General Rondon's great-great uncle—who had seized power the year before with the support of the Murtinhos, had previously made a number of public pronouncements favoring opening the area to settlement. Ponce would not renegotiate the contract and it was not until after his death that the company brought up the matter again.[7]

In 1912 a second attempt to revise the contract along lines suggested by the company was defeated in the state legislature by partisans of "Colonel" Pedro Celestino Correia da Costa, a pharmacist and "intuitive physician" who had won fame leading revolutionary troops under Ponce. The company, alarmed by this unexpected defeat, mobilized its resources to ensure that in 1916, when the original contract was due to expire, the state government would be receptive to its proposals for a new arrangement. The pro-company forces prevailed in 1916 and a

contract was approved giving Laranjeira Mate a ten-year lease
on 1,440,000 hectares for an annual payment of 350,000 milreis.
The company was to have absolute control of this vast area during the tenure of the contract, the signing of which sparked an
armed revolt against the state government by Pedro Celestino
and his followers.[8]

The Mato Grosso civil war was ended in 1917 by federal intervention. Under pressure from Rio the pro- and anti-company
factions agreed to a compromise governor, the Bishop of Pru-
siade, and resolved their differences: Pedro Celestino gave up
his harassment of Laranjeira Mate in return for his uncon-
tested election as governor in 1921 as the Fusion candidate.
With the Fusion well entrenched in power in Mato Grosso, and
with Governor Pedro Celestino faithfully honoring the state's
commitments to Laranjeira Mate, the company could look forward to sympathetic treatment when its contract came up again
for renewal in 1926. In the meantime, Laranjeira Mate consoli-
dated its control over 440,000 hectares of land beyond what it
was legally entitled to.[9]

As the company strengthened its hold on southern Mato
Grosso, the flow of settlers into the area slowed to a trickle. The
company generally came to terms with those gaúcho immigrants
who had already established themselves there, hiring some as
private policemen to prevent the encroachment of others on its
domain, and even buying mate from a few who had set themselves up as independent producers. But for gathering the mate
leaves on its own vast lands, the company preferred to import
Paraguayan laborers, whom it exploited under a system of peon-
age that was little better than slavery. The same vicious system
was employed in the gathering of mate across the river in
Paraná, where rebel Major João Cabanas, the son of a Spaniard,
was so incensed by the mistreatment of the Paraguayans that he
had four foremen of a company contractor shot by a firing
squad.[10]

Other revolutionary leaders were surprisingly tolerant toward the Laranjeira Mate Company and its suppliers. The company's supervisors were largely successful in the efforts they
made to get along with the rebel officers whose troops occupied

their railroad and port facilities in Paraná from September 1924 to April 1925. Laranjeira Mate's managers in Mato Grosso were spared potential trouble when João Cabanas and his followers—many of them liberated Paraguayan peons—deserted Miguel Costa's division as it crossed the Paraná River. Miguel, Prestes, and Távora did not intend to free Guarani-speaking serfs or exploit any animosity the other inhabitants of southernmost Mato Grosso might have for the Laranjeira Mate Company.[11] They were merely passing through this fertile land of hills, woods, and fields—ideal for guerrilla warfare—on their way to challenge the federal troops in Ponta Porã, to continue their feud with the government of Artur Bernardes in faraway Rio. They could not be distracted by opportunities for social revolution.

The rebels clashed with federal troops in Mato Grosso for the first time at a place called Panchita on May 6, when João Alberto's detachment ran into a motorized light infantry company that had been sent south from Ponta Porã to investigate reports that some bandits had crossed the border from Paraguay. About thirty federals were killed, wounded, or captured before the rest of the company fled in trucks to the village of Amambai, from whence the alarm was spread to the rest of the state. João Alberto pressed his attack the next day and the federals fled across the Amambai River, where they linked up with a group of mounted irregulars who had ridden south from Ponta Porã. The two forces soon parted company, however, with the federals resuming their flight to the north while the irregulars, under "Colonel" Mário Gonçalves, set fire to the bridge over the Amambai River.[12]

Mário Gonçalves was a landowner and political leader in the county (*município*) of Ponta Porã. His title denoted political power rather than military attainment, although Gonçalves, unlike the average Brazilian "colonel," was not without the latter. Most of these colonels had received National Guard commissions, which were passed out as favors to influential men during the empire period and, especially, after the proclamation of the republic, when titles of nobility were no longer available for this purpose. By 1917 the National Guard had 8,778 brigades and

231,044 officers, but no troops. The National Guard, supposedly the federal army reserve, existed only on paper. It was
abolished in 1918, as part of Brazil's World War I military reforms, and replaced by the Army of the Second Line. Those National Guard colonels and lesser officers who were serious about
part-time soldiering could transfer to the second-line army and
by 1920 more than forty-four thousand had done so.[13] The
others who had held rank in the defunct National Guard—and
those whose commissions were self-conferred—did not forfeit
what was really important to them: Respectful neighbors still
addressed them by their military titles. *"Coronelismo"* could not
be eliminated by federal law.

The Army of the Second Line was never systematically
organized in accordance with the law of 1918 that decreed its existence. During the 1920's, however, reserve units of the federal
army were created on the spot in response to local revolutionary
situations. One such unit was the Fiftieth Independent Cavalry
Regiment, commanded by Reserve Lieutenant Colonel Mário
Gonçalves, which was raised to help put down a mutiny of regular federal troops in Bela Vista, Mato Grosso, in July 1924.
Gonçalves and his men served along the Paraná River during
August and September 1924 and in October were assigned to
guard the Mato Grosso—Paraguay border in the vicinity of Ponta
Porã. The "regiment" was comprised of somewhat more than
one hundred men when it rode south from Ponta Porã on May
7, 1925, to try to stop the rebel advance at the Amambai
Bridge.[14]

Gonçalves' reservists set fire to the bridge and then took up
ambush positions on the Ponta Porã road, as the revolutionaries
occupied the south bank of the river. The bridge was extensively
damaged by the fire, but João Alberto decided it was worth
repairing—a job that would take two days—since it would enable
him to employ some trucks, which he had captured at Panchita,
in the advance on Ponta Porã; also, the pause at the river would
allow Siqueira Campos' detachment to catch up and take part in
the final drive on that town. Mário Gonçalves' patrols observed
from afar as João Alberto's men went to work on the bridge over

the Amambai River, while sixty-five kilometers to the north fear gripped the federal troops in Ponta Porã. Tales of the ferocity of the rebels at Panchita apparently unnerved officers and men alike; on the night of May 7 the regulars began to abandon their garrison at Ponta Porã.[15]

On the night before Mário Gonçalves was sent out to fight the invaders, the regular officers had entertained the reservists at the federal barracks. At the party the regulars swore before the Brazilian flag that they would fight to the death against the rebels. The circular trenches that were being dug around the barracks appeared as concrete evidence of a determination to resist. Gonçalves was duly impressed and agreed to try to delay the rebel advance south of Ponta Porã, while the regulars strengthened the town's defenses. But after Gonçalves had departed on his combat mission, the garrison commander, Colonel Péricles de Albuquerque, noticing the weakening resolve of his officers and men—and perhaps fearing a mass defection to the enemy—consented to the evacuation of Ponta Porã. Péricles could not immediately inform general headquarters in Campo Grande of his decision, because somebody had cut the telegraph line. So, after the retreat was under way, the colonel sent a captain to Campo Grande by automobile to inform general headquarters of the action he was taking and to justify it. The captain, before he reached Campo Grande, fired his revolver through the car's windshield, so that he could arrive at headquarters with visual evidence of the desperateness of the situation at Ponta Porã.[16]

The evacuation that began on the night of May 7 was completed by the morning of May 9. Mário Gonçalves, his men still posted on the road to Amambai, learned of the flight of his allies when he rode into Ponta Porã that day. He then called in his outposts, and early in the afternoon of May 9 his men passed through Ponta Porã on their way north. The civil government retreated to Paraguay with the town records, leaving public buildings at the mercy of looters from both sides of the border— a wide street that separated Ponta Porã from the Paraguayan town of Pedro Juan Caballero. Order was restored on the Brazil-

ian side of the street the next morning when Ponta Porã was occupied by João Alberto's rebel detachment.[17]

Colonel Mário Gonçalves' 133 irregular cavalrymen caught
up with the 518 retreating federals, who were accompanied by
25 state militiamen, about thirty kilometers from Ponta Porã on
the road to Campo Grande. The convoy moved slowly, at the
pace of the oxcarts that were loaded down with ammunition and
unit property. The regular officers were dispirited, their troops
in disarray; they seemed concerned only with putting more distance between themselves and the rebels. But on the afternoon
of May 12 an automobile drove up to the loyalists, now sixty-five
kilometers from Ponta Porã, bringing a major from Campo
Grande with orders from general headquarters. Major Bertoldo
Klinger presented himself as Colonel Péricles' new chief-of-
staff. General headquarters did not agree with the decision to
abandon Ponta Porã, Klinger explained as tactfully as he could,
but what was done, was done; there would be no recriminations.
General headquarters had sent him to help Colonel Péricles organize his new defensive position, Klinger declared; the loyalists
would not retreat one more step. Major Klinger obviously was
going to be more than just chief-of-staff, and Mário Gonçalves
was delighted. Klinger's arrival, the rustic colonel declared, "was
like a star fallen from the sky." [18]

João Alberto's detachment, followed closely by that of
Siqueira Campos, entered Ponta Porã on May 10, 1925. It was
about eleven o'clock in the morning when João Alberto's men
moved into the Eleventh Cavalry Regiment barracks, taking
over from some army deserters and civilian revolutionaries who
had crossed over from exile in Pedro Juan Caballero to occupy
the vacant installation the day before. The returning exiles had
not prevented looters from stripping the barracks of furniture,
dishes, and other items, which were carted off to Pedro Juan
Caballero prior to the arrival of the rebel troops. The rebel colonel felt it necessary to make arrangements with the mayor of
Pedro Juan Caballero for the maintenance of law and order in
the sister towns. The Paraguayan official was amenable to João
Alberto's suggestions for joint policing and invited the Brazilian
to his home to drink some beer. As João Alberto was leaving the

Paraguayan's home, his host presented him with a bill for the beer he had drunk there.[19]

Pedro Juan Caballero was a much more lively place than Ponta Porã. On the Paraguayan side of International Avenue there were about ten mud-hut cabarets where guitars and violins played all night long and there was no shortage of Guarani girls eager to dance native polkas on the clay floors. Brazilian rebel soldiers invaded the cabarets on the night of May 10 and, though they had practically no money, ordered and drank large quantities of liquor. Anger against the Brazilians mounted among the cabaret owners and their regular patrons, who resented the foreigners' moving in on their women. It was not long before the first gunfights broke out, and the shooting continued through most of the night. The noise, however, was greater than the effect: Only three men were killed—one a Paraguayan—and about ten wounded.[20]

João Alberto was glad to get his troops out of Ponta Porã the next day, when he resumed the pursuit of the enemy. Siqueira Campos followed João Alberto on May 12, after Prestes moved his brigade headquarters to Ponta Porã. General Miguel Costa arrived in the town on May 13. Both Miguel and Prestes were eager for the lead detachments to attack the retreating loyalists while they were still in a state of panic. João Alberto had some doubts about continuing the pursuit, but Prestes insisted that an easy victory was within their grasp: He had information from loyalist deserters that the government forces that had fled Ponta Porã were leaderless and in utter confusion.[21]

But Major Klinger had taken over as *de facto* commander of the six hundred and eighty loyalists on the road to Campo Grande and was entrenching them at the crossroads near the headwaters of the Apa River—at Cabeceira do Apa—on May 13. While the bulk of his forces were digging in, constructing a defense in depth, Klinger sent mounted reconnaissance patrols down the road toward Ponta Porã. These were the loyalists that João Alberto's advance guards fired on as the rebel detachment approached Cabeceira do Apa on May 13. The rebels camped that night about two kilometers south of Klinger's lines; they numbered fewer than three hundred, as many of those who had started out from Ponta Porã had been posted at strategic points to secure João Alberto's rear and maintain liaison with Siqueira Campos' detachment, a day's march behind.[22]

At 6:30 in the morning of May 14 João Alberto attacked Klinger's position at Cabeceira do Apa. The rebels assaulted the loyalist first line of defense, manned by about forty infantrymen, on the front and left flank. The revolutionaries advanced, cavalry mixed with infantry, shouting insults at the loyalists, who soon broke and ran for the second line of defense, eight hundred meters to the north. This line, held by some one hundred soldiers, withstood the initial rebel assault by fire, and, at ten o'clock, Klinger loosed Mário Gonçalves' irregular cavalry on the enemy. The counterattack was conducted by one of the two squadrons that comprised Gonçalves' regiment—about sixty horsemen. Three times they charged the rebel positions; on the third try they broke the enemy line and the revolutionaries disbanded and fled in disorder to the south. But Klinger did not reinforce the counterattack and João Alberto was able to reassemble most of his men, near their previous night's camp, and turn back Gonçalves' cavalry. One of João Alberto's squadrons, however, did not stop running until it reached Paraguay, where its members sought political asylum. The action at Cabeceira do Apa, in which fewer than a dozen men lost their lives, "frightened a fair number of revolutionaries." [23]

Siqueira Campos linked up with João Alberto on the afternoon of May 14 and helped him stabilize his position south of Cabeceira do Apa. Together the two rebel commanders had almost as many men as Klinger, but they decided against renewing the drive up the Campo Grande road. Miguel Costa wanted to resume the attack, but Prestes sided with his detachment leaders. While Klinger might receive reinforcements at any minute (one thousand militiamen from Rio Grande do Sul, it was rumored, were expected momentarily in Campo Grande), Miguel had no one else to throw into the fight: Távora's São Paulo Brigade was camped south of Ponta Porã, between Amambai and Campanário, and wracked by desertions, while Cordeiro de Farias' Rio Grande detachment was even farther away, near the Paraná River, guarding the division's rear.[24]

The division could not attack but neither could it remain where it was: The proximity of the Paraguayan border made the temptation to desert hard to resist. In Ponta Porã General Miguel's chief-of-staff, Major Coriolano de Almeida Júnior, and two lieutenants walked out on the revolution. It was decided to march the division to the northeast, away from the international border, toward the Brazilian state of Goiás. The São Paulo Brigade and Cordeiro's detachment would rendezvous at Dourados, and proceed from there to the vicinity of Ribas do Rio Pardo, on the Northwest Railroad, east of Campo Grande; João Alberto and Siqueira would break contact with Klinger, swing to the east, and cover the division's left flank in the march toward Ribas.[25]

João Alberto and Siqueira had some trouble shaking off Mário Gonçalves' irregular cavalry, but contact was broken by the night of May 15. Klinger remained at Cabeceira do Apa for another week, integrating into his forces fresh regular units from Campo Grande and new groups of civilian volunteers from the surrounding area. On May 22 he sent two columns marching on Dourados: one directly on the road from Cabeceira do Apa and the other via Ponta Porã. Before launching the offensive, Klinger addressed a letter to "Major Miguel Costa, Captain Prestes and the other chiefs of the revolutionaries in Mato Grosso." The letter, dated May 21, was dispatched by automobile under a flag of truce and was delivered to Miguel Costa at his headquarters near Dourados.[26]

"My fearless comrades," the letter began, "I present my compliments with the purpose of inviting you to put an end to the inglorious armed struggle." The situation of the rebels was hopeless, Klinger explained; they were being surrounded by loyalist units from all parts of the country, "including Rio Grande do Sul." The number of troops in Klinger's detachment, only one of several operating against the revolutionaries, was alone equivalent to the total rebel strength. The government forces inevitably would triumph, but in the meantime the country would suffer. Klinger appealed to the rebels' patriotism, "which certainly has been the supreme motive of your action," to terminate immediately "this useless struggle that . . . can only add to the

disgrace of the country and her sons and deepen the division
and increase hatreds." Klinger said he was in a position to guarantee the safe conduct of all the rebel officers and a tenth of
their enlisted men to the nearest international border. He would
do this if the rebels would surrender to him all the arms, ammunition, horses, and other matériel in their possession. The details
could be arranged by representatives of their two forces. The
letter was signed "Your comrade, Bertoldo Klinger." [27]

Major Klinger was a chubby little man with a bald head and a
bristly moustache. He was forty-one years old, a native of Rio
Grande do Sul. His father was born in Austria and his mother
was the daughter of German immigrants whose family owned
the beer brewery that employed his father. The father cherished
his major's commission in the National Guard and the son was
attracted to military life by the parading of bands and troops in
his hometown of Rio Grande. Young Klinger obtained an appointment to the Praia Vermelha Military Academy in Rio, but
was expelled, along with the rest of the student body, for taking
part in the vaccination revolt of 1904. Nine months later Klinger
and the others were granted amnesty and allowed to resume
their studies at the new military academy at Realengo. [28]
Commissioned a second lieutenant of engineers in 1907
Klinger switched to the artillery in 1908. At that time the Brazilian army was buying 75-mm. guns from the Krupp factory and
Klinger was sent to Germany for two years to study their employment with the Kaiser's army. Returning to Brazil at the end
of 1912, Klinger became an energetic proponent of the "professionalization" of the Brazilian army. He was a fiercely ambitious
man, but promotions came slowly. He was only a captain, stationed in São Paulo, at the time of the 1922 revolt in Rio. He was
not implicated in that subversive movement and he received his
promotion to major in 1923. Nevertheless, he could hardly ignore the proposition that his advancement would be much more
rapid if he took part in a successful revolution. At any rate, he
was in touch with a number of revolutionaries, including the
fugitive Távora brothers, prior to the outbreak in São Paulo on

July 5, 1924. At that time he was stationed on the coast, at Santos, where he was arrested on July 7.

Major Klinger was held incommunicado on various ships of
the Brazilian navy for more than four months, during which he
read, for the third time, Graf von der Goltz' *Wars of Napoleon.*
The charges against him were dropped in November, and the
next month he was assigned to the field artillery regiment in
Campo Grande, Mato Grosso. Also in this city was the headquarters of the military region of Mato Grosso, commanded by
General Malan D'Angrogne, whose confidence Klinger soon
won. In May 1925 when the rebels invaded Mato Grosso and
federal resistance crumbled at Ponta Porã, Klinger was sent to
restore the situation. He was chosen chief-of-staff of the "Péricles Detachment"—so named for its commander, federal Colonel Péricles de Albuquerque—which included all loyalist forces
along the Paraguayan border from the Paraná River to Bela
Vista. Brazilian military custom would not allow the assignment
of that many troops to a mere major, so the incompetent Colonel
Péricles was retained as their nominal commander. Klinger
doubtlessly remembered the World War I role of General Erich
Ludendorff, whom he had met in Germany, and was quite willing to play Ludendorff to Péricles' Hindenburg.

At Cabeceira do Apa on May 14, 1925, Klinger won an important victory, "reminiscent of Joffre's Frenchmen at the
Marne, and of Pétain at the invincible bastion of Verdun"—or so
it was said at the dedication of the monument to the two loyalist
soldiers who were killed there.[29] A few days after the battle Colonel Péricles was recalled and Klinger—left in temporary command and perhaps fearing that a more assertive officer would
soon be placed over him—decreed that the outfit would henceforth be known as the "Mário Gonçalves Detachment." Regular
officers could not bear the thought of this unschooled provincial
commanding their soldiers—even nominally—but General
Malan could not afford to offend him and run the risk of alienating the Mato Grosso power structure, which, in turn, might
deprive the federal government of the only troops in that state

who had proven themselves in combat with the rebels. So Mário Gonçalves replaced Péricles as Klinger's "Hindenburg" and remained as "commander" of the detachment until June 1, when he accepted an appointment as Civil and Military Governor of Ponta Porã.[30]

In the meantime Klinger had a free hand to pursue his campaign against the rebels. He launched his two-pronged drive on Dourados after learning, on May 20, that the rebels had abandoned Ponta Porã and were marching north from the vicinity of Campanário. Klinger hoped to catch the rebels in his pincers, but he was most concerned with blocking their path to the north: He could not allow them to threaten General Malan's headquarters in Campo Grande. It would be better to let them emigrate to Paraguay—and Klinger wrote to the rebel officers offering to help them do that if they would surrender all of their arms and 90 percent of their men. He dispatched the letter with a sergeant in a government automobile driven by a civilian. Not only did the rebels refuse to answer the letter, but they made prisoners of the sergeant and the chauffeur and kept the car.[31]

General Miguel could not let the messengers return, because they would report that his forces were much farther to the north than Klinger suspected. When Klinger's pincers closed around Dourados on May 27, the revolutionaries had escaped. While the loyalists reassembled at Dourados, in preparation for the chase to the north, Klinger wrote another letter to the revolutionaries, reiterating his offer of May 21, but upbraiding them for their bad manners in keeping his car and arresting his messengers. The second letter was to be delivered by a man whom the rebels liked and respected and, presumably, would not detain—a Laranjeira Mate Company administrator who had become a great friend of the revolutionary officers when they were camped on company land. But neither the civilian nor the sergeant assigned to escort him had the will to carry out the mission, and the letter was never delivered.[32] Had it been delivered, it would not have been well received; the leaders of the "Unvanquished Column" (*Coluna Invicta*) were determined to continue the struggle on Brazilian soil.

The emergence of the Unvanquished Column from the ruins of Isidoro's Paraná front boosted the sagging morale of the revolutionary underground in Brazil and even inspired a few military conspirators to take action. In Rio de Janeiro, on the night of May 21, some fugitive army officers tried to seize control of the Third Infantry Regiment, stationed at the old military academy barracks on Praia Vermelha. They planned to arrest the loyalist officer in charge, rally the soldiers to the revolution—with the help of some of the regiment's sergeants, with whom they were in touch—and march to the aid of another group of revolutionaries who would be simultaneously attacking the presidential palace about five kilometers away. The attack on the palace did not occur, because the civilian revolutionaries assigned to that job never showed up. The fugitive officers, however, did appear at the gates of the barracks in three automobiles a few minutes after 9 P.M. Armed with revolvers, they quickly overpowered the sentries and had the bugler-of-the-guard sound assembly. The officer-of-the-day was in the latrine when the bugler began to play; when he emerged he was seized and disarmed by the revolutionaries.[33]

The troops fell in on the barracks' illuminated quadrangle, facing the revolutionary officers, the disarmed officer-of-the-day, and the bugler. Suddenly the bugler bolted and disappeared into the shadows at the edge of the quadrangle. Then a soldier in the ranks did the same. Within seconds the formation dissolved, with soldiers scurrying in every direction from the quadrangle, where the revolutionary officers continued to stand in the harsh electric light, ordering the men to return, threatening them with their pistols. The sergeants who were supposed to help the revolution vanished into the darkness with the rest of the enlisted men. The officer-of-the-day escaped from his captors during the confusion and soon was directing rifle fire at the frustrated revolutionaries standing alone in the quadrangle. After one was killed, the other rebels carried his body to their cars and fled into the city and disappeared.[34] That was the last attempted barracks revolt in Rio de Janeiro during the 1920's, but there would be others in states approached by the revolutionary column of Miguel Costa and Luís Carlos Prestes.

Before Miguel Costa's division headquarters left Ponta Porã on May 15, the general had a pontoon bridge built with some barrels that were found there. The bridge was hauled in sections by truck to the Dourados River, south of the town of that name. Using this portable bridge the São Paulo Brigade crossed the river and passed to the west of the town of Dourados, which Cordeiro's Rio Grande detachment occupied on May 19 and held for several days until the rest of the troops had cleared the area. Continuing the march north across lush grasslands reminiscent of the southern pampas, the rebel column arrived at the Vacaria River on May 26, the day before Klinger's loyalists reached Dourados, eighty kilometers to the south. The government troops were nearly a week's march behind the revolutionaries. Both sides made some use of trucks, which were ideally suited to the terrain now that the rainy season was ending, but neither force had enough motor vehicles to transport all of its men, more than one thousand in each case. Also, gasoline and oil were scarce in this frontier area, and many trucks had to be abandoned for lack of fuel. The horse was still the fastest means of transportation for large bodies of troops, and the rebels were well mounted, thanks to the work of their foraging parties, which requisitioned the local ranchers' best animals.[35]

The detachments of João Alberto and Siqueira Campos, driving northeast from Cabeceira do Apa, crossed the Vacaria River a day ahead of the São Paulo Brigade and formed the division's vanguard for the march across the Northwest Railroad. João Alberto reached the railroad on May 30 and cut the telegraph line near Ribas do Rio Pardo. Neither that town's garrison nor the loyalist troops in Campo Grande came out to fight the rebels, who completed the railroad crossing on the night of June 1, swung to the left, and occupied the town of Jaraguari, on the motor road sixty-eight kilometers north of Campo Grande, on June 4.[36]

At Jaraguari, the open country, or *campo limpo,* across which the rebels had marched since leaving Ponta Porã, gave way to *campo cerrado:* grasslands dotted with shrubs and stunted trees. The topsoil here was thinner and the pastures poorer; this land would not provide the rebels with the abundance of food and mounts that they had enjoyed south of Jaraguari. João Alberto, in his memoirs, would write about the beauty of the southern Mato Grosso landscape and recall that "the plentiful cattle and herds of easily caught horses delighted our men." Except for the fight at Cabeceira do Apa, the march from Ponta Porã to Jaraguari "seemed like an excursion." [37] Lourenço Moreira Lima, a captain on Miguel Costa's staff, remembered southern Mato Grosso's "marvelous grasslands, that unfolded like a sea of unbroken green, beneath a sky forever blue," and the "immense quantity of cattle, mate, and other resources that provided good nutrition" for the rebel troops. The people from whom these goods were taken did not bear their losses with magnanimity: "We were received with gunfire by the inhabitants of the places through which we passed, as if we were enemies," Moreira Lima noted.[38]

"We had no money at our disposal to buy what was indispensable to our troops," Moreira Lima wrote. What the troops needed, they took. "There were some excesses at the beginning of our march through Mato Grosso," the captain admitted. The women who accompanied the Rio Grande Brigade were especially greedy: "At the beginning of the invasion of Mato Grosso they deemed themselves to have the right to invade private homes" and take what they wanted. Local residents sustained much greater losses, however, at the hands of rebel foraging parties, called *potreadas*. These patrols of five to fifteen men rode along the flanks of the division, rounding up horses and other private property useful to the rebels. The members of a potreada from Siqueira Campos' detachment were ambushed in Mato Grosso by the Malaquias, a Negro ranching clan, as the rebels were catching horses in a Malaquias corral. Two of the foragers were killed and the others were chased away, but they returned later in much greater strength, headed by Lieutenant Colonel Siqueira Campos himself, who was determined to teach the Malaquias a lesson. In the second fight at the ranch, several of the Malaquias men were killed before the rest were driven off. One of their women was seized inside the ranch house as she poured kerosine on the family's stocks of flour to render it useless to the invaders. The rebels proceeded to burn down her house.[39]

The people of the towns occupied by the rebels were not spared personal injury and property loss. Substantial damage was sustained by the townspeople of Jaraguari, where the division spent the night of June 4, 1925, when about one hundred drunken rebels went on a rampage. The revolutionary command did not condone such behavior and a few of the rioters, fearing punishment, deserted the division at dawn on June 5. On that day the division's two brigades left Jaraguari and entered, by separate routes, a region of campo cerrado known as the "Desert of Camapuã." The two brigades were reunited five days later near the headwaters of the Camapuã River. It was there that the First Revolutionary Division underwent an important transformation.[40]

The authority of the division commander, General Miguel Costa, had steadily declined since the crossing of the Paraná River in April. Miguel had wanted to commit the division to decisive combat in Mato Grosso, and, for a while, his desire was shared by Colonel Luís Carlos Prestes, commander of the Rio Grande Brigade. The concurrence of Prestes was essential, as his troops accounted for nearly two-thirds of the division's strength. But after the defeat at Cabeceira do Apa, Prestes' two principal detachment commanders argued against further offensive operations and the colonel accepted their point of view. Miguel Costa had no choice but to go along with Prestes' plan to break contact with the enemy and withdraw to the northeast. In his rivalry with Prestes, Miguel received little effective support from his São Paulo comrades: The Paulista troops, though resentful of the Riograndense ascendency, were stultified by the uncertain leadership of Juarez Távora. The vital elements of the division responded to Prestes and not to Miguel—a fact the general acknowledged when he approved the reorganization of the rebel forces on June 10, 1925.[41]

While Miguel Costa remained as nominal commanding general, Prestes became chief-of-staff, with full powers to direct military operations, "completely controlling the commander in chief." The Rio Grande and São Paulo brigades were replaced by four detachments. The first, second, and third detachments were commanded, respectively, by lieutenant colonels Cordeiro de Farias, João Alberto, and Siqueira Campos, all members of the extinct Rio Grande Brigade. Some São Paulo troops were integrated into these units, while others were placed in a fourth detachment, commanded by Major Djalma Soares Dutra, an ex-federal cavalry officer who had been with the Paulistas since the beginning of the revolution. Lieutenant Colonel Juarez Távora became Prestes' assistant chief-of-staff.[42]

The total number of troops in this force, no more than twelve hundred, and the fact that there were no other revolutionary units in the field, made a mockery of the designation "First Revolutionary Division." In any case, the outfit soon became known to friends and foes alike as the "Prestes Column." Most of the revolutionary troops were armed with Brazil's standard military rifle, a 7-mm. Mauser. The column had four 7-mm. machine guns and about the same number of serviceable automatic rifles of that caliber. For all of these weapons there was a total of only about twenty thousand cartridges. Prestes had no artillery, no mortars, and no grenades.[43] The column, however, was highly mobile, and Prestes intended to employ it in a "war of movement."

When Prestes was in the Contestado he had written to Isidoro that "war in Brazil, whatever the terrain might be, is war of movement." Prestes was not suggesting that Isidoro might better protect his Paraná base area by adopting a system of mobile defense—or that he could best wear down and ultimately defeat the government army by abandoning positional warfare, dividing his forces, and setting them in motion about a central focus. What Prestes wanted Isidoro to do in February 1925 was to send him arms and ammunition so that he and his seven hundred men could march off toward Rio de Janeiro.[44] War in Brazil, Prestes seemed to think, was not so much "war of movement," as just "movement." The "war" he proposed to fight amounted to an armed protest demonstration. Its objectives would be to dem-

onstrate the continued intransigency of the men of the column
and to inspire other Brazilians to take more concrete action
against the government of President Artur Bernardes.[45]

Colonel Prestes was not concerned with the destruction of
the government's army or even of its will to fight. He was not interested in controlling terrain or in building a base of popular
support in some part of Brazil. The column would not remain in
any one place long enough to create a rebel infrastructure or to
set up a pipeline for receiving money and arms from revolutionary sympathizers in Brazil or in exile. By avoiding combat
whenever possible, the column could probably get by for a long
time on the little ammunition it had. Money was not necessary
for horses, food, and other necessities of life, as these could be
taken at gunpoint from defenseless civilians. This would not en-
dear the rebels to the people of the areas through which they
passed—especially since the column would not remain in any
place long enough to tailor its requisition policies effectively to
local conditions and exploit popular grievances. As it turned
out, the people of Brazil's poorest regions were called upon to
pay for this demonstration against the government in Rio de
Janeiro. The interests of the revolutionaries lay in Rio: That was
where they wanted their protest to be felt. In June 1925 the column veered to the east, following the path of least resistance, but
responding to the desire Prestes had expressed four months earlier of "directing myself toward Rio de Janeiro, perhaps through
Minas Gerais." [46]

Before the revolutionaries left Mato Grosso, Prestes admitted
the possibility that the column's protest might fail to rouse
others to decisive action—that they might be forced to turn away
from their march on Rio and, eventually, have to seek refuge in
some foreign country.[47] State and local forces posed a real threat
to the column, but the rebels did not expect much opposition
from the federal army. In fact, the federal army was the main
target of the revolutionaries' "armed propaganda," the institution which, they hoped, could be inspired to rise up and strike
down the hated government of Artur Bernardes. In June 1925
there were not many federal officers willing to commit themselves to a coup in Rio, but neither were there many who had

any stomach for operations in the countryside against their former comrades. One of the few who was eager for action was Major Klinger, whose detachment of federal troops and Mato Grosso irregulars was disbanded in Campo Grande on June 10. Two days later Klinger left Campo Grande as chief-of-staff of a new outfit composed of state troops from Minas Gerais and Rio Grande do Sul to hunt down the Prestes Column.[48]

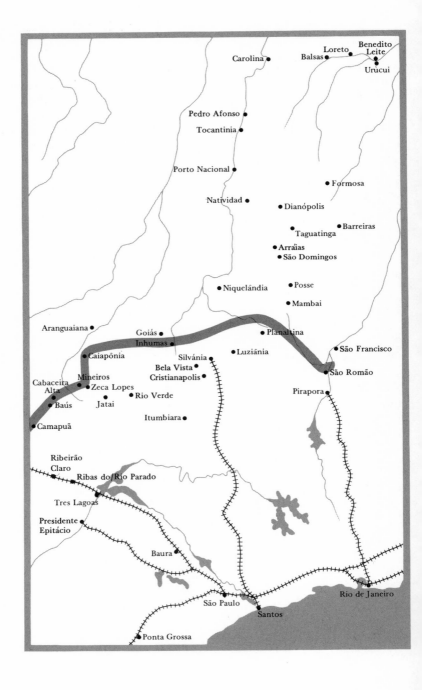

Klinger and Totó

I In 1914 the government of Mato Grosso gave "Colonel" Antônio Manuel Moreira the exclusive right to exploit the recently discovered diamond fields along the Garças River near the Goiás border. But Moreira's legal monopoly was ignored by several thousand prospectors who poured into the area, many from the Chapada Diamantina, or Diamond Plateau, of Bahia, where the mines were playing out. The Bahians were a rough crew, schooled in the private warfare of the Chapada Diamantina and inclined to disregard any authority other than that of family or clan. But, in their defiance of Colonel Moreira and the Mato Grosso government, the illegal miners saw the need of banding together under strong leadership. The man whom most of them accepted as their chief was "Doctor" José Morbeck, an agronomist from Bahia, who, like them, had come to the diamond fields to seek his fortune— though not necessarily by panning pebbles in the stream beds.[1] Morbeck pledged to champion the cause of the small miners, or *garimpeiros,* in the courts, in the state and national political arenas, and, if necessary, on the battlefield.

The Fusion Government installed in Mato Grosso in 1921 was eager to come to terms with Morbeck and his garimpeiros. The state government was in a financial bind at a time when the garimpeiros were extracting perhaps 16 million milreis' worth of diamonds annually and escaping all Mato Grosso taxation (the stones were sold to Morbeck and his associates who shipped them out across the nearby Goiás border). In 1923 the Mato Grosso government annulled Colonel Moreira's monopoly grant and announced that the garimpeiros could now apply to the state for ten-year leases on claims they were working. The cost of the leases was fairly low, as were the production taxes that the legal miners would be liable for, but the garimpeiros saw in this little advantage over the old illegal system under which they paid nothing.[2]

In the meantime the state government was courting Morbeck, trying to get him to join the Fusion and facilitate the collection of taxes in the mining district. Morbeck was persuaded to give up the idea of seeking federal recognition of an independent territory of Garças and to accept the authority of the Mato Grosso government in his domain. State tax collectors were sent into the region, whose isolation from the power centers of Mato Grosso was ended in 1924 with the hasty construction of two motor roads to Alto Araguaia, a town on the Goiás border where Morbeck had his headquarters. One road cut across the mining district from the west, from Cuiabá, the state capital, and the other reached Alto Araguaia from Ribeirão Claro, a station on the Northwest Railroad east of Campo Grande. With feeling among the garimpeiros running strong against the encroachments of the government, Morbeck declined to join the Fusion and, in July 1924, counseled his followers to refuse to pay state taxes.[3]

By this time the revolution had broken out in São Paulo and Morbeck's agents were soon in touch with Isidoro. But Morbeck played both sides of the street: He appealed to the federal government for arms so that he could raise a Patriotic Battalion to fight the rebels. The garimpeiro chief had some important friends in the federal service, including General Rondon, who offered to mediate between Morbeck and the state government. The Mato Grosso government, determined to force a showdown with Morbeck, declined the mediation offer and urged the federals not to send him any weapons. The garimpeiros, however, already were pretty well armed. On May 19, 1925, the government sent a force of thirty state policemen up the motor road from Ribeirão Claro to Alto Araguaia. Their attempt to establish the first state police station in Morbeck's town was frustrated by the garimpeiros, who attacked them in Alto Araguaia on May 24 and 25, killing several and chasing away the rest.[4]

Federal General Malan D'Angrogne, commander of the military region of Mato Grosso, believed that the struggle between Morbeck and the state government was unrelated to the Isidoro-Miguel Costa-Prestes rebellion against the federal government. After all, Morbeck had offered to fight against the revolutionaries and his loyalty to the federal government was vouched for by such eminent legalists as General Rondon. But early in June, after the rebels crossed the Northwest Railroad, heading in the general direction of the mining district, Malan decided to send an emissary to Alto Araguaia to confer with Morbeck and make sure that the garimpeiro chief's attitude toward the federal government had not changed. While Malan's emissary was on his way to the mining district, the federal government, on June 6, received an interesting telegram from its minister in Asunción. Marshal Isidoro, then residing in a boardinghouse in the Paraguayan capital, had just told a Bernardist informer that "Morbeck had left the Garças River with his armed following to attack Cuiabá" and was "trying to link up with the revolutionaries."[5]

The Prestes Column seemed to be heading for Alto Araguaia and General Malan had to get his troops there first, to prevent the rebels from joining forces with the garimpeiros, should that be their intention, or, if not, to intercept them before they could invade the state of Goiás. General Malan offered command of the drive on Alto Araguaia to federal Colonel Álvaro Mariante, but he turned it down. Major Klinger was eager for the job, but did not have the requisite rank. Malan never formally appointed a commanding officer for the troops he ordered to Alto Araguaia; he named Klinger chief-of-staff and kept him as "acting commander" for the life of the detachment. Klinger left

Ribeirão Claro on June 14 with his "vanguard" of three hundred Minas Gerais state militiamen in eighteen trucks, carrying enough gasoline to get them to Alto Araguaia, five hundred kilometers to the north. The rest of Klinger's detachment, another seven hundred Mineiros plus about one thousand state troops from Rio Grande do Sul, remained at Ribeirão Claro awaiting the arrival of transportation and further orders. Klinger wired Malan for more gasoline and a minimum of twenty-five additional trucks.[6]

Since Klinger's eighteen trucks were of a light-duty, civilian type and could carry a total of only one hundred eighty men and their equipment over the unimproved road at one time, the major had to move his three hundred troops in shuttles. He and about half of his men were camped a few kilometers short of the village of Baús when some of the others, nearly one hundred kilometers behind, were shot at on June 18. The enemy force was Djalma Dutra's Fourth Detachment, covering the right flank of the Prestes Column in its advance from Camapuã to Baús. For two days Dutra harassed Klinger's forces on the road south of Baús, firing on trucks and tearing up bridges, as he made his way north to join Prestes. By June 20 Klinger and slightly more than two hundred Mineiro militiamen were surrounded in two positions near Baús by the twelve hundred rebels of the Prestes Column. Before the rebels closed in around him, Klinger met briefly with a major from General Malan's staff, who was en route to Campo Grande from Alto Araguaia, where he had conferred with Doctor Morbeck.[7] The federals had nothing to fear from the garimpeiros.

In two days of skirmishing around Baús, June 19–20, losses on each side were about a dozen men killed or wounded. Klinger had the advantage of prepared defensive positions, but otherwise the terrain favored the attackers. The land was rent by gullies and defiles and covered with brush, providing concealment and fairly safe avenues of approach for the attackers, while limiting the fields of fire of the defenders. But after several rebels were killed in an unsuccessful attack by Cordeiro's detachment on the afternoon of June 19, the revolutionaries lost what taste they had for offensive operations against Klinger. The loyalists were kept under siege for another day, however, as the Prestes Column prepared to move up the road toward Alto Araguaia. In the meantime, rebel Captain Moreira Lima was sent ahead to that town to see José Morbeck, who "we were told . . . was our friend and was ready to join the column." [8]

The rebels did not press their attack on Klinger, General Miguel Costa explained to the troops, because "the expulsion of the enemy or his annihilation in the positions that he occupied would have cost a great sacrifice in lives in addition to a dangerous expenditure of ammunition," which would have been unnecessary, since the loyalists were no obstacle to the column's movement to the north or to the east.[9] The column withdrew to the north on May 21 and the next day was rejoined at Cabeceira Alta by Moreira Lima, who was returning from his meeting with Morbeck in Alto Araguaia. The garimpeiro chief had given Moreira "some truly idiotic excuses for not being able to accompany us at that time." [10]

The fact was that Morbeck and his garimpeiros had their own war to fight against the state of Mato Grosso and could not afford to get involved in an armed protest against the federal government. Morbeck gave these nomadic revolutionaries little chance of overthrowing the regime in Rio and felt that he could best serve his own cause by trying to win the favor—or at least the neutrality—of the federal government. The visiting rebels, for their part, had no desire to fight for the garimpeiros. It would be another year before Luís Carlos Prestes would see the utility in making common cause with the diamond miners of the Garças River, but by then the military power of the garimpeiros would be broken by the forces of the state of Mato Grosso. On June 23, 1925, the Prestes Column veered off the road to Alto Araguaia and headed east into the state of Goiás.[11]

The Prestes Column took the trail that ran along the ridgeline of the Serra do Baús, a range of hills extending to the village of Mineiros, Goiás. The trail was impassable for motor vehicles, so Prestes did not have to worry about Klinger falling on his rear. Besides, past experience indicated that Klinger would be

slow to venture from his defensive positions near Baús; he had
remained in his trenches at Cabeceira do Apa for nearly a week
after the last rebel forces had withdrawn from that area. The
serra along which the rebels rode formed part of the watershed
dividing the Brazilian subcontinent. To their left the streams
flowed into the Araguaia and, ultimately, into the Amazon,
while on their right the drainage was into tributaries of the
Paraná. From the top of the serra for as far as the eye could see,
there was campo cerrado. The terrain was more open at the
higher levels, with the shrubs growing thicker toward the bot-
tom of the slopes, where, along the stream beds, there were
stands of hardwoods and other full-sized trees.

About thirteen kilometers west of Mineiros the trail from
Baús merged with a road from Alto Araguaia. This was a motor
road that had been built by Morbeck and his associates to facilitate their diamond trade; it ran east through Mineiros to Jataí
and beyond. Between the intersection and the town there was a
bridge, at the Verdinho River. The rebel vanguard, João Alberto's detachment, crossed this bridge and occupied the town
of Mineiros on June 26. There were a few prorevolutionary civilians on hand to welcome João Alberto, but most of the town's
inhabitants had fled down the road to Jataí. The rebels made
their usual requisitions in and around Mineiros and picked up at
least one truck. On June 27 the column's main body crossed the
bridge heading for Mineiros and Jataí.[12]

Prestes was now moving in the direction of Rio de Janeiro.
Extended eastward, a line drawn through Mineiros and Jataí,
Goiás, would pass through the south of the state of Minas Gerais
and come very close to the federal capital. No insurmountable
natural obstacles lay ahead—no great rivers, like the Uruguay or
the Paraná, too wide for the column's horses to swim. There
were innumerable federal and state garrisons to the east, but
these could be bypassed, just as the column had ridden around
Campo Grande. It seemed unlikely that the loyalists would make
any serious attempt to run the rebels down. It had taken them
more than a month to follow Miguel Costa's brigade from São
Paulo to the Paraná River, and even longer to follow Prestes
from Rio Grande do Sul to the Contestado. The highly mobile

Prestes Column could literally ride circles around the government forces. By avoiding combat the column could remain in the field indefinitely, defying the government of Artur Bernardes and, perhaps, eventually inspiring the people of Brazil to rise up and overthrow the tyrant. Such calculations, however, would be upset by a storm that was brewing on the western horizon.

Colonel Prestes and his staff were with the column rearguard, Cordeiro's detachment, at the Verdinho Bridge outside Mineiros, Goiás, on the afternoon of June 27 when Klinger's touring car and five truckloads of Minas Gerais militiamen appeared from the direction of Alto Araguaia. The major had not dallied at Baús after the rebel withdrawal on June 22; he had plunged on up the road to Alto Araguaia without waiting for reinforcements from Ribeirão Claro. He learned the rebel's direction of march when he reached Cabeceira Alta, but since his vehicles could not negotiate the trail his quarry had taken, he continued north to Alto Araguaia, repairing a damaged bridge on the way. With insufficient gasoline to shuttle his three hundred troops east on the road to Mineiros, Klinger had to leave about half of them in Alto Araguaia. Several hours behind the five trucks that approached the Verdinho Bridge at 4 P.M. on June 27 were eight more, but Klinger did not wait for them: He attacked Cordeiro's detachment with the force at hand, fewer than one hundred men.[13]

Surprised by Klinger's arrival, Prestes and Cordeiro soon perceived his weakness. They stopped his advance and then forced him back from the bridge, which they set on fire. The action at the bridge cost the revolutionaries one dead and one wounded; Klinger had no casualties. The rebel rearguard maintained contact with the loyalists west of the burned-out bridge throughout the night, while the rest of the column moved through Mineiros and headed toward Jataí. Also during the night, the remainder of Klinger's motorized force arrived, increasing his strength to one hundred twenty riflemen and five machine-gun crews.[14]

Early on the morning of June 28 the rebel rearguard waded across the shallow river and withdrew to the east, giving the loyalists possession of the ruined bridge. Should Klinger decide to continue his pursuit, he would have to expend much time and effort in preparing a crossing for his trucks. But the major was undaunted; immediately he set his men to work digging cuts into opposite banks of the river and making a ford between them, using timbers salvaged from the bridge to span the deepest channels of the clear green watercourse. By nightfall the militiamen had managed to get five of their trucks across. By seven o'clock the next morning thirteen government vehicles, including Klinger's staff car, were in Mineiros. Klinger paused in the village long enough to write a letter to the rebel officers, which he dispatched with his chauffeur in his car, and then climbed aboard one of his trucks to resume the pursuit down the road to Jataí.[15]

About seventy kilometers east of Mineiros, at noon on June 29, Klinger overtook the rebel rearguard, now Djalma Dutra's detachment. Upon sighting the enemy, Klinger's men dismounted and formed a skirmish line. There was a brief exchange of fire, after which some of the revolutionaries fled into the thicket on the side of the road, abandoning two machine-gun tripods, while a rebel truck drove off rapidly to the east. Klinger was quick to give chase. From the middle of his motorized column the major contemplated the clouds of dust raised by his lead trucks: "They seemed to be unfurled banners, swiftly conveying throughout those backlands the word of order, the presence of the law." [16]

Klinger's trucks were stopped by rebel fire at two o'clock and again at four o'clock. The second time the resistance was determined and the fighting was close-in and confused. An eighteen-year-old revolutionary lieutenant, Aldo Manenti, an Italian from São Paulo, mounted the cab of Klinger's lead truck, perhaps thinking it was a rebel vehicle, and was killed at the steering wheel. Four other revolutionaries were killed inside the line Klinger's men formed when their trucks halted at four o'clock. The loyalists had two men wounded in the late-afternoon encounter and their commander decided to camp on the spot for the night.[17] The rebel main body was just four kilometers away, at the Zeca Lopes ranch.

There was consternation at revolutionary headquarters on the afternoon of June 29. Klinger's staff car arrived at the Zeca Lopes ranch around noon with a letter advising the rebels that the major was "very close" to them and urging them to surrender and avoid useless bloodshed. Not long afterward news arrived of Djalma Dutra's first encounter with the loyalists—confirming that Klinger's trucks had crossed the Verdinho River and the major's troops were serious about doing battle with the column. But the rebels could easily avoid being run down by Klinger's trucks: All they had to do was get off the road. They could turn off the Jataí road at the Zeca Lopes ranch and take the oxcart trail to Caiapônia, which was impassable to motor vehicles. At first, most of the rebel officers were inclined to take this route, but the eloquent Juarez Távora thought differently; at a council of war on the afternoon of June 29 he convinced his colleagues that they should make a stand at the Zeca Lopes ranch.[18]

The rebels either had to smash Klinger, making an example of him, or give up all hopes of operating closer to Rio de Janeiro, where there were many motor roads. Klinger had taken the initiative away from the revolutionaries and shaken their confidence, but the column, which outnumbered his forces nearly ten to one, was still capable of striking back. Juarez Távora's plan would, "if . . . carried out to the letter, oblige the enemy troops to surrender or, at least, disperse into the bush, leaving in our hands the trucks that transported them."[19] The attack was to be executed by two detachments, João Alberto's and Siqueira's, under the direction of Colonel Távora. The action was planned to commence at dawn on June 30 with an infantry attack on Klinger's front by João Alberto's detachment and a simultaneous assault on his rear by two dismounted companies from Siqueira's detachment, which were to infiltrate through the woods north of the road during the night. The attacking riflemen were issued twenty-five rounds of ammunition apiece.[20]

But the plan could not be carried out to the letter: The night was dark and the brush on the right flank was thick and it took Captain Modesto Lafayette Cruz's company longer than Távora had calculated to get into place. In fact, dawn had broken and

Modesto's men were spotted by Klinger's sentries before they reached their attack position. Although the element of surprise was lost, the rebels, on Távora's command, rushed Klinger's front, rear, and left flank. The gallant Captain Modesto, a civilian who had joined the revolution in São Paulo, was cut down as he charged the enemy firing an automatic rifle. He and eleven other revolutionaries were killed near Klinger's lines before the rest of the attackers took flight. The loyalists had eight men wounded, one mortally. The rebels kept Klinger under siege after the attacks failed, but the firing slackened and finally stopped at midday, as both sides were running low on ammunition.[21]

At Zeca Lopes, Juarez Távora demonstrated that he had learned little from his defeats at Três Lagoas and Alegrete: He was much too willing to send infantrymen through unfamiliar terrain to attack an entrenched enemy. Of course, he could argue that there was no time for reconnaissance and that the overwhelming superiority of rebel numbers should have been sufficient to carry the day, even if their avenues of approach were covered by the enemy. But the numerical superiority of the rebels was insufficient to compensate for their relatively low level of discipline and morale. With a few notable exceptions, the men Távora sent into battle lacked the spirit of Klinger's loyalists. Revolutionary ineptitude had allowed Klinger to shape the Mineiro militiamen into a disciplined and aggressive force. Apparently the rebels did not consider striking at Klinger's troops when they were most vulnerable—ambushing them as they moved down winding, brush-bordered roads bunched up in their trucks.

The attack on Klinger's position near Zeca Lopes was not pressed after the morning of June 30, it was said, because revolutionary tactics required that the rebels avoid combat except "when material necessities impose upon them the duty of throwing themselves forward to capture munitions." A victory over Klinger would have been worthless, since after two days of combat "the enemy certainly would have expended almost all of his ammunition."[22] At any rate, the tacit cease-fire on the afternoon of June 30 allowed the rebels to collect their wounded and bury some of their dead. Klinger's Mineiros, after throwing back the rebel attacks, had not rushed out to cut the throats of the enemy wounded, as was the custom in Rio Grande do Sul. Instead, the loyalists allowed rebel stretcher-bearers to come close to their lines to pick up their wounded. Klinger's adherence to the rules of war and the "humanity" of his troops impressed both João Alberto and Siqueira Campos.[23] The major even sacrificed some of his "precious gasoline" for the cremation of twelve rebel bodies that were not carried away, to avoid "possible insults" to the dead by "wild animals."[24]

The rebel wounded, more than a dozen, were taken to the Zeca Lopes ranch house where they were treated by the column's medical section: Medical Doctor José Ataíde da Silva, Veterinary Doctor Aristides Corrêa Leal, a pharmacist, and several orderlies. The section was ill-prepared for the work at hand: Bandages and antiseptics were in short supply, important surgical instruments were missing, and there was no anesthesia. One of the soldiers operated on was a sixteen-year-old boy who had been shot in the left hand in a previous day's action; gangrene had set in and the hand had to be amputated. With the patient conscious, smoking a cigarette, occasionally letting out a piercing scream, the doctor cut into the wrist with a bistoury and completed the amputation "with a saw improvised from a knife."[25]

The heaviest casualties on June 30 were suffered by Siqueira's detachment, which was pulled out of the line around noon and replaced by Cordeiro's. While Cordeiro and João Alberto held Klinger at bay, other rebel officers shifted their troops onto the Caiapônia oxcart trail and began the withdrawal to the north. To delay any reinforcements that might be sent to Klinger from Jataí, rebel headquarters dispatched a patrol east on the motor road to tear up the bridge over the Claro River—a mission that was accomplished despite the desertion of the group's commanding officer.[26] Another matter that was attended to before the revolutionaries abandoned the Zeca Lopes ranch was the drafting of a reply to Major Klinger's letter.

In his letter of June 29 Klinger said that he could no longer offer the generous terms of the month before, but if the rebels would surrender to him, he would guarantee their lives and, as their comrade, make as many concessions to them as possible. The reply, signed by Miguel Costa, "Commander of the men of dignity," was nailed to a fence post in front of the ranch house. (Klinger's messenger of June 29, like his predecessors, was forced to accompany the rebels as a prisoner, in this case for about a month.) Miguel Costa advised Klinger, "ex-comrade of revolutionary ideals," that if he wanted to earn some respect from those who justly considered him a traitor, he should not annoy them any more with his letters telling them how proud he is to be leading "valiant constables of Bernardes." The revolutionaries were not interested in the "pompous guarantees" offered them by this federal army officer and his aggregation of policemen from the tyrant's state of Minas Gerais. "The curse for the blood spilled," the letter concluded, "will fall one day on the conscience of traitors." [27]

Nevertheless, the rebels had enough faith in Klinger and his men to leave a wounded officer in the Zeca Lopes ranch house where the loyalists would find him. Also abandoned inside the ranch house were maps, letters, and other papers belonging to Juarez Távora, and a severed human hand. Other indications of a precipitous rebel withdrawal were ten slaughtered steers, left uneaten in the yard near the house. Prestes and the rebel headquarters group took off up the Caiapônia trail about 8 P.M. and did not stop to camp until they were twenty-five kilometers from the Zeca Lopes ranch. The night was dark and travel was difficult. The horse Prestes was riding fell into a hole and the chief-of-staff was badly shaken.[28]

The state of Goiás stretches over fifteen hundred kilometers from south to north and includes some of the oldest geological formations on earth. Ancient masses of crystalline rock have been eroded by heavy tropical rains to form the rounded hilltops, convex slopes, and narrow valleys typical of almost every part of the state. Only in the extreme north do the valleys widen to any extent, as the great rivers Araguaia and Tocantins approach the greater Amazon, forming alluvial plains. In 1925 there were broad tropical forests in the far north and thin strands of evergreen and semi-deciduous trees along the sparkling green watercourses that crisscrossed the rest of the state, but most of the surface of Goiás was covered by campo cerrado. The grass that grew among the shrubs was thick, but not particularly nutritious; the land would not support as many grazing animals per square kilometer as would, for example, the coxilhas of Rio Grande do Sul.

Men of European descent—it would be a mistake to call them white (most were mestizos), Portuguese-speaking (many preferred a form of the Guarani tongue), or civilized—first settled in the area in the 1720's to exploit the gold mines they discovered near what became the city of Goiás. By the beginning of the twentieth century the gold around Goiás city was long gone, although there were still a few placers, as well as some diamond washings, being worked elsewhere in the state, especially in the north. The production of these mines was meager. Livestock raising, despite poor pastures, had superseded mining as Goiás's principal economic activity. The cruelty and greed of the early settlers, the bandeirantes, was handed down over the generations and scarcely modified by the shift from mining to pastoral pursuits.

At the turn of the century the state of Goiás was the fiefdom of Senator Leopoldo de Bulhões, an illustrious statesman who served twice as federal finance minister. A hard-money man like Joaquim Murtinho, his colleague from neighboring Mato Grosso, Bulhões was absorbed in the great political and economic issues of the republic and could spare little time for his home state. Anyway, Goiás, the collection of rancher despotisms that provided the votes necessary to keep Bulhões in the federal senate, was best left alone. "There," said Bulhões in Rio, referring to his native state, "the worse the better." He opposed the extension of railroads into Goiás because "adventurers would begin to enter and then there would be opposition" to his political machine.[29]

But opposition developed anyway and by 1912 Antônio

"Totó" Ramos Caiado had emerged as Goiás's new strong man. Despite initial promises of reform, Totó Caiado turned out to be as beholden to the big landowners as Bulhões had been. After rising to power, Totó, like Bulhões, refused to serve as state governor, preferring Rio de Janeiro to the wretched little capital of Goiás. He took his seat in the federal Senate in Rio and left the state government in the hands of relatives. Senator Caiado did not wield nearly as much power on the national scene as Bulhões had exercised, though he did have enough influence in Rio to persuade the federal government to send troops to northern Goiás in 1919 to help state forces put down a rising of ranchers. But the federals had neither the capacity nor the will to deal effectively with the backcountry rebels and, after a few months, the intervention was called off. The state forces, however, carried on the struggle against the recalcitrant ranchers with single-minded ruthlessness, and within a few years most of Totó's enemies in northern Goiás had either been killed or driven across the state line into Bahia.[30]

Totó Caiado's constituency was a turbulent one, but the senator managed to hold on to power for nearly two decades, a period in which there was little progress. In all of the state of Goiás, which had a total population of more than half a million, there were only about seven thousand children in elementary schools in 1925. By contrast, the neighboring state of Mato Grosso, with less than half Goiás's population, had nine thousand children attending classes. Labor, not education, was the chief concern of the big landowners upon whom Totó depended to keep him in power. Workers were scarce in this sparsely settled land and extraordinary measures were required to deal with the labor shortage. One of these, a "special law" carried over from the empire period, allowed employers to physically restrain "contract employees" and apprehend any worker who might flee from his "patron" before fulfilling his contract obligations. Senator Caiado not only supported this medieval law but publicly defended a landowner who went a step beyond it and castrated a runaway ranchhand.[31]

Goiás provided plenty of hiding space and sustenance for

fugitive indentured servants and for criminals as well. Even without a gun it was not hard to live off the land: Eggs of the ostrich-like rhea were easy to find on the ground; armadillos could be dug out of their holes; and fish could be stunned by poison extracted from certain vines. But most of the fugitives had guns, which allowed them to take the deer and peccaries that roamed the campo cerrado, as well as a wide variety of edible fowl. The countryside was haunted by gunmen, who were often protected by certain landowners, rivals of those against whom the criminals transgressed. In the wide spaces between the ranching settlements were innumerable solitary mud huts, the homes of bandits, hired killers, or more-or-less peaceful hunters, fishermen, subsistence farmers, and prospectors.

Although all of Goiás lay in the tropics, most of the land was high—five hundred to twelve hundred meters above sea level—and mosquito-borne diseases like malaria were a problem only in the deepest valleys. A much greater threat to the health of the people of Goiás was Chagas' disease, which was endemic from one end of the state to the other. This disease, discovered in 1909 by Dr. Carlos Chagas, was caused by mites that infested the walls of the wattle-and-daub dwellings that housed the great majority of Goianos. The bloodsucking mites would emerge from the walls at night to feast on sleeping humans, causing infections that killed children and debilitated adults, leaving them lethargic and prone to heart failure. Another menace to health on the Goiás plateau came from snakes—including the bushmaster, a cousin of the rattlesnake, that grew to a length of more than three meters and packed enough venom to kill one hundred men. Plagued by illiteracy, disease, and vermin, the Goianos also had to endure Totó Caiado.

Senator Caiado happened to be in Goiás to attend his brother's inauguration as governor when word was received that the Prestes Column was marching in the direction of the state capital. Totó's friends, among many others, fled the town of Caiapônia (then known as Rio Bonito) when the rebels entered it on July 5. But enough townspeople remained to constitute a fair-sized welcoming party for the Prestes Column. Among these were two priests: One said mass for the rebel troops in celebration of the anniversary of the revolution, and the other, Padre Manuel de Macedo, a determined enemy of the Caiado dynasty, accompanied the column on July 6 as it left Caiapônia "simulating . . . an advance on the Goiano capital." [32]

By July 10 Senator Caiado had raised a force of some eight hundred volunteers and posted it south of Goiás city, where he said he expected to intercept the rebels. But shortly afterward the senator withdrew his men to the state capital to parade them at the inauguration of his brother on July 14, and the Prestes Column passed unmolested south of Goiás city, heading east. Totó's Patriotic Battalion picked up the rebel trail a few days later, but never came close to overtaking the Prestes Column. The senator's "patriots" seemed less interested in pursuing the revolutionaries than in rounding up the horses the rebels had cast off. Many of these animals, it was said, were sent to Goiás city where they were sold at auction for the personal profit of the senator. This practice prompted the revolutionaries to begin killing their exhausted horses instead of turning them loose. Nevertheless, Totó and his officers were still able to pick up horses—and other property—as they rode across southern Goiás. The poorest farms and ranches were stripped of their useful animals and their men were pressed into the service of the Patriotic Battalion. [33]

"In all frankness," Major Klinger wrote to Senator Caiado on July 25, "I consider the mission of your forces terminated, for any further effort to overtake the revolutionaries is useless." Klinger begged the senator's permission to suggest that he "hurry to discharge his volunteers in order to end as soon as possible the grim complaints of the families from whom they were uprooted through the abuses of Your Excellency's delegates." The major went on to state that "the suffering of the poor people of Goiás, victims of the fury of these alleged patriots, is indescribable." [34] The letter would cause Klinger trouble later.

When Major Klinger crossed into Goiás from Mato Grosso, he left the jurisdiction of General Malan D'Angrogne and entered the military district of São Paulo and Goiás, commanded by General Eduardo Sócrates. The two-thousand-man force that had been assembled at Ribeirão Claro, Mato Grosso, with Klinger as chief-of-staff, was thereupon disbanded, its three-hundred-man "vanguard" passing to General Sócrates' command as the Klinger detachment. After the fight at the Zeca Lopes ranch, when the Prestes Column struck out to the north where Klinger's trucks could not follow, Klinger advised his new commanding general that there was little more that his forces could do to combat the rebels and requested that he be returned to General Malan's jurisdiction. The major went on to venture his opinion that any further military operations against the rebels would be futile, since, after the drubbing they received at Zeca Lopes, it would no longer be possible to lure them into combat, and they could evade pursuers indefinitely in Brazil's roadless backlands. Klinger suggested that the time had come for the government to give up trying to overpower the revolutionaries and switch to a policy "based on national harmony." [35]

For this last suggestion Klinger received a rebuke from the minister of war. His request to be transferred back to Mato Grosso was denied and he and his three hundred Mineiros were assigned to guard the motor road that ran from Alto Araguaia through Mineiros and Jataí to Rio Verde, in case the rebels should return to that area. Finally, on July 19, Klinger was allowed to shift his troops to Itumbiara, on the Minas Gerais border, and from there he was sent north on the motor road to Goiás city to intercept the rebels who were being "driven" eastward by Senator Caiado's battalion. About half of Klinger's three hundred Mineiros were left behind at Rio Verde or Itumbiara, but his detachment was brought back up to strength on the road to Goiás city by the addition of several units of state troops from Rio Grande do Sul. Arriving at Bela Vista on July 22, Klinger learned that the revolutionaries had already crossed the road to Goiás city near Inhumas. The major then shifted his men to a more easterly road that went to the town of Anápolis. [36]

The main body of the Prestes Column halted about fifteen kilometers northwest of Anápolis at midday on July 23. That afternoon a delegation of five merchants from Anápolis arrived at the rebel camp and offered the revolutionaries a ransom—in goods, money, or both—if they would bypass their town, which, they said was defenseless. While the rebel officers were considering the offer, a civilian messenger arrived at the camp from Anápolis to report that a large government force had arrived in the town—and to save the merchants from an embarrassing, if not deadly, situation. The revolutionary leaders were convinced that the merchants were sincere in their offer and had not intended to lure them into a trap, but they could not afford to remain in the area to collect the payment. Early the next morning the Prestes Column began its march around Anápolis, swinging about ten kilometers north of the town.[37]

Klinger arrived in Anápolis on the afternoon of July 23 with about one hundred Mineiro militiamen, one hundred fifty gaúcho state troops, and eight machine guns. He posted the Rio Grande contingent two kilometers outside Anápolis on the road to the west and the Mineiros at the edge of town on the road to the north. On the morning of July 24 Klinger sent thirty Mineiros in three trucks to make a reconnaissance twenty-five kilometers to the north. After covering the distance and seeing no signs of the enemy, the patrol turned around and headed back toward Anápolis. The trucks were spotted around 11 A.M. by the rebel vanguard, Cordeiro's detachment, as it was emerging from a thicket near the road, ten kilometers north of the town. Cordeiro's men fell back into the bushes and ambushed the government trucks as they drove in front of them. One loyalist was killed and several were wounded as the trucks ground to a halt and their occupants piled out and fled into the bushes on the opposite side of the road from the rebels. The jubilant revolutionaries took possession of the three trucks, four thousand rounds of ammunition, and an automatic rifle.[38] The rebels finally realized that Klinger's mechanized forces were not invulnerable.

The firing could be heard in Anápolis and Klinger immediately ordered a captain to take about fifty Mineiros and go to the aid of the ambushed patrol. The motorized relief force was fired upon as it approached the scene of the earlier action. The sight

of the disabled trucks and the sudden aggressiveness of the
enemy unnerved the captain, who swung his own vehicles
around and dashed to the rear. The detachment of João Alberto, which had moved to Cordeiro's right, emerged from the
bushes and gave chase. The rebel horsemen galloped after the
trucks firing pistols and shouting gaúcho war whoops.[39]

The road was riddled with holes and washouts and it was
with difficulty that the motorized Mineiros outdistanced their
mounted pursuers. One truck broke down on the road and its
occupants scurried into the bush, out of the way of the charging
calvalrymen. The loyalist captain finally stopped running about
two kilometers north of Anápolis, where he organized a defensive line and sent a request to Klinger for reinforcements. João
Alberto did not try to overrun this line; his men kept the loyalists
under sporadic fire as the other rebel troops crossed the road
and resumed the march to the east. About 2 P.M., before Klinger
could mount a counterattack, João Alberto's men broke contact
and disappeared with the rest of the column into the campo cerrado. The revolutionaries marched away toward Luziânia, their
spirits soaring like the columns of smoke from the government
trucks they had captured and set afire.[40]

While the casualties acknowledged by the two sides were
comparable—one killed and two wounded by the rebels, and
one killed and two captured by the loyalists—the losses of matériel and the deflation of loyalist morale made the encounter at
Anápolis a rebel victory. Klinger, although he had long since
given up any hope of destroying the Prestes Column or forcing
it to surrender, was determined not to let his campaign end on
this sour note. Leaving thirty-one men at Anápolis, Klinger
loaded the rest of his troops onto his remaining trucks and
drove south to Silvânia. From there he took the motor road to
the northwest, toward Luziânia, where he hoped to intercept the
revolutionaries. Klinger arrived at Luziânia with two hundred
twenty-one men in nineteen trucks on July 26. Deploying most
of his men around the town, the major organized a mounted patrol of twenty men from his gaúcho contingent and sent it west
into the campo cerrado to look for the enemy. The patrol lo-

cated the Prestes Column on the morning of July 28, about forty
kilometers from Luziânia, but was soon discovered and chased
away by the rebels. Before the gaúchos lost contact with the revolutionaries, they took four prisoners, whom they presented to
Klinger for questioning.[41]

Acting on information supplied by the patrol and its prisoners, Klinger left Luziânia with about half of his men and took the
road that ascended to the high pleateau of Goiás, the area set
aside by the federal Constitution of 1891 as the future capital of
Brazil. At Planaltina, on August 1, Klinger received some reinforcements from Luziânia, but decided that, because of the poor
condition of the roads on the high plateau, additional troops
would only slow him down. Keeping one hundred fifty Mineiros
with him at Planaltina, Klinger sent his gaúchos back down the
road to Luziânia and ordered the troops in that town to begin a
withdrawal to the railhead at Silvânia on August 3. The major
considered his Goiás campaign to be nearing its end; with his
one hundred fifty Mineiro militiamen he would make one last
effort to overtake the rebels and fire some parting shots at
them.[42]

The road gave out completely about fifty kilometers north of
Planaltina. Assured by local ranchers that the rebels were only a
few kilometers away, moving across his front, Klinger mounted
some of his Mineiros on horses and requisitioned two oxcarts to
move his machine guns and ammunition. On the afternoon of
August 5 Klinger was about twenty kilometers north of where he
had left his trucks when a rancher rode up to report that the
rebels had just rustled some of his cattle. As they drove off animals, the revolutionaries told the rancher that they were going
to Bahia and asked him for directions to the town of Posse, near
the border of that state.[43]

Before dawn on August 6 Klinger set up an ambush on the
trail to Posse. But the Mineiros aimed poorly in the early morning light and the first rebels to appear, about fifteen men from
Siqueira's detachment, survived the loyalist fusilade and escaped
apparently without injury. The Prestes Column spent the rest of

the day maneuvering around Klinger's positions. There were still some rebel stragglers in the area the following day, and one of these was wounded and captured by the Mineiros. Klinger's only casualty in his last fight with the Prestes Column was one man wounded. After he returned to Silvânia he was court-martialed for his unauthorized withdrawal from Luziânia and the high plateau. The Supreme Military Tribunal found him guilty of disobeying orders and sentenced him to seven months in prison but, on appeal, reversed itself and overturned his conviction on November 7, 1925.[44] Klinger's quarrel with Senator Caiado, his suggestion that the rebels be offered amnesty, and the freewheeling manner in which he conducted his military operations had offended important segments of the "constituted regime." He would be neutral in the next revolution and join the rebels in the one after that.

About a week after their bruising encounter with Klinger at the Zeca Lopes ranch, the leaders of the revolutionary column, then in the vicinity of Caiapônia, Goiás, resolved to head for Bahia and the other states of the Brazilian Northeast. But no matter where they went—except, perhaps, the Amazonian wilderness—they knew they would have to fight. Klinger's actions had dispelled the notion that they could avoid combat simply by moving fast and bypassing garrisoned cities and towns. If Prestes was to "direct himself toward Rio," he could only do so at the head of a mighty army. In the populous Northeast the one-thousand-man column could grow into such a force: Federal army garrisons as well as the civilian followings of local leaders were expected to join ranks with the column in this neglected and poverty-stricken region of Brazil. But President Bernardes, for all his slighting of the Northeast—he had drastically reduced federal spending there—was sure to resist the rebel invasion of the region with all the forces he could muster. To effectively combat these forces, the revolutionaries would need additional arms and ammunition. Around July 11, 1925, they sent a messenger to Paraguay with a letter for Isidoro, explaining their plans and asking the marshal to try to get them some munitions, which "should be deposited at some point in the Northeast or in Bahia." [45]

The letter was delivered, but Isidoro, who was working on plans for an exile invasion of Rio Grande do Sul, was unable to provide any munitions to the Prestes Column. The marshal referred the request to a "certain coreligionist who was in Rio and in a position to act," but the Prestes Column never received any arms shipments from this or any other source. Had it not been for the shortage of munitions, Captain Moreira Lima would later lament, "we would have dominated all the Northeast; we would have been able to invade Minas Gerais with a respectable army, and, finally, we would have arrived at the gates of Rio de Janeiro, from whence we surely would have expelled the Bernardist gang." [46] In any case, the failure of the column's leadership to devise an effective system of arms resupply greatly reduced the military and political potential of the wandering revolutionaries.

The column's first destination in its drive on the Northeast was the hinterland of Bahia, where a civil war had erupted in March 1925. Should they be unable to take advantage of the political situation in that important coastal state, which was exceeded in population only by Minas Gerais and São Paulo, they could march on into the other northeastern states, "where there was said to be great sympathy for our cause." [47] Along the way they would hope to receive the support of some federal army garrisons and pick up an arms shipment from Isidoro.

From Caiapônia the best route to Bahia seemed to be through Anápolis and Posse, Goiás. But after their contact with Klinger's men (whom they mistook for Goiás state troops) north of Planaltina on the trail to Posse, the revolutionaries decided to detour to the south and approach Bahia through the northwestern bulge of Minas Gerais. By swinging to the south they would avoid a possible enemy concentration at Posse, now that the loyalists had learned that they were heading toward that town, and put themselves in position to cross the São Francisco River closer to its source. The population centers of Bahia all lay east of this great river, which originated in central Minas Gerais and flowed north for more than a thousand kilometers before turning east to empty into the ocean. In Bahia the rebels would need barges to get their horses across the river; in Minas Gerais they might be able to swim them across. The Prestes Column entered Minas Gerais near Serra Bonita on August 11, and eight days later a patrol from João Alberto's detachment reached the São Francisco River at São Romão.[48]

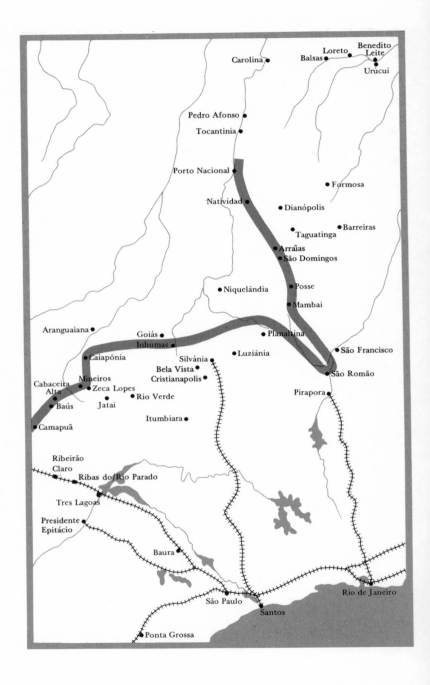

North Toward the Northeast

VI In Mato Grosso and southern Goiás the Prestes Column averaged about fifty kilometers of travel a day. The distance covered by the headquarters, at the center of the column, was estimated and recorded daily by Captain Moreira Lima. The unit of measure used was the *légua*, or league, the value of which varied from place to place in Brazil, as the term originally denoted the distance a horse walking at a steady pace would cover in an hour; terrain and vegetation affected what was considered a league in different localities. In Moreira Lima's calculations, however, the league was used as the constant equivalent of 6,666 meters. A "normal" day's march was eight leagues, which, in the campo cerrado, did require about eight hours in the saddle. On a typical day the rebels would ride from 5 A.M. until 10 or 11 A.M., rest themselves and their horses during the hottest part of the day and resume the march for two or three hours in the late afternoon. At this rate a horse would last for about fifteen days. A faster pace would require more fresh horses than the Goiás countryside could provide.[1]

Combat conditions, or the lack of adequate pasture or water at the end of a "normal" day's march, might compel the column to cover more than eight leagues in one twenty-four-hour period.

Also, marching schedules might be rearranged to take advantage of moonlit nights, when passage through the campo cerrado could be made in greater comfort than during daylight hours. In central Goiás, after the threat from Major Klinger ended, the column often marched only during the mornings, as the bandeirantes of the seventeenth and eighteenth centuries had done. Horses became increasingly scarce as the column moved away from the relatively settled areas of southern Goiás, and, at times, a substantial number of rebels, like the bandeirantes before them, had to proceed on foot. Under these conditions a day's march might amount to less than three leagues. Sometimes the column would halt for as long as four days, to rest men and horses, repair equipment, and allow stragglers to catch up. During these periods, however, patrols were constantly moving on the column's flanks and front, rounding up cattle and horses and gathering intelligence.[2]

The column's vanguard detachment usually camped at about a day's march from the rearguard detachment. The other two detachments and the column headquarters would be grouped together about midway between the front and rear. The detachments normally rotated positions every twenty-four hours. The old vanguard would be relieved shortly before dawn by a detachment from the center and would remain camped as the rest of the column moved past it, leaving it, at the end of the day, in the rearguard position. The men of the vanguard detachment moved forward on a wide front, gathering the information upon which the column's leadership would base the marching orders for the next morning. Each afternoon the vanguard commander would ride back to the column headquarters to meet with Prestes, Miguel Costa, Távora, and with the other detachment leaders. These high officers would discuss the sketch maps and other intelligence supplied by the vanguard commander and, collectively, they would decide on future operations.[3]

The meetings were held in or near one of the two tents that housed Miguel Costa and the officers of his personal staff. Prestes and his aides did not pitch tents; usually they slept on the ground close together with a huge tarpaulin lying over them. The general was not inclined to self-flagellation and saw no reason to give up all the comforts and amenities of civilization. He was always clean shaven and correctly dressed. Many horses served him during the march, each carefully selected, well-groomed, and properly saddled. In addition, the general had a mare mule—an amazing animal that packed his belongings for nearly two years before she disappeared one night in the campo cerrado. Besides the two tents, Miguel's baggage included both a field cot and a hammock and a variety of other useful things, such as fishing gear, scissors, needles, thread, pencils, writing paper, maps, rulers, books, leaf tobacco and corn husks for making cigarettes, matches, shoe polish, brushes, aspirin, balsam, and bicarbonate. The general willingly shared his possessions with comrades in need, although he regularly chided them for not having the foresight to pack such necessary items in their own baggage.[4]

Besides General Miguel and colonels Prestes and Távora, the column headquarters included about a dozen lesser officers and perhaps thirty orderlies, baggage masters, and cooks. Prestes wryly observed that the Brazilian tendency toward bureaucracy could not be overcome even in a revolutionary column in the middle of the wilderness. There were two officers' messes at column headquarters, Prestes' and Miguel's. At Prestes' mess the fare was meager and simple and did not attract visitors; the chief-of-staff's cook doubled as his baggage master and was not inclined toward the culinary art, which suited Prestes, who considered eating a vice. The best provisioned and most hospitable mess in the column was Miguel's, which employed several cooks. Visiting detachment commanders gravitated to the general's table at mealtime. For a while Assistant Chief-of-Staff Juarez Távora had his own mess, where the food was prepared by Tia Maria, an elderly black woman who had been with the revolutionaries since São Paulo. Tia Maria was a good cook, but was also an alcoholic and would go on a binge whenever the column passed through a place where strong drink, including patent medicines, was to be had. Távora, unwilling to go without meals while Tia Maria sobered up, eventually dismissed her and joined Miguel's mess. He was one of the column's heartiest eaters and the major consumer of the general's bicarbonate.[5]

During halts revolutionary officers congregated at Miguel's command post to play chess or backgammon or just to talk. Prestes and Djalma Dutra were avid chess players, as was João Alberto, who also was a frequent winner in backgammon. João Alberto's versatility amazed his comrades: This tall, dark, and lean son of a Pernambuco schoolteacher played the violin and the piano, butchered and dressed steers, performed minor surgical operations, piloted sailboats, was a whiz at mathematics, and could even fix watches. He said that after the revolution he wanted to raise pigs on some land he owned in the state of Alagoas. Miguel Costa wanted to plant eucalyptus trees near São Paulo.[6]

When the intellectuals of the column gathered in Miguel's hospitable tent, "various and interesting subjects were discussed, which gave rise to animated polemics, real spiritual gymnastics, reminiscent of the student debates of a time not long past."[7] Questions of science, mathematics, philosophy, and religion were frequently debated, while politics was less often discussed, since the revolutionaries were agreed on the goal of replacing the government of Artur Bernardes with a regime of true representative democracy. Except for the effusive Colonel Távora, no one seemed disposed to elaborate on this goal. When Juarez Távora brought up his ideas for restricting the powers of the state governments and establishing a unitary national regime, "Siqueira, an incisive and critical spirit, made rubbish of the plans of organization of Juarez." Miguel Costa, a fervent Paulista patriot, was likely to object to any political proposal on the grounds that it gave insufficient attention to São Paulo.[8] Djalma Dutra, a Carioca with "big brown eyes and the features of an Arab," had a "splendid sense of humor" and was "a terrible contrary spirit";[9] he was more likely to support "Siqueira in his satires than Juarez in his political arguments." The youthful Cordeiro de Farias would laugh merrily at it all; an accommodating soul, he was for everything. "Only Prestes maintained any reserve."[10]

Religion was another matter on which Prestes remained silent. The chief-of-staff, the son of a positivist, would not state his own religious beliefs, if any, in open discussion. However, it was said in the column that he had studied Catholicism as a youth and had been baptized at the age of eighteen; later he was supposed to have left the church. At any rate, the only practicing Catholic among the seven top leaders of the column was Juarez Távora. "João Alberto, Siqueira, and Cordeiro gave the impression of not being concerned with the existence of God or of the soul." Miguel Costa and Djalma Dutra were spiritists.[11]

Kardecian spiritism had thousands of devotees among the middle and upper classes of São Paulo and Rio de Janeiro, the home cities of Miguel Costa and Djalma Dutra. Middle-class devotees thronged the spiritist temples of the great urban areas to consult mediums and study the works of Alain Kardec, while the very wealthy "followed the doctrine" at home, reading the texts and holding séances in the privacy of their own mansions. Spiritist rites had been practiced by lower-class Brazilians and their ancestors, blacks and Indians, since time immemorial, but not until the late nineteenth century was the white elite given a respectable doctrinal basis for belief in spirits. The works of the Parisian Hippolyte Leon Denizard Rivail, written in the 1850's and 1860's under the pen name "Alain Kardec," went through more editions in Portuguese than in any other language, including the original French. Kardec's teachings, transmitted to him by superior spirits through mediums, set forth a scheme of progressive reincarnation that appealed both to the scientific evolutionist spirit of the age and to man's mystical tendencies, so denigrated by Comte's positivism. Also, in acknowledging the existence of troublesome "disincarnate" spirits—which sometimes entered the bodies of living persons, causing physical and mental illness—Kardec reasserted the healing function of faith. Kardecian practitioners, like witch doctors and medicine men, quite often relieved the afflictions of people whom physicians had treated in vain.

Padre Manuel de Macedo, the priest who joined the column in Caiapônia, tried to reconcile Catholicism with spiritism. Many lower-class Brazilians had already effectively fused the two in *macumba* and *candomblé*—voodoo rites celebrated in various parts of Brazil where there were large black populations. While none of the higher officers of the Prestes Column were blacks or mulattoes, there were a number of persons of African descent in the lower commissioned ranks and among the enlisted men. Lieutenant Hermínio, the mulatto commander of the headquarters machine-gun section, was both a professed Catholic and a determined placater of ghosts, headless mules, werewolves, and other supernatural beings. The men of the column lived in terror of the dark; they huddled around campfires even on the warmest nights, and when rains put out the fires they lit candles to ward off the demons lurking among the shrubs of the campo cerrado. Rebel foraging parties stripped stores and homes of candles to insure an adequate supply for themselves and their comrades.[12]

Newspapers, magazines, and books were eagerly sought by the officers of the column. Reading material confiscated in towns and from the homes of educated ranchers was passed from hand-to-hand among the literate revolutionaries. They would read during breaks and even in the saddle, as their horses plodded through the campo cerrado. Often a book would be torn up into chapters so that several readers could enjoy the volume simultaneously. Under this system the chances of anyone finishing the book were remote, as the temptation to use the chapters for cigarette paper was hard to resist. Major Ary Salgado Freire, executive officer of Dutra's detachment, consumed an entire Bible, lent to him by Moreira Lima, in making cigarettes. Printed matter might also be used for toilet paper, but more often toilet paper was used to roll cigarettes.[13]

The column's enlisted men entertained themselves by swapping stories around their campfires and by singing and dancing to the accompaniment of accordians, guitars, flutes, drums, and trumpets. The night of St. John, June 23, 1925, was an especially festive occasion. Huge bonfires illuminated the campo cerrado as the men celebrated into the early hours of the morning. At other times, when the rebel soldiers were on the move, they amused themselves by setting the grass ablaze. "Many times the column marched within an immense circle of fires, whose smoke could be seen from far away." [14]

Some of the rebels from Rio Grande do Sul were very young, twelve to twenty years old. Young, long-haired, beardless rebels were often mistaken for women by the inhabitants of the areas through which the column marched, leaving the impression that the revolutionary forces included a large number of female warriors. Actually, the revolutionaries were accompanied by no more than fifty women, few of whom carried firearms—except to relieve their men—or took any part in combat. Almost all of the women were from Rio Grande do Sul. In southern Mato Grosso about twenty Paraguayan women, dressed as men, infiltrated João Alberto's ranks and accompanied the rebels for about ten kilometers before they were discovered and expelled by the detachment commander. Nevertheless, João Alberto tolerated the camp followers who had been with the column since Rio Grande do Sul, as did Cordeiro and Dutra.[15]

Siqueira Campos did not permit women in his detachment. Furthermore, Siqueira made life miserable for camp followers wherever he found them. Encountering a woman on horseback, he would force her to dismount, appropriate her mount for his own cavalhada, and leave her stranded in the trail with all her belongings. The distaff members of the column feared and detested him and scattered when they saw him coming. Perhaps Siqueira dealt harshly with the camp followers because they fell so short of his standards for women, based on his recollections of his mother, who died of a snakebite when he was sixteen years old.[16] More likely, Siqueira, who was developing into the column's best soldier, was motivated by military considerations: The women were inimical to discipline.

Some of the women flitted from man to man and provoked bloody fights among the soldiers. Others, however, remained more-or-less faithful to a single mate: "Monkey Face" stayed with her man even though he frequently beat her and once tried to shoot her with his automatic rifle. She gave birth during the march, as did Santa Rosa, a white girl with regular features who would have been pretty had she been cleaned up. A few hours after Santa Rosa's baby was born, the mother mounted a horse, took the child in her arms, and resumed the march. More pampered was Elza, Major Manuel Lira's mistress, who was carried in a stretcher after she gave birth. Lira, a mulatto from Pernambuco who had made his fortune as a steamboat pilot on the Amazon, was in São Paulo when the revolution broke out in 1924 and joined it out of a spirit of adventure; he rose to become João Cabanas' executive officer, and after the Prestes Column was reorganized in June 1925, he served João Alberto in that capacity. But Lira's efficiency was reduced by his liaison with Elza, a pretty, blonde German who left a husband of that nationality to live with the mulatto officer. To please his woman, the major acquired a tent, a bed, and other luxuries. He was killed defending his baggage when the column was attacked at a river crossing.[17]

A liaison that survived the march of the Prestes Column was that of Hermínia, an Austrian nurse who joined the revolution in São Paulo, and the mulatto Lieutenant Firmino. Hermínia was brave, hardworking, and practical—she had a dog which she trained to catch chickens. As a nurse she ministered to the wounded with energy and dedication and was held in high regard by all. After the end of the march Hermínia and her lover settled down on a farm in Bolivia. More typical of the women of the column was Alzira. About eighteen years old, Alzira was not bad looking but she was half crazy. She would fly into a rage when the men teased her, which was often, and would do such things as stripping off her clothes on the street of a town through which the column was passing. Prestes, learning that one such performance was under way, sent a three-man patrol to arrest Alzira and bring her to him. One of the members of the patrol returned to ask Prestes for reinforcements: The three men were insufficient to catch and clothe Alzira, who "said that she would only come nude." [18]

Colonel Prestes normally kept his distance from the rebel women, clothed or not. But Prestes was no woman-hater, as Siqueira often appeared to be. The chief-of-staff did not mistreat the female members of the column, and he regarded those who committed sexual crimes against women as perhaps the most despicable of all criminals. Prestes, who found it relatively easy to pardon robbers and murderers, once declared that a man accused of seducing a virgin deserved to be shot.[19]

The colonel's puritanical notions did not prevent him from achieving rapport with the soldiers of the column. Habitually smiling, he was accessible to all; he spent much of his free time with the enlisted men, sometimes entertaining them with riddles. He ate no better, and with less regularity, than the common soldiers and, like them, seldom slept in a tent. When there were not enough horses to go around, the colonel would not hesitate to give up his own mount to a wounded soldier. He was not feared; he was respected by officers and men alike. He was strong-willed—"to desire is to be able to," he would say—and decisive: "A decision that is quick but wrong," he believed, "is worth more than one that is correct but late." [20] In combat situations his quick decisions were seldom wrong, and after the fiasco at the Zeca Lopes ranch, when he had let himself be swayed by the reasoned arguments of Juarez Távora, he relied almost exclusively on his own instincts. The rebel soldiers trusted him implicitly and only rarely did the column's collective leadership reject his recommendations.

The route indicated by Prestes turned out to be one of few triumphs and much hardship and suffering. The wounded and the sick were deprived of the services of the column's only medical doctor when Captain José Ataíde da Silva was sent to Rio de Janeiro on an "important mission" after the fight at the Zeca Lopes ranch. His successor as column medical chief, Aristides Corrêa Leal, the veterinarian, was reluctant to treat humans and, for the most part, left the care of the wounded to Lieutenant Aquino, a pharmacist, and Hermínia, the nurse. On two occasions, however, Aristides was prevailed upon to perform surgery: He amputated the gangrenous forearm of one soldier and sewed up another man whose abdomen had been ripped open. The first patient recovered after a second amputation was performed by a medical doctor in a town through which the column passed and the other died. The wounded who survived the enemy bullets and the treatment of the column's medical section endured great pain as they were jostled about on stretchers lashed fore and aft between horses. One soldier, whose leg was smashed by a bullet at the Zeca Lopes ranch, spent more than four months on one of these painful conveyances. Shortly after he was pronounced cured he fell off a horse and refractured his leg; he had to spend three more months on a stretcher.[21]

The medical section concerned itself mainly with the wounded; the sick were generally left to cure themselves or seek treatment from one of several *curandeiros,* eclectic healers, among the soldiers of the column. The curandeiros prescribed herb remedies for some ailments and performed voodoo rituals for others. They were especially successful in dealing with toothaches. With the patient lying on his back, the curandeiro would say some incomprehensible words over him and then plunge a knife into the ground; the patient would feel a sharp surge of pain, which would quickly subside, leaving him free of suffering. The offending tooth, it was said, would then crumble in his mouth. The performances of the curandeiros "shook the skepticism of the unbelievers," according to Captain Italo Landucci. João Alberto and Moreira Lima also testified to their prowess.[22]

Diseases that caused deaths in the column included tetanus, uremia, erysipelas, pneumonia, and acute anemia. Unknown afflictions carried away some, including a young man who steadily lost strength as his body withered away above his legs, which had swollen to enormous proportions, until he died of exhaustion. Another soldier was unable to urinate and suffered lingering and excruciating pain before he finally died. A catheter would have saved him, but that was one of the many medical instruments that the column lacked. When the rebels occupied a town with a pharmacy, Lieutenant Aquino and Nurse Hermínia would be sent to requisition medical supplies. The backcountry drugstores were often poorly supplied with bandages and antiseptics, but were usually well stocked with Humphrey's Marvelous Curative, an all-purpose balm that was applied to wounds with some success. For internal problems, there was the ubiquitous Nogueira's Elixir, which had a high alcoholic content and was quickly snatched off the shelves by foraging soldiers. Some rebels would guzzle any medicine suspected of containing alcohol—including laxatives and menstrual regulators.[23]

The provision of food, like that of medicine, was the responsibility of the individual soldier. To facilitate the collection of food and the preparation of meals, the men of each detachment formed free associations called *fogões.* The *fogão*—literally "big fire"—was a gaúcho institution: an eating cooperative formed by a dozen or so comrades, about the number that could be expected to consume the best parts of one steer before the meat went bad. In the Prestes Column the fogão quickly evolved as the basic administration unit, whose elected chief often dealt directly with the detachment commander, bypassing the formal company or squadron structure. (Djalma Dutra, a cavalry officer, divided his detachment into squadrons; his colleagues, all artillerymen without artillery, used the company designation.) The men of the fogão selected, in addition to their chief, a steward, who was excused from combat and was responsible for safeguarding the group's food stocks, cooking equipment, and pack animals, as well as for directing the preparation of meals. The fogão chief represented his comrades in dealing with the command structure and ensured that his group received its fair share of the goods brought back by the potreadas, the detachment's authorized foraging parties.[24]

Within each detachment were certain men especially attracted to foraging, and it was from them that the initiative for organizing a potreada usually came. A group of five to fifteen men would go to the detachment commander with a proposal and, if he approved it, would receive written permission to ride away from the column and requisition horses, cattle, and other goods needed by their comrades. No one was supposed to separate from the column or enter any building without written authorization from a detachment commander or from general headquarters. Potreadas, however, could be authorized to go anywhere and appropriate anything in the name of the revolution—except for a few items like personal clothing, jewels, and money belonging to individuals. If asked, a forager might give a receipt for confiscated property. Although potreadas were usually expected to return to their detachment in a day or two, some never came back and others were away for periods as long as several months. Changing combat situations or other circumstances beyond their control would be blamed for their tardiness.[25]

The value of livestock requisitions far exceeded that of any other category of property confiscated by the Prestes Column. The gaúcho eating habits adopted by the revolutionaries entailed a great deal of waste, which increased the resentment of the frugal ranchers of Goiás, whose cattle they appropriated. Hindquarters of beef, which did not make good churrasco, were left for the vultures, leading some of the less sophisticated Goianos to believe that the rebels ate the front portions only to give themselves speed. Goianos were especially incensed by the seizure of their horses: The relative scarcity of mounts in Goiás caused the rebels to take horses even from religious pilgrims and members of wedding parties, leaving them stranded on back-country trails. Mules and donkeys were also confiscated, even if they were too small to ride, to pack supplies and personal belongings.[26]

On many occasions Goianos fought desperately to protect their property. Winchester hunting rifles in the hands of irate property owners took an increasing toll of rebel foragers. In Goiás the potreadas began to ransack private homes for Winchesters, not only to prevent their victims from ambushing them later, but to provide themselves with serviceable weapons when their own Mauser rifles ran out of ammunition. While 7-mm. military ammunition was rare in the backlands, .44-caliber Winchester cartridges were available practically everywhere. By depriving farmers and ranchers of their rifles and ammunition, the potreadas left them at the mercy of the bandits who followed in the wake of the Prestes Column.[27]

The potreadas had a secondary mission of gathering intelligence. The foragers would make sketch maps of the terrain they crossed, which they would give to their detachment commander along with any significant information elicited from the people whom they encountered. Potreadas, as well as reconnaissance patrols, might force civilians to accompany them back to their detachment or to column headquarters for questioning. Those civilians who seemed to be most familiar with the trails in the area would be pressed into revolutionary service as guides— and sometimes tied up at night to prevent them from escaping. Others would be freed after the rebels interrogated them, a job that was not easy. "We struggled with the greatest difficulties to obtain information," Captain Moreira Lima noted, "not only because of the bad will of almost all the guides . . . but also because of the incredible ignorance of the poor backcountrymen, who hardly knew how to speak, and the fear that we inspired." The interrogators were further hindered by "the timidity that overcame these humble and rustic people when they found themselves in the presence of persons whom they recognized to be their superiors," at times causing them "to lose their faculties of expression." Even when they did speak, their language "was almost incomprehensible to most of the officers." [28]

Juarez Távora, General Miguel, Prestes, and João Alberto were the column's best interrogators. Siqueira, Dutra, and Cordeiro "always ended up getting irritated," causing the rustics to lose their tongues. Many of those questioned feigned ignorance of the trails in their area or deliberately gave the rebels erroneous information. Some were impressed, and perhaps persuaded to tell the truth, upon learning that a priest was with the column. One headquarters officer went beyond exploiting the presence of Padre Manuel de Macedo to claim that the rebels were escorting a bishop. He directed some Goianos to where Miguel Costa was lounging in his hammock; upon gazing at the middle-aged, blue-eyed, clean-shaven general, the countrymen were convinced that they were in the presence of a bishop and fell down on their knees and kissed his hand. There was little in the revolutionary program that could appeal to these people. Once a rebel captain was asked if the revolution favored the "old law" or the "new law." To please the rustics he said that the revolutionaries were for the "old law" of Emperor Dom Pedro, which had required only a religious ceremony for legal marriage. The "new law" of the republic called for a civil ceremony, which cost from 60 to 100 milreis—compared with the 5 or 10 milreis charged for a church wedding in the backlands. [29]

On occasions the column leadership punished rebels who committed offenses against civilians. One soldier who assaulted a Goiano without justification was forced to walk fifty leagues on foot; others were expelled from the column for such crimes as robbery and attempted murder. Harsher penalties were imposed on rare occasions: A sergeant died before a firing squad for the especially brutal rape of a housewife. Proscriptions against the consumption of alcohol were regularly proclaimed, to avert incidents like the ones that occurred in Jaraguari, Mato Grosso. When towns were occupied, guards were posted around stores to prevent looting and also to stop soldiers from buying alcoholic beverages. Enlisted men were, in fact, forbidden to carry money: A soldier with money was presumed to have stolen it. The revolutionary command approved no requisitions of money in Goiás, and in Mato Grosso the only authorized confiscation of funds was in Campanário, where the Laranjeira Mate Company turned over to the column headquarters 61,000 milreis in Brazilian and Argentine currency, together with some animals and supplies. In return for this payment the revolutionary command refrained from interference in Laranjeira Mate's relations with its Paraguayan peons; the rebels and the company managers parted on good terms.[30] This money, earmarked for the purchase of munitions in Rio or in a neighboring republic, was not used to pay for supplies requisitioned during the march nor was any of it disbursed to the troops.

Throughout the march of the Prestes Column rebel soldiers would ransack homes and stores for alcoholic beverages, or find money with which to buy drinks when effective measures were taken to prevent looting. Eventually, their officers would resort to forcing store owners to pour all their liquor onto the ground, and pharmacists to empty their bottles of Nogueira's Elixir. Despite these efforts by their leaders, some rebels would always find something to drink. In fact, a certain amount of drunkenness was tolerated in the Prestes Column. "Many times drunks had to be tied onto their horses to prevent them from falling off during the march."[31]

From the high plateau of Goiás the Prestes Column descended into the valley of the São Francisco River. On August 13, 1925, the rebel headquarters camped in a forlorn and forgotten corner of Minas Gerais, the home state of President Artur Bernardes. João Alberto, with ninety men from his detachment and a machine-gun section, continued toward the São Francisco to investigate the possibilities of the column's crossing the river near São Romão, Minas Gerais, and going north from there into

Bahia. In a forced march, João Alberto reached São Romão on
the night of August 19. When the rebels entered this river town,
which they had been told was ungarrisoned, they were surprised
to find some soldiers from the Bahia state militia drinking at a
bar. Confused gun battles broke out as the revolutionaries discovered that São Romão was full of government troops. João Alberto quickly pulled his men out of town, but not before they
had taken a couple of prisoners. From the prisoners the rebels
learned that the government force in São Romão was a battalion
of Bahian troops that was on its way home from the campaign in
Paraná. These were the Bahians who, with a state unit from Rio
Grande do Sul, had spearheaded the pincers movement that
forced the surrender of the rebels at Catanduvas. After General
Rondon's command was dissolved, the Bahians were sent by rail
to Pirapora, Minas Gerais, where they boarded the steamboats
and barges that were to take them down the river to Bahia.[32]

The Bahians were due to resume their voyage down the São
Francisco on the morning of August 20, but after the events of
the previous night, João Alberto guessed that they would delay
their departure from São Romão in order to defend the town
against a possible revolutionary attack. The rebel commander,
his forces camped two kilometers outside São Romão, decided to
take advantage of this time to send about thirty men with his two
machine guns along the left bank of the São Francisco to a point
just beyond the mouth of the Urucuia River, where they would
lay an ambush for the boats. João Alberto and the rest of his
troops would make their presence felt around São Romão during the day of August 20, after which they would leave the area
in time to rejoin the machine gunners at the ambush position
before the enemy appeared there.[33]

João Alberto's plans went astray. Two rebel officers—including Major Nestor Veríssimo, a gaúcho revolutionary who had
been João Alberto's right-hand man since Rio Grande do Sul—
were captured while probing around São Romão, and the machine-gun section did not reach the ambush position until the afternoon of August 21, because of the difficulty of the interven-
ing terrain. The machine guns had not yet been emplaced when
the boats were spotted coming down the river; João Alberto and

the rest of the rebel force were still struggling along the bank of the São Francisco south of the Urucuia. The machine gunners hastily positioned their guns on a bluff above the São Francisco and opened fire on the lead steamboat and the barge it was towing. Many loyalist soldiers on the unprotected craft seemed to be struck down by the rebel's raking fire before the crafts veered to the bank and found cover beneath the bluff on which the machine guns were emplaced. The loyalist battalion disembarked and chased away the thirty rebels, who withdrew along the left bank of the Urucuia River toward the encampment of the column headquarters. The Bahians, instead of pursuing, boarded their boats and steamed away toward home.[34]

João Alberto and the machine-gun section were reunited later in the day on the left bank of the Urucuia River. The colonel immediately dispatched a messenger upstream with a letter for Prestes, informing the chief-of-staff of the latest developments on the São Francisco. After reading João Alberto's letter, Prestes decided to send one more probe to the river, to a point opposite the town of São Francisco, seventy kilometers downstream from São Romão, to see if a quick crossing could be made there. This mission was assigned to Djalma Dutra's detachment. Dutra's men, however, found a large deposit of *cachaça*—liquor distilled from fermented sugarcane juice—on a farm en route and were immobilized there when "a great number of them got drunk." Nevertheless, Dutra managed to complete his reconnaissance and return to headquarters to report that there were no large boats to be captured around São Francisco and that the river there was too wide to swim horses across.[35]

With all the shooting by João Alberto's men and drinking by Dutra's, the government was well aware of the presence of the bulk of the rebel forces near the west bank of the São Francisco and was able to guess their intention. No matter where the revolutionaries might attempt a crossing, they could expect resistance; loyalist forces had been alerted up and down the river. Deciding that it would be inopportune to try to cross the São Francisco at this time, Prestes proposed that the column return to Goiás and march north, in order to enter the Northeast through the states of Maranhão and Piauí. The other members of the high command accepted the plan and the column turned to the northwest and marched off in the direction of the Goiano town of Posse. Between the rebel camp on the Urucuia River and the settled area around Posse there were two hundred kilometers of uninhabited wilderness, including a stretch of dry, sandy wasteland belonging to the state of Bahia. The rebels and their horses experienced great suffering in crossing this terrain; on September 7, when the column reached Mambaí, a town in Goiás fifty kilometers south of Posse, almost all the revolutionaries were on foot. The rebels occupied Mambaí without resistance and the column's main body remained there for three days while potreadas scoured the nearby ranches for fresh horses.[36]

There was much grumbling in the column during the march through the desert to Mambaí, and the decision to plunge into the wilds of northern Goiás was not popular with some rebel officers. Mário Geri—former commander of the Italian company in São Paulo, now a major on Miguel Costa's staff—decided the time had come to put an end to this bootless adventure. Geri enlisted one other officer and some soldiers in a conspiracy to "exterminate" the column's general staff, seize the rebel treasury, and march off to the south with those rebels who cared to join them in pursuit of more profitable employment for their arms. Padre Manuel de Macedo, approached with the proposition that they attack Goiás city and overthrow the Caiado dynasty, seemed to go along with the conspirators. Geri and his associates were undone when they tried to recruit Lieutenant Agricola Batista, a chronic griper, but a man incapable of treason. Agricola informed headquarters of the conspiracy and the plotters were arrested. An investigation quickly determined the guilt of Geri, a lieutenant, and several soldiers, all of whom were promptly expelled from the column. Padre Manuel, who said that he only pretended to agree with the conspirators, would remain with the rebels for a few more months.[37]

Having expelled the traitors and remounted the troops, the Prestes Column moved on to the town of Posse, which it occupied on September 12. There was no federal or state garrison in Posse and the townspeople made no attempt to resist the revolutionaries. The mayor and a number of notable residents of Posse, including a French medical doctor, were on hand to welcome the column and receive assurances from rebel officers that their troops would be held in check. In fact, the revolutionary soldiers spent most of their two days in Posse engaged in such innocuous activities as picking ticks off their bodies and boiling their clothes to get rid of lice. The French doctor treated some of the rebel sick and wounded and the town's intellectuals seemed willing to help in informing the Brazilian people of the column's ideals and objectives. In Posse arrangements were made for the transmission of a letter from Miguel Costa, Prestes, and Távora to Congressman João Batista Luzardo.[38]

A partisan of Assis Brasil, Batista Luzardo was one of the Liberators elected to the federal Congress from Rio Grande do Sul in accordance with the peace agreement that ended the gaúcho civil war of 1923. Short and fat, Luzardo had served as a colonel in the Liberator army and was notorious for personally cutting the throats of Chimango prisoners. He was also known, among the Chimangos at least, as a coward.[39] But Luzardo was an educated man; he was both a physician and a lawyer, and he won the confidence of Assis Brazil, the white-haired ex-diplomat, agronomist, and political thinker who headed the Liberator movement—and who remained remote from the fields of battle. When the revolution of 1924 broke out, Assis Brasil fled into exile, but Batista Luzardo, secure in his congressional immunity, remained in Brazil. President Bernardes, for all his authoritarian ways, did not interfere with the rights of the tiny opposition minority in Congress. While newspapers were censored, Luzardo and the other oppositionists were free to speak out in Congress and their words were circulated throughout Brazil by the official publication *Diário do Congresso,* or *Congressional Daily.*

Through Luzardo and the *Diário do Congresso* the rebel leaders hoped to make their positions clear to the Brazilian people and to the administration of President Bernardes. Within the column high command at least one officer, Juarez Távora, was personally acquainted with Luzardo: The two had posed together for photographs during one of the congressman's "peace missions" to Isidoro's headquarters just before the collapse of the revolutionary front in Paraná. About the same time that a messenger was dispatched to Paraguay with a letter asking Isidoro for arms and informing him of the column's decision to march to the Northeast, following the combat at the Zeca Lopes ranch, Dr. José Ataíde da Silva was relieved of his duties as medical section commander and sent to Rio with a letter for Luzardo, which described the rebel campaign in Mato Grosso and southern Goiás, so that he and the Brazilian people would not be misled by government claims of victory over the revolutionaries. Two months later the rebel chiefs wrote a second letter to Luzardo, bringing him up to date on military operations and also stating their conditions for laying down their arms.[40]

"As the minimum limit of our liberal aspirations," the revolutionaries insisted on "the repeal of the Press Control Law and the adoption of the secret ballot." These measures, together with "a normal amnesty" and an end to the state of siege, could constitute the basis for a peace "gratifying for us, honorable for the government, and advantageous for the country." [41] Batista Luzardo spoke out repeatedly in Congress in favor of these "liberal aspirations" and he was a consistent advocate of amnesty—not only for the men of the Prestes Column, but also for the revolutionaries in exile and the rebels imprisoned in Brazil. This last group was increased in October 1925 as a result of an attempt by Honório Lemes to revive the revolution in Rio Grande do Sul. General Honório rode across the border from Uruguay around the first of the month, but on October 8 the doughty old Maragato and several dozen of his gaúchos were run down and captured by the Chimangos of Flores da Cunha. A proposal by Batista Luzardo for a general amnesty was defeated in the Brazilian Congress in December 1925. President Bernardes stood firm against amnesty and would not permit his partisans to consider the liberal reforms advocated by the opposition while rebels were in arms against his government.[42]

The Prestes Column, after stating its political objectives in the letter to Luzardo, resumed its march on September 15. The route north from Posse was not as difficult as many rebels had feared it would be. The trails they took were old ones, blazed by the gold seekers of the eighteenth century. The town of São Domingos, eighty kilometers north of Posse, lay on the main route between Salvador, Bahia—until 1763 the capital of Brazil—and Goiás city. Arraias, one hundred kilometers northwest of São Domingos, was on the trail between Goiás city and the gold fields around Pôrto Nacional, or Pôrto Real as it was called in colonial times. Both of these routes were in use as early as 1740. Most of the gold mining settlements originally served by the trails had vanished long before the advent of the twentieth century, but the principal towns remained, though greatly reduced in size. The area between Posse and Pôrto Nacional was thinly populated, decadent, and almost completely ignored by both the federal and state governments. With no government troops in this area to contend with, the Prestes Column could devote a maximum of effort to the search for horses and cattle; under these circumstances, the region's relatively meager resources were sufficient to satisfy most rebel needs. While the gaúchos of the column lamented the lack of erva mate, they learned to appreciate the fruit of the stately mango trees planted by the area's early settlers. These and other vestiges of past glory fascinated the revolutionaries, and the march from Posse to Pôrto Nacional was almost idyllic. The ranchers of the area seldom fought to protect their livestock and the only combat with government forces occurred far out on the column's right flank, as Siqueira's detachment scouted a reported enemy concentration along the Goiás-Bahia border.[43]

Forces of the Goiás state militia had been stationed in Dianópolis, then known as Duro, since the backlands war of 1919–1922. The war was set off by the murder of "Colonel" Joaquim Wolney by some state policemen who had come to Dianópolis from Goiás city with a judge who was supposed to try the colonel for stealing his neighbors' cattle. Apparently the state authorities decided to spare themselves the trouble of a trial by wiping out the accused and the rest of his troublesome family. Colonel Joaquim Wolney, who was around eighty years old, was killed at his ranch near Dianópolis on December 23, 1918, on the eve of the scheduled trial, along with several of his kin—but his wife and son, Abílio, escaped the massacre. "Colonel" Abílio, whose political ambitions had earlier been thwarted by the Caiado dynasty, now declared war on the state government and proclaimed his determination to avenge the death of his father. But the state authorities and the local enemies of the Wolney clan—which was of Dutch descent, like many others in northern Brazil, once a colony of the Netherlands—acted quickly and rounded up most of Abílio's surviving close relatives and locked them up in the Dianópolis jail, where they were held as hostages.[44]

Undaunted, Abílio crossed the border into Bahia to raise his avenging army from among his friends and associates in that state, where the Wolneys allegedly marketed the cattle they rustled in Goiás. Near the village of Formosa do Rio Prêto he assembled a force of Bahian gunmen, or *jagunços*. This was a fearsome crew, composed, it was said, of men who filed their teeth to make them resemble those of the piranhas of the São Francisco River, of men who had *corpos fechados*, bodies invulnerable to bullets—or thought they had, which had the same effect in augmenting their ferocity in battle. Deeply religious, sober, almost chaste, the jagunço took his pleasures in fighting and killing and derived a maximum of gratification in exacting cold vengeance. He was quiet, introspective; his speech was soft and rhythmical, deliberate and truly elegant. Abílio Wolney's Bahian jagunços did not use lights at night and some of them slept in a squatting position, their Winchesters at the ready. They had an uncanny ability to see in the dark and their aim was reputed to be infallible in nighttime ambushes.[45]

The terrified enemies of the Wolneys around Dianópolis begged the state government to do something to forestall the anticipated jagunço invasion. In February 1919 Senator Totó Caiado arranged for federal intervention in northern Goiás. Federal troops were ordered from Salvador, Bahia, to Dianópolis, but the terrain west of the São Francisco River was too difficult for them and they stopped short of Goiás. In the meantime, Abílio Wolney moved his jagunços to the outskirts of Dianópolis and demanded that his relatives be released immediately from jail. The police chief replied that he would kill every

one of the prisoners the minute Abílio or any of his jagunços set
foot in the town. Abílio's sister was released and sent to persuade
her brother that his enemies meant business. But Abílio ignored
the pleas of his sister and launched his attack anyway. There was
some furious fighting, from house to house, before the anti-
Wolney forces gave up the struggle and fled the town. Abílio
found his relatives locked in the stocks of the ancient dungeon,
all stabbed through the heart. The young colonel lost most of his
family, but he gained Dianópolis—and a lot of sympathy in Rio
de Janeiro when reports of the latest atrocity reached the national capital.[46]

An officer from the federal expeditionary force that was
stalled at Barreiras, Bahia, was sent without troops to Dianópolis
to investigate the situation and confer with Wolney. Major Álvaro Mariante reached Dianópolis in June 1919 and determined
that the area was effectively under Wolney's control. On
Mariante's recommendation the federal intervention was called
off and the government of the state of Goiás was left to deal with
Wolney as best it could. There was some talk of a negotiated settlement, but, in the end, the Caiado regime decided that it could
not afford to temporize with the jagunço chief. Governor
Eugénio Rodrigues Jardim, Senator Caiado's brother-in-law,
pressed the struggle against Wolney with great vigor. A company of state militia was raised in the Araguaia River region and
sent to the Dianópolis area to join the fight against Wolney. By
1922 the state forces and their local allies had retaken Dianópolis and driven Wolney and his jagunços back to Bahia. They
wreaked a terrible vengeance on those who had cooperated with
Wolney during his occupation of the area; the slightest suspicion
of collaboration was grounds for summary execution. Northern
Goiás was effectively pacified and Abílio Wolney seemed to turn
his back on the area as he embarked on a new career as a
rancher and politician in the state of Bahia. Nevertheless, the
state of Goiás retained a garrison in Dianópolis, in case he
should attempt a comeback.[47]

The state troops at Dianópolis were shifted to Taguatinga
when it was reported that the Prestes Column was approaching

that town. The militiamen, probably fewer than one hundred, dug trenches in the streets of Taguatinga and were in good defensive positions when Siqueira Campos' detachment approached the town on the afternoon of September 29, 1925. The rebels withdrew after three probing attacks, in which they expended much valuable ammunition and lost one man killed, one wounded, and one captured. Siqueira had located the enemy troops on the column's right flank and determined that they would indeed fight—at least to defend their positions. The militiamen did not pursue Siqueira's detachment when it withdrew to the northwest to rejoin the rebel main body.[48]

A week before Siqueira's fight at Taguatinga the column headquarters had occupied the town of Arraias, whose citizens received the revolutionaries with some enthusiasm. The rebel main force went from there to the town of Natividade, which they found to be almost completely deserted. While the revolutionaries occupied the abandoned town and ransacked its vacant buildings, Siqueira's men and a patrol from João Alberto's detachment, sent to explore the column's left flank, rejoined the rebel main body. From Natividade the reunified column marched on Pôrto Nacional. En route a message was received from the prior of the Dominican missionaries in Pôrto Nacional: Friar José M. Audrin declared that the column would meet no resistance in his town and invited the rebel officers to be his guests at the monastery. The revolutionary chiefs replied, assuring the prior of their peaceful and honorable intentions and urging him "to counsel the people not to abandon their homes or take out and hide objects of their property." It was indispensable, they said, that the head of each household remain "to help us prevent any outrage against his property that some bad soldier might try to commit." The friar agreed, but, contrary to his advice, most of the people of Pôrto Nacional locked up their houses and fled into the bush with all the belongings they could carry.[49]

Pôrto Nacional was on the Tocantins River, about seventy kilometers downstream from the limit of navigation. Although it had fewer than six thousand people, it was officially a "city," the urban center of northern Goiás. Its communications with the outside world were mainly via the river, which emptied into the Amazon not far from the city of Belém. The closest telegraph station was at Carolina, Maranhão, more than four hundred kilometers downstream. Pôrto Nacional's elevation was much less than the average for Goiás, only about 230 meters, and malaria, rather than Chagas' disease, was its major health problem. The city was the seat of a bishop—who happened to be out of town when the Prestes Column arrived—and, in addition to the monastery, boasted a convent of nuns, who operated a school for local children. The Dominican friars provided religious services for the faithful of the area and did some proselytizing among the Indians who lived downstream. The Indians—Xerentes, Caraós, and Apinajés—belonged to the Tapuya (or Ge) group, a family of tribes that once dominated much of central South America and were implacable enemies of the Tupi Guarani of Paraguay and the Brazilian coast. Pôrto Nacional had a newspaper, *Norte de Goiás,* which was printed on an ancient press, made in 1860, whose type was so worn that its print was hardly legible.[50]

Advance elements of the Prestes Column arrived in Pôrto Nacional on October 12 and the rebel headquarters moved into the monastery on October 16. The city's mayor and police chief had fled, but a judge remained, as well as a state legislator—who claimed he had broken with Totó Caiado because the senator had physically abused him in Goiás city when he refused to join his Patriotic Battalion as a private. (Among the people of Pôrto Nacional it was said that Totó had taken a bullwhip to their representative.) Friar Audrin, a forty-six-year-old native of France, treated the rebel officers with great courtesy and said mass for the troops; he even baptized the babies of the camp followers. His kindness was repaid by the revolutionaries, who generally refrained from looting abandoned houses; the good conduct of the occupiers encouraged some of the refugees in the nearby woods to return to their homes. Some residents who had lost their fear of the rebels asked to see "Princess Isabela." It was rumored in the backlands that the daughter of the last emperor of Brazil was accompanying the column, but the only Isabela among the revolutionaries turned out to be an alcoholic camp follower who was better known by her nickname *Pisca-Pisca*— "Blinky." [51]

Three members of the Prestes Column—Captain Lourenço Moreira Lima, Dr. José Damião Pinheiro Machado, and Padre Manuel de Macedo—took over the printing plant of *Norte de Goiás* and put out the seventh issue of *O Libertador*. The first six issues of this revolutionary newspaper had been published by Pinheiro Machado in São Luís, Rio Grande do Sul, while Captain Prestes' railroad battalion occupied that town late in 1924. *O Libertador* published information to refute the government contention that the rebels were common malefactors and to show that the democratic revolution begun in the south was alive and well in the north. Besides publishing a newspaper, the revolutionaries engaged in other civic activities in Pôrto Nacional, such as demonstrating their automatic weapons to the girls of the convent school and paroling convicts in the local jail. One of the inmates they released was an old Negro, who had been sentenced to thirty years, of which he had served eleven by 1925, by a drunken judge even though a jury had found him innocent of murder—at least those were the facts of the case as determined by lawyer Moreira Lima. Also, the rebels removed from the jail or destroyed its stocks, fetters, and ferules. Receipts were given for private and church property appropriated for revolutionary use. [52]

For all the goodwill he displayed toward the rebels, Friar Audrin was compelled after a week of occupation to point out to them, in writing, the suffering they were causing: "The passage of the Revolutionary Column through our backlands and through this city has been a lamentable disaster, which will remain for some years irreparable. In a few days our people, in the majority poor, have seen themselves reduced to almost complete misery." While the cleric realized that the rebels were motivated by high ideals rather than by greed, the distinction meant little to their victims. Friar Audrin suggested that the time had come to put an end to this destructive crusade, and he offered to try to communicate with certain persons in Rio or São Paulo who might be able to arrange "an understanding between the Government and the Revolutionaries." [53]

The rebels replied expressing regret for the measures they had been forced to take by the necessities of war and reminding the friar that the men of the column, no less than the civilians he spoke of, were enduring great deprivation. But they welcomed his offer. "We believe, with our esteemed chiefs, Marshal Isidoro Lopes and Senhor Assis Brasil, that the best and easiest means of pacifying the country would be a loyal and dispassionate understanding between the Government and the Revolution. Therefore, and in view of the sincere patriotism of your proposals, we impose no conditions in accepting them." [54] Audrin and the rebel leaders then got together and selected the names of three men in the Rio–São Paulo area—two churchmen and a congressman from Goiás—whom they would ask to serve as mediators. But then difficulties arose: To the friar, an "understanding" meant that the rebels would lay down their arms in return for amnesty, while to the revolutionaries, it meant that the government would make additional concessions. Audrin envisioned a drawn-out series of negotiations, perhaps through the telegraph office in Carolina, during which the rebel troops would remain quartered in Pôrto Nacional, "consuming the few possessions of the townspeople while many families remained apprehensive and hidden in the woods," suffering privation and exposure during the rainy season, which was just beginning.[55]

Then, suddenly and mysteriously, the revolutionaries evacuated Pôrto Nacional on October 22. Friar Audrin was glad to see them go—and not just because it meant an end to their demands on his flock. The Frenchman still respected their idealism but found their gasconades irritating. The rebels had no right to the title "Unvanquished Column" Friar Audrin believed, although he would not object to their calling themselves "The Column of Death." Their passage through the backlands "was essentially malign." The rebel leaders went about the country "freeing criminals, tearing up jails, burning archives and public records, thus giving an imprudent example of contempt for laws and for the authorities." After the rebels departed, many of their victims tried to recoup their losses at the expense of their neighbors. The rebels "left behind them an epidemic of robberies." Many times Friar Audrin would have to raise his voice against those who followed the example of the revolutionaries and seized the property of others. Nevertheless, the friar could not help but admire the column's austere chief-of-staff: "Of all the members of the revolutionary army . . . Colonel Luís Carlos Prestes was the most considerate and attentive toward our backlanders." [56]

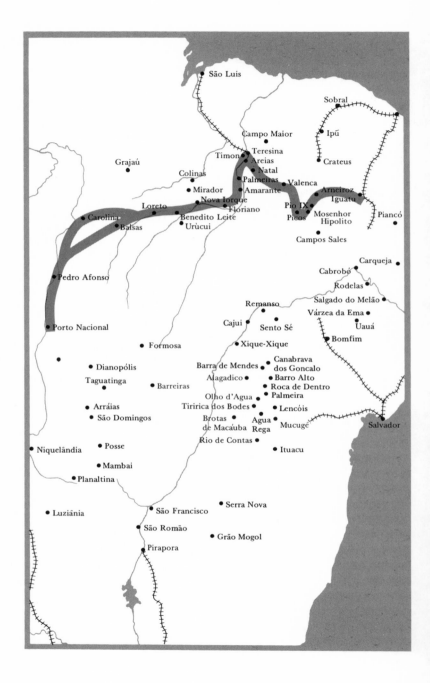

São Luis

Sobral

Campo Maior   Ipú

Teresina
Grajaú   Timon   Areias   Crateus
             Colinas   Natal
                    Palmeiras
         Mirador   Amarante   Valenca
       Loreto   Nova Iorque   Arneiroz
                  Flóriano   Pio IX   Iguatu
   Carolina   Benedito Leite   Picos   Mosenhor   Piancó
     Balsas   Urùcui   Hipolito

                        Campos Sales

                                        Carqueja
                              Cabrobó
Pedro Afonso   Rodelas
                         Remanso Salgado do Melão
                                  Várzea da Ema
                    Cajui   Sento Sé   Uauá
Porto Nacional   Bomfim
          Formosa   Xique-Xique

     Dianopólis   Barra de Mendes   Canabrava
                            Alagadico   dos Goncalo
   Taguatinga   Barro Alto
                     Barreiras   Roca de Dentro
                          Olho d'Agua   Palmeira
   Arráias   Tiririca dos Bodes   Lencóis
   São Domingos   Brotas   Agua
                     de Macáuba Rega Mucugé   Salvador
                     Rio de Contas
Niquelândia   Posse   Ituacu

         Mambai
   Planaltina

   Luziânia   São Francisco   Serra Nova

           São Romão
                      Grão Mogol
           Pirapora

Golden Days in the Middle-North

VII Luís Carlos Prestes could not swim and he almost drowned while bathing in the Tocantins at Pôrto Nacional. The colonel was swept up in the current of the river and would have perished had it not been for the quick action of Major Manuel Lira, the former steamboat captain on the Amazon. Despite his narrow escape, Prestes refused to be intimidated by the river and, on October 22, 1925, left Pôrto Nacional on a raft made of palm-tree trunks, as his soldiers marched along the right bank of the Tocantins toward the village of Tocantínia. After exchanging a few shots with a small enemy force, probably the policemen who had fled Pôrto Nacional two weeks before, the rebels occupied Tocantínia on October 28. It was from this village that the revolutionaries, nine hundred strong, launched their invasion of the state of Maranhão.[1]

The people of Maranhão were historical malcontents. They had engaged in long and bloody revolts against the Dutch colonial regime, against the Portuguese, and against the Brazilian Empire. Since the proclamation of the republic, however, the Maranhenses had fought only among themselves. Nevertheless, the leaders of the Prestes Column felt they had a good chance of

rekindling the traditional Maranhense ire against the central
government in faraway Rio. The government in São Luís was
firmly allied with President Bernardes, but it had some powerful
enemies in the backlands, who, unlike José Morbeck in Mato
Grosso, seemed to have no qualms about joining the column in
an armed movement aimed at the federal regime as well as at the
state oligarchy. Furthermore, Maranhão was a coastal state, the
gateway to the populous Northeast. Control of Maranhão would
be of far greater value to the revolution than dominion over
the empty spaces of landlocked Mato Grosso or Goiás, hundreds
of kilometers from any important centers of population or
power.

From Pôrto Nacional the revolutionary headquarters had
sent a circular letter to the "responsible men" in the Maranhense
city of Carolina, informing them that the column might be coming their way and urging them to remain calm and advise the
local residents not to flee or hide their belongings, for it was impossible for the rebel leaders "to guarantee the property rights
of anyone over objects which our soldiers might find hidden outside homes." Later, from Tocantínia, Major Paulo Kruger da
Cunha Cruz was sent incognito down the river in a canoe to
Carolina. From there he was to proceed overland to São Luís,
sounding out opposition leaders along the way. He would be
followed, as far as Carolina, by Cordeiro's detachment, accompanied by Juarez Távora and some other staff officers. João Alberto's detachment struck out due west from Tocantínia to
screen the rebel right flank and check on reports that a loyalist
force was advancing on the column from the São Francisco valley in Bahia. The detachments of Cordeiro and João Alberto
were to rejoin the rebel main force in the vicinity of Balsas,
Maranhão, where the revolutionary chiefs would pool their intelligence and decide how to proceed with the campaign.[2]

The column's main body followed the Tocantins as far as
Pedro Afonso before veering to the right in the direction of Balsas. Between Tocantínia and Pedro Afonso the rebels were approached by a band of Indians, whose arrival was announced by

one of their number blowing on a native trumpet. The Indian chief spoke to the revolutionary leaders through his interpreter, a member of the tribe who had spent some time in Teresina, Piauí, and wore a straw hat as a symbol of his status. The rebel officers respectfully acceded to the interpreter's request that they join the Indians in forming a semicircle around the chief, who then launched into an hour-long discourse in the Xerente tongue. The chief spoke in a loud voice, frothing at the mouth, periodically thrusting his hands into the air and stamping his feet. When the speech was over the rebels waited for the natives to begin the applause, but there was none; instead, the interpreter turned to Miguel Costa and said:

"General, chief is saying that Christian takes much from Indian—he does not let Indian hunt, he kills Indian—that Rondon does not care about Indian. He is asking you to give tired horse to him; give hoe; give musket; give old clothes; and give money.

"General, these things you give to chief, but money you give to me, for I am no longer a wild Indian." [3]

The revolutionaries must have been good to the Indians, for they accompanied the column headquarters for about three hundred kilometers. The Indians on foot were always able to reach a campsite before the staff officers on horseback. While the Indians were around, the rebels had to take extra precautions to secure their horses. The Xerentes, it was said, would rather eat horseflesh than the meat of any other animal. They would slip off during the night with horses or anything else that their revolutionary friends left unguarded. [4]

The rebels and the Indians parted company as the column entered the settled areas of southern Maranhão. Cordeiro's detachment, on the rebel left flank, was a day's march short of Carolina when it received a messenger from that city. The emissary bore a letter from three politicians welcoming the revolutionaries to the area and assuring them that they would meet no resistance in Carolina, where the majority of the people were awaiting them "with open arms." The rebels were not disappointed: Their entrance into Carolina—on November 15, the

thirty-sixth anniversary of the proclamation of the republic—
was a festive occasion. Most of the people of the city, which was
considerably larger than Pôrto Nacional, were on hand to cheer
the rebel troops and join them in a round of patriotic celebrations. Juarez Távora, who was accompanying Cordeiro's detachment to rally civilian support for the revolution, treated the
crowds to his oratory, which was received with great enthusiasm.
Carolina, "The Princess of the Tocantins" was an oasis of culture
in the backlands: It had a high school, a library, a philharmonic
orchestra, a convent, Catholic and Protestant churches, a spiritist center, and two newspapers. Captain Moreira Lima took
over the offices of one of the newspapers and put out the eighth
issue of *O Libertador*.[5]

Lourenço Moreira Lima was known among his Tenente
comrades as the "Ferocious Bacharel." The term *bacharel,* meaning college graduate, was sometimes used as a synonym for lawyer, which Moreira Lima was, while the plural, *bacharéis,* was
employed by military men as a collective pejorative for all the
selfish and pusillanimous civilian politicians, attorneys, kept jour-
nalists, and bureaucrats who were ruining the country—a category to which he emphatically did not belong, as the qualifier
"ferocious" made clear. Moreira, who appeared to be about fifty
years old in 1925, had spent more than a decade as a lawyer in
the Amazonian rubber country before moving to Rio de Janeiro
in 1920. Having witnessed the rubber cycle from boom to bust—
with all its attendant evils, including the brutal exploitation of
semi-enslaved labor—Moreira was fanatically devoted to the
overthrow of the political system that permitted such abuses. He
was involved in the conspiracies of 1922 and 1924 and spent five
months in prison for his revolutionary activities; he was a captain on Isidoro's staff when the Paraná front collapsed, and despite the precarious state of his health, he volunteered to join the
Prestes Column, which he served as "secretary." The captain
suffered greatly from a strangulated hernia and wore a truss
fashioned from rope and wire; he did not complain, but often
was seen clutching his stomach while marching on foot.[6]

Moreira Lima was a true believer, a man of courage and zeal.

His rage against the prevailing regime was as limitless as his compassion for its victims—including most convicted criminals, who, he believed, had been forced into antisocial behavior by the corrupt system he was fighting to destroy. It was on his recommendation, strongly endorsed by Prestes, that jails were emptied and stocks and chains ripped out of them. An abhorrence of corporal punishment led Moreira and his colleagues to destroy the ferules they found in jails and in public schools as well. There were, however, few public schools in the backlands through which the rebels passed; Moreira Lima blamed this deplorable fact on the state governments, which siphoned off much of the revenue collected in the local communities. In Carolina, Maranhão, the revolutionaries burned the local tax lists, not only to relieve the local property holders, at least temporarily, of an onerous burden, but also to strike at the financial base of the malevolent oligarchy in São Luís, the state capital.[7]

While the rebels destroyed Carolina's tax lists, they encouraged local residents to register in the public records office the receipts they received for the property they gave up for revolutionary use. In addition to food, animals, and supplies, money was requisitioned by the rebels in Carolina: A total of perhaps 10,000 milreis was collected from the merchants of the city. The requisitions were not greatly resented at the time, possibly because the people of Carolina believed that the Prestes Column and the Maranhense opposition would soon seize São Luís, set up a revolutionary government there, and pay off their obligations from the state treasury. It was not inconceivable that President Bernardes would be forced to come to terms with the revolutionary movement in Maranhão, just as his predecessors had accepted extra-constitutional changes of government in other peripheral states. With the Prestes Column and Maranhense insurgents in control of Maranhão, the federal government might well be persuaded to recognize a *de facto* government in São Luís and grant amnesty to the rebels from the south to prevent the spread of the revolution to the states of the Northeast. Upon entering Carolina, colonels Távora and Cordeiro had sent a telegram to the president "informing him of the occupation of the city and urging him to abandon the attitude of hate and vengeance that inspired his actions." [8]

The leaders of the Prestes Column fully realized that "the effective and lasting possession" of Maranhão by the revolution "would put us in a most advantageous position *vis-à-vis* the federal government." From northern Goiás the rebels had sent Major Paulo Kruger as an emissary to the opposition leaders in Maranhão to persuade them to foment "a serious uprising in our favor." [9] Kruger made some contacts, but he did not reach the opposition chiefs in São Luís. He was discovered and arrested by the authorities in the town of Grajaú. Learning of this event while he was in Carolina, Juarez Távora, "without consulting the Division Command," sent letters, via a civilian messenger, to two prominent opposition figures in the state capital, one of whom was an appeals court judge. In view of "the lamentable disaster," the capture of Kruger, Távora suggested that earlier plans would have to be changed. In the letters he called for civilian uprisings in the center of the state, not in São Luís, to support rebel operations in the Parnaíba valley, along the border between Maranhão and Piauí. Most important, he said, was for the revolution's Maranhense friends to cut the railroad between São Luís and Teresina, the capital of the state of Piauí and the principal city of the Parnaíba valley. After dispatching these letters, Távora left Carolina on November 23 with Cordeiro and his troops to rejoin the column headquarters at Balsas.[10]

The other members of the rebel high command agreed with Juarez Távora that the failure of the Kruger mission virtually precluded a statewide popular revolt in Maranhão. Whatever local forces might come over to their side would be employed in operations in the Parnaíba valley, which the rebels intended to use as a base for an invasion of the Brazilian Northeast. Juarez Távora's brother, Fernandes, was at the time preparing an uprising in Ceará, and the column leaders resolved to invade that northeastern state "at the earliest possible date." [11] To get there they would have to cross the two middle-north states of Maranhão and Piauí.

The campos cerrados of northern Goiás extended across southern Maranhão to the Parnaíba valley, but other aspects of the landscape changed, with rolling country giving way to flat plains as the rebels marched eastward. The rains were heavy and the rivers were high, but the revolutionaries could always round up enough canoes to take them across, and none of the streams was too wide for their horses to swim. During this time of year there were practically no passable motor roads in Maranhão beyond São Luís, which was on an island, and the state's only extensively navigable rivers were the Tocantins and the Parnaíba, on its borders. The São Luís–Teresina railroad was the only route of rapid transportation in the interior of the state. The rebels did not have to fear a Klinger-type pursuit in Maranhão.

João Alberto's detachment, which had linked up with the column main body in Balsas on November 21, was sent north to Grajaú to rally the local revolutionaries and to try to rescue Paulo Kruger. Grajaú was on the edge of the *mata*, or forest zone, of central and northern Maranhão. The most powerful local chief in that area was "Colonel" Manuel Bernardino, an immigrant from Távora's home state of Ceará, who was an outspoken foe of the Maranhão oligarchy and had a large following among the small farmers around Grajaú. Manuel Bernardino, who billed himself as "The Lenin of the Mata," and two hundred of his partisans, all armed with Winchesters, joined João Alberto outside Grajaú on December 2. This was the first significant reinforcement that the Prestes Column had received since it left Paraná. But before the combined forces of Joáo Alberto and Manuel Bernardino could lay siege to the town of Grajaú, its loyalist defenders fled to São Luís, taking Paulo Kruger with them. From Grajaú, João Alberto and Manuel Bernardino marched toward Mirador to rendezvous with the column headquarters, picking up fifty more Maranhense volunteers along the way. "Maranhão was the state that contributed the most in men and resources," Captain Ítalo Landucci would recall; "there the column had its golden period." [12]

Before the column headquarters reached Mirador, there was

an incident that threatened to dissipate some of the goodwill that the rebels had built up among the people of southern Maranhão. A group of soldiers from João Alberto's detachment who, for some reason, had not followed their commander to Grajaú, entered the town of Loreto on the night of December 3 and began "perpetrating a ruckus." Prestes, who happened to be in the town attending a birthday party for Miguel Costa, confronted the disorderly soldiers and demanded that their leader, a sergeant, hand over his sidearm. Instead of submitting, the sergeant drew his pistol and pointed it at Prestes, and his followers assumed the same menacing attitude. The mutineers, however, were immediately set upon and disarmed by the headquarters personnel and locked up in the town jail. General Miguel wanted to punish them severely, but Prestes sensed that the real culprit was their company commander, Benício dos Santos, an unruly gaúcho himself, who abetted the unsoldierly conduct of his men. The next morning Prestes released the men from jail and told them to return to their camp, a short distance outside town, and tell Benício to prepare his company for a march on the column's flank. Prestes, accompanied by only one aide, rode out to Benício's camp, put himself at the head of his company, and led the gaúcho commander and his men on a twenty-four-hour punishment march, which effectively tamed some of the wildest spirits of the column.[13]

Among the detachment commanders, Siqueira Campos was the most resolute in enforcing military discipline. A few days after the episode in Loreto, Siqueira's men, the column's vanguard, occupied the village of Mirador. Word was received there that armed civilians, led by a pro-government police chief and by a deserter from the Prestes Column, were assembling in nearby Colinas. Although Siqueira had not planned to go beyond Mirador, he immediately set out for Colinas with most of his detachment, arriving there, after an all-night march, on the morning of December 9. By this time the enemy had fled to the north, but Siqueira was determined to run down the deserter, who had committed innumerable robberies since slipping away from the column on the Tocantins, and punish him. Siqueira's weary troops pushed on until they arrived at a ranch twenty kilometers from Colinas, where they caught the enemy napping. The deserter was killed in his hammock and his band was wiped out.[14]

While the detachments of Siqueira and Cordeiro were on their way to Mirador to link up with João Alberto, coming from Grajaú, Dutra's men were marching toward the town of Benedito Leite on the Parnaíba River. The rebels had learned of an enemy concentration on the river at Benedito Leite and Uruçuí, its sister town on the Piauí side. Djalma Dutra's mission was to fix these forces by feigning an attack on Benedito Leite, while the rebel main body approached the river for a crossing farther downstream. About dusk on December 7, Dutra's two hundred rebels began trading shots with the loyalists entrenched at Benedito Leite. These forces, together with supporting troops across the river in Uruçuí, totaled 946 men, about a third of whom were federal light infantrymen. The rest were regular Piauí militiamen (140), volunteers incorporated into the Piauí militia (196), a company from the Ceará militia, and a group of 50 armed civilians. During the night, as the firing continued and a thick mist rose from the river, spreading a shroud over the battlefield, terror gripped the government soldiers. In the early morning hours there was a blind scramble for the river, as panic-striken troops stumbled over one another trying to get aboard the steamboats that stood near the banks with engines churning and lights ablaze in the translucent gloom. When the sun rose and the fog lifted, the loyalists were gone. Without trying, Djalma Dutra had won the Prestes Column's greatest victory. He occupied both towns on December 8, took possession of the war matériel abandoned by their erstwhile defenders, and dispatched a messenger to inform rebel headquarters of the loyalist movement downriver. Then he began a march along the river toward Nova Iorque.[15]

The column headquarters, which was monitoring government telegraph transmissions at Mirador, learned of the unexpected victory at Benedito Leite/Uruçui before Dutra's messenger arrived. The rebel chiefs decided to move their forces immediately to the river and strike some more blows at the reeling enemy. And, with both the federals and the Piauí militia in a state of panic, the possibility of capturing Teresina, the Piauiense capital, could not be ignored. João Alberto crossed the river at Nova Iorque and joined Dutra in marching toward the capital along the Piauí side; Cordeiro, Siqueira, and Manuel Bernardino closed in on the city from the Maranhão side of the river.[16] While Manuel Bernardino's interests lay in São Luís, he supported the attack on Teresina, apparently hoping that revolutionary control of the Piauí city could facilitate his operations across the river in Maranhão.

The loyalists managed to regain some of their composure after fleeing Benedito Leite and Uruçui. They lined their steamboats and barges with sandbags and cotton bales, which enabled them to run the rebel gantlet to Teresina without suffering significant casualties. Their spirits were boosted somewhat by their escape, but in the Piauí capital their morale, and that of the city's other defending troops, sank abysmally. General João Gomes Ribeiro Filho, commander in chief of all government forces in the Middle-North and Northeast, with headquarters in São Luís, made plans to evacuate Teresina—which were strongly protested by Governor Matias Olímpio de Melo of Piauí. The governor's determination to hold Teresina was shared by President Artur Bernardes, who began rushing reinforcements to the north, including seven hundred and eighty Chimango provisionals from Rio Grande do Sul. The debacle at Benedito Leite/Uruçui had demonstrated once again the unreliability of federal troops and had indicated that the Piauí state militia was not much better. To defend Teresina from the Prestes Column, Bernardes was willing to arm enemies of the Piauí oligarchy, including alleged bandits. The president's policy of raising Patriotic Battalions from among the Piauí opposition was resisted by both General João Gomes and Governor Matias Olímpio, but it effectively undercut the Prestes Column's appeal in the state. While about one hundred sixty volunteers joined the revolution in Piauí, no leader of the stature of Maranhão's Manuel Bernardino was among them. "Colonel" José Honório Granja, who had waged a bloody campaign against the state government in 1922, sided with President Bernardes in 1925–1926.[17]

Piauí was the poorest state in Brazil. The principal economic activity of its six hundred thousand people was tending to the state's million cattle and half million sheep and goats.[18] The pastures were fairly good in the northern half of the state and along most of the Maranhão border, where the land was campo cerrado and well watered. The southern half of the state received less rainfall, and much of it was covered by *catinga,* thickets of thorny shrubs and cacti, characteristic of the semi-arid interior of the Brazilian Northeast; here cattle were also raised—though the vegetation was better suited for goats—and cotton planting could be profitable, except in time of severe drought, which occurred about every seventh year. The northern half of the state, where most of the people lived, was a transition region, combining the humidity of the Amazon with the heat of the interior Northeast. The land was low, most of it below two hundred meters, and generally flat. Reaching above the dwarf trees of the campo cerrado were the pinnate fronds of fat-trunked babaçu palms, whose nuts yielded an oil that could be sold to soap manufacturers. Along the banks of the Parnaíba, once covered by forest, the soil was quite fertile and a variety of tropical crops could be raised. But there—as elsewhere in Piauí, except for the semi-arid south and a range of small mountains along the Ceará border—endemic malaria drained the strength of the population and impeded the exploitation of the state's resources.

The Prestes Column invaded Piauí in force on December 12, 1925, as the detachment of João Alberto joined that of Djalma Dutra and crossed the Parnaíba River from the town of Nova Iorque in Maranhão. Dutra's men had been in Nova Iorque since December 9, when they discovered one of the steamboats from Benedito Leite tied up there and killed two of the Piauí militiamen on board before the vessel could get under way again. João Alberto and Dutra advanced along the right bank of the river toward Floriano, Piauí's second largest city, which had been abandoned by government forces on December 10. Terrified residents of Floriano followed the soldiers down the river toward Teresina, their belongings piled onto rafts or canoes, a number of which overturned in the rapids downstream. After the substantial citizens had fled, mobs of looters roamed the streets of Floriano, breaking into homes and stores and making off with much of the merchandise and personal property that had been left behind. One building that was spared was the state customs house. After the rebels occupied Floriano on December 18, they opened the customs warehouse, took what goods they needed and distributed the rest to "the people." The total property loss in Floriano was calculated at more than a million milreis, a figure the rebels did not dispute. Juarez Távora pointed out, however, that had Floriano's propertied class not fled the city, or tried to ship their property downriver, their total losses, as a result of rebel requisitions, probably would have amounted to no more than 10,000 milreis.[19]

In Floriano, Captain Moreira Lima, Dr. Pinheiro Machado, and Padre Manuel de Macedo put out the ninth issue of *O Libertador*. The newspaper headlined the "Formidable Victory of Revolutionary Arms" at Uruçui and Benedito Leite, where, it was claimed, Djalma Dutra's detachment overran the loyalist trenches in a furious assault on the night of December 8—when, in fact, the rebel attack was limited to the firing of a few shots toward the government positions by a small patrol at a great distance early in the evening. The falsification was necessary, Moreira Lima felt, to satisfy the demands of psychological warfare. The editors also took poetic license in reporting a strange phenomenon observed during the fighting: The stars of the southern cross turned red and shone with a brilliance never before seen. Actually, the stars were not visible on that foggy night, nor on many other evenings in the Parnaíba valley during the rest of the month of December 1925 when the rains were unusually heavy even for that time of year; in Teresina it rained every day and almost every night.[20]

The government forces in the Parnaíba valley were under
the immediate command of federal army Colonel Gustavo Fre-
derico Beuttmuller, who had arrived in Teresina from General
João Gomes' headquarters in São Luís on December 11. One of
the colonel's first acts as commander was to order a halt to the
flight of loyalist forces down the river from Uruçui. The troops
were made to disembark, regroup, and dig in at the town of
Amarante, one hundred seventy kilometers above Teresina. But
rumors flew through the rainy days and dark nights that the revolutionaries had bypassed Amarante and were gathering on the
outskirts of Teresina for an assault on the city; rebel patrols
were reported as far west as Caxias, threatening to cut the São
Luís railroad. Finally, on the night of December 17, Beuttmuller
ordered the troops in Amarante to evacuate that town and come
to Teresina to assist in the defense of the capital. Actually, the
most advanced rebel element, Siqueira Campos' detachment,
was only about sixty kilometers downstream from Amarante.[21]
On the morning of December 18, as the loyalists descended
the Parnaíba from Amarante, Siqueira's men began scouting
both banks of the river for possible ambush positions. They did
not expect the loyalists to flee Amarante before the other detachments attacked the town—Cordeiro from Maranhão and
Dutra and João Alberto from the Piauí side—which was not supposed to occur until December 21. Thus, Siqueira's ambush was
not prepared when the enemy appeared three days earlier. The
loyalists proceeded cautiously and learned of the rebel presence
when they paused and sent a patrol ashore just above Palmeiras.
The government officers then disembarked half of their five
hundred men and sent them in two columns along both banks of
the river to clear the way for the boats. One of the loyalist columns surprised a group of rebels at lunch in a ranch house near
the river; the revolutionaries fled into the brush, abandoning
some rifles, a poncho, and a pair of gold-framed eyeglasses.
There was some confused fighting for about eighteen kilometers
along the river, but before the day was over, all of the government soldiers were back on their boats, which carried them the
rest of the way to Teresina without further incident. When the

soldiers disembarked in the capital on December 19 they boasted of winning a great victory and produced "Prestes'" eyeglasses and poncho to support their claim. Between Benedito Leite and Teresina nearly half their number had been lost. Almost all of the casualties, however, were "missing in action"; only four had been killed: one by hostile fire near Palmeiras, two at Nova Iorque, and one by drowning in the scramble for the boats at Benedito Leite. The rebels, apparently, had no one killed in these actions.[22]

The detachments of Cordeiro, João Alberto, and Dutra converged on Amarante, as planned, on December 21, and the next day the final drive on Teresina was launched. The advance was resumed on both banks of the river, with Prestes on the Maranhão side, coordinating the operations of Siqueira, Cordeiro, and Manuel Bernardino, which were aimed at the town of Timon, across from Teresina, and the São Luís railroad. On the Piauí side, the movements toward Teresina by João Alberto and Djalma Dutra were to be coordinated by Juarez Távora. Some of João Alberto's troops were detached to guard Miguel Costa's headquarters, which was to move from Floriano to Amarante. Similarly, Dutra's executive officer, Ary Salgado Freire, was sent to the east with a small force to screen the rebel rear and right flank and watch for a loyalist column that was supposed to be moving north from the São Francisco valley. In all, the rebels numbered about thirteen hundred, of whom probably fewer than a thousand were involved in operations around Teresina and Timon. The loyalist troops in the Teresina–Timon area in late December totaled some four thousand, about half of whom were federal army regulars. The government forces were abundantly supplied with ammunition, while the rebels had an average of about ten rounds per man.[23]

Teresina, a city of some sixty thousand people, was situated on a gentle rise between the muddy Parnaíba and the intermittent Rio Poti, which ran parallel to the great river four or five kilometers to the east. There was no bridge across the Parnaíba in those days and the railroad from São Luís ended at Timon.

When the people of Teresina learned of the government retreat from Floriano, they began to abandon their own city. Much property and a few lives were lost as local residents took to the swollen river with their belongings piled high on rafts and canoes. On December 14 Colonel Beuttmuller declared that henceforth no one would be allowed to leave the city without his permission. By this time, however, all but a tenth of the city's population had already fled. The soldiers in Teresina were as jittery as the civilians, and on the night of December 23 they began firing into the darkness at the edge of the city. Surrounded by barbed wire, standing in trenches with water up to their knees, the government soldiers maintained a heavy volume of fire throughout every night for the rest of the month; until the night of December 27, when the rebels began their probing attacks on Teresina and Timon, the loyalists were shooting exclusively at phantoms. The federal officers were convinced, however, that they had been withstanding strong enemy attacks since December 23. On December 26, General João Gomes in São Luís wired Governor Matias Olímpio in Teresina that military considerations would probably require him to withdraw his troops from the city to induce the rebels to congregate there, where he could then surround and destroy them. Teresina was not much, but it was the only capital the governor had, and he refused to give it up. The obstinacy of Matias Olímpio helped save Teresina from the fate of São Paulo.[24]

The revolutionaries ran into strong resistance when they launched simultaneous probes at Timon and Teresina on the night of December 27. The rebel hope that the panic of Benedito Leite–Uruçui would be repeated at Teresina-Timon evaporated on the following night. Two of João Alberto's men were killed by machine-gun fire and left hanging on the barbed wire at the edge of Teresina. Outside Timon the rebels managed to cut the São Luís railroad, but the action cost the life of one of Cordeiro's captains. The attacks were resumed with less intensity on the next night. Then, on the morning of December 30, Juarez Távora sent a messenger across the Parnaíba in a canoe to deliver to Prestes a plan for withdrawing all rebel forces to the Piauí side of the river. By the end of the day the rebel chiefs had agreed to lift the siege of Timon and Teresina and retire to the east.[25]

The Prestes Column's next objective would be the state of Pernambuco. When the revolutionaries first approached Piauí from southern Maranhão, they were on their way to Ceará, where Manuel do Nascimento Fernandes Távora, brother of Juarez, was preparing an uprising in the state capital. But the emergence of the rebels in northern Brazil had prompted President Bernardes to crack down on suspected subversives in the Northeast. In Fortaleza the opposition newspaper, *A Tribuna,* was closed, and its editor, Fernandes Távora, was forced into exile in Europe, dealing a severe blow to the conspiracy in Ceará. As the rebel leaders in the Parnaíba valley pondered the diminishing prospects for the revolution in Ceará, Waldemar de Paula Lima arrived late in December with news of a new opportunity. Waldemar was a former navy petty officer who had left the column in Mato Grosso to go to Rio de Janeiro and make contact with the revolutionary underground in the national capital. Eventually, Waldemar got in touch with Cleto Campelo, a fugitive federal army lieutenant who had an idea for a barracks revolt in Recife, the capital of Pernambuco and the largest city in the Northeast. Waldemar journeyed to Recife, conferred with Cleto and other revolutionaries there, and when it was learned that the rebels had entered the Parnaíba valley, he went to Piauí to enlist the support of the Prestes Column for the planned uprising in Pernambuco. By December 28 Waldemar was at Miguel Costa's headquarters in Amarante. The plan to march to Pernambuco could not be finally approved, however, until the detachment commanders got together after the withdrawal from Timon and Teresina had been virtually completed.[26]

The decision to leave the Parnaíba valley was generally welcomed by the rebel troops, who were shorn of all hope of an easy victory at Teresina, depressed by the constant rains, and wracked by malarial fevers. Perhaps half of the revolutionaries had contracted malaria by the end of December. Only Manuel Bernardino and the Maranhão and Piauí volunteers might be expected to oppose the movement to the east. Yet the "Lenin of the Mata" had little choice but to join the exodus; to refuse would be to leave himself at the mercy of his resurgent enemies in Maranhão. He and most of his men would cross the river with the detachments of Siqueira and Cordeiro. Juarez Távora, already on the Piauí side, had located several canoes and a flatboat to bring the men and their horses across.[27]

Távora's headquarters—at Angelim ranch on the Parnaíba ten kilometers south of Teresina—maintained contact with Prestes across the river by means of canoe-borne couriers. This line of communications was threatened by a government motor launch, which, on two occasions, captured one of Távora's canoes. On the morning of December 31, after the second incursion, Colonel Távora went forward from his command post with two officers to select a position from which the enemy boat could be ambushed the next time it came out of Teresina. At this time the rebel troops in Maranhão were beginning to cross the river more than twenty kilometers upstream from Távora's headquarters at Angelim ranch. Most of Djalma Dutra's detachment was deployed in the vicinity of the ranch on the morning of December 31, while João Alberto and his men were on their way to the eastern outskirts of Teresina, via the Rio Poti, to make a demonstration that night and maintain the illusion of a siege. Between the Poti and the Parnaíba was a road that went to the village of Natal, which had been selected as the column's reassembly point, about sixty-five kilometers from Teresina. On this road, about one kilometer north of the rebel camp at Angelim ranch, was the hamlet of Areias, six hundred meters from the riverbank. A combat outpost, some thirty revolutionaries with a machine gun, was at Areias, while a few hundred meters farther up the road, where it intersected a telegraph-line trail, also coming from Teresina, there was a rebel observation post. Directly to the west, on the riverbank, was another observation post. It was beyond this second observation post that Juarez Távora and two officers went in search of an ambush position on the river. The area was covered with dense brush.[28]

In the meantime, loyalist troops were making their first sally from Teresina along the road to Natal. Two federal army majors had persuaded the torpid Colonel Beuttmuller to allow them to take one hundred twenty picked men on an armed reconnaissance south of the city. The soldiers, selected from three federal light infantry battalions, had three automatic weapons. They left Teresina at seven in the morning and came upon the rebel observation post at the intersection of the road and the telegraph line shortly before ten o'clock. There was a brief exchange of fire, after which the rebels disappeared into the brush on the side of the road. The loyalists then proceeded to assault Areias, loosing a tremendous volume of fire on the unfortunate hamlet. The thirty or more rebels who had been there were able to escape into the woods. The "numerous" dead and wounded later found in Areias turned out to be local residents. Soon after the firing stopped a lone horseman came down the road. Sitting tall in the saddle, he wore gaúcho pants, a white shirt, and, on his hat, a red cockade. As a soldier pointed a rifle at him, he tossed a pistol and a knife to the ground, looked at a federal army major, and declared in a clear and firm voice: "I am Juarez Távora and I turn myself in as a prisoner." [29]

Instead of attacking the rebels at Angelim ranch, the loyalists returned to Teresina with their prisoner. Távora would later write that he had no choice but to give up. His horse, he claimed, refused to move during the firing, while his two companions were making good their escape. When the shooting stopped and his mount consented to move again, he returned to Areias, which he found under enemy control. "Ordered to surrender," Távora described his predicament, he "refrained from the insane adventure of a futile resistance and surrendered." Yet, the rebel colonel had heard the heavy firing at Areias and certainly realized that a large government force was in or around the hamlet. He had no reason to believe that he could ride straight down the road into Areias without being apprehended by the enemy. Had he chosen to escape, he could have done so easily, by taking to the brush on either side of the road, even without his horse. Many rebels abandoned their horses at Areias and made it through the woods on foot to the rebel camp at Angelim ranch.[30] Távora, it seems, was the only revolutionary lost that day.

One of the kindest explanations for Távora's behavior was offered by Hygínio Cunha, a Piauiense who knew the Areias area well and was in Teresina during the siege. In the months that followed he wrote, in the earnest if turgid prose of a provincial litterateur, a surprisingly objective and balanced account of the events in the Parnaíba valley. At the army barracks in Teresina, according to Hygínio Cunha, Távora declared "that he was suffering from cystitis and needed surgery. Now, it is known that horseback riding aggravates afflictions of the bladder and is, indeed, insupportable with them. The rebel chief, then, was rendered incapable of making the long return journey through the backlands across which he had come in vertiginous forays. Between dying in the painful throes of disease—crippled, abandoned in the savage woods—and surrendering, expecting to obtain medical treatment, to recover his health and return to the coterie of his comrades, the second alternative seems more human." [31]

During the first days of January 1926 the detachments of the Prestes Column converged on the village of Natal, Piauí. By the morning of January 3 only Siqueira's outfit, accompanied by Colonel Prestes, had not reached Natal. While the government forces in Teresina had made no move from the city since their sally of December 31, the rebel chiefs at Natal were concerned that the enemy might attack them there before Siqueira and Prestes arrived from Maranhão. To dissuade the loyalists from leaving Teresina, it was decided at Natal that João Alberto would make another feint against the city from the east, and then march directly for the Ceará border. After Prestes and Siqueira reached Natal, the column main body would take a more southerly route to Ceará and link up with João Alberto in

the Cearense town of Arneiroz. This town was far from the state
capital at Fortaleza, but with the imprisonment of Juarez Távora
the rebels had lost their last hopes of setting off a general uprising in Ceará. At Arneiroz the column would be in a good position to invade Pernambuco and support the revolt that was
being prepared in Recife. When Prestes and Siqueira reached
Natal they would ratify the Pernambuco plan.[32]

In the meantime, the Bishop of Piauí appeared in Natal on
the afternoon of January 3 with a letter from Távora to Prestes.
The letter was delivered to the chief-of-staff when he arrived
that night. The imprisoned Távora suggested that the time had
come to withdraw the rebel forces from around Teresina and
spare its innocent citizens the hardships and dangers of a prolonged siege or an all-out assault on the city. In Távora's opinion, the revolutionary conquest of Teresina would not be worth
its cost in lives. A rebel withdrawal from Teresina, he indicated,
would not be obstructed by Colonel Beuttmuller, who was confining his troops to their positions while he awaited Prestes' reply
to Távora's letter, which was written on January 1. Three days
later Prestes gave the bishop his answer: The rebels would suspend their attacks on Teresina for humanitarian reasons if Colonel Beuttmuller would keep his forces out of the rebel-
controlled areas of Piauí, "which take in almost all of its territory." [33]

The bishop, who had spent two days on horseback riding
from Teresina to Natal, was well aware that the rebels had already lifted the siege. Perhaps, he suggested, the revolutionaries
would like him to mediate for them with the authorities in Teresina to arrange a rebel surrender. Prestes insisted that the revolutionaries had no intention of laying down their arms. The
rebels had not really been retreating during the last few days,
Miguel Costa added smoothly; they had been concentrating
some of their troops at Natal in order to draw the enemy south
from Teresina, so that a rebel striking force, now in the Poti
valley, could take the city from the east. In fact, this movement
against Teresina had begun before the bishop arrived in Natal

with Távora's humanitarian proposal. The revolutionary command might not be able to get in touch with the striking force in time to stop the first attacks of the suspended offensive. The bishop was urged to explain to Colonel Beuttmuller that, should his troops be attacked that night from the east, this should not be taken as a sign of bad faith. João Alberto's men were indeed on the eastern outskirts of Teresina, and their presence there apparently convinced the city's defenders that the deal brought back by the bishop was a good one. Colonel Beuttmuller kept his part of the bargain and for two weeks the rebels were unopposed as they marched across Piauí toward Ceará.[34]

The government of Piauí suspected that Colonel Beuttmuller and most of his federal troops sympathized with the rebels and wanted them to get away. One officer, who started off with his battalion toward Campo Maior in pursuit of João Alberto, was called back and severely reprimanded by Beuttmuller. The pursuit of the Prestes Column in the Northeast would be left to state troops and to the forces of backcountry warlords. The most prominent of the warlords—who coexisted with the governments of their states, often under the conditions of an armed truce—dealt directly with the federal administration through their congressional representatives in Rio. When the rebels first threatened Bahia, in August 1925, Congressman Francisco Rocha of Bahia's Middle São Francisco valley offered President Bernardes the military services of his constituents. The offer was accepted and federal uniforms, arms, and salaries were provided for the men of "Colonel" Franklin Lins de Albuquerque, who were formed into a Patriotic Battalion. "Colonel" Franklin's interstate associates, José Honório Granja of Piauí and Abílio Wolney of Goiás, both sometime refugees in the Middle São Francisco, were also mustered into the federal service with their bands of jagunços.[35]

In Ceará, as the Prestes Column marched through the adjacent state of Piauí, Congressman Floro Bartolomeu secured federal aid for the gunmen of the Cairiri valley. On December 31, 1925, a special train left Fortaleza for the Cairiri town of

Joàzeiro, loaded with war matériel and carrying Floro and a million milreis in federal funds.[36] Joàzeiro was the Mecca of the northeastern hinterland, the seat of Padre Cícero Romão Batista, spiritual and temporal chief of thousands of jagunços and political partner of Floro Bartolomeu. Padre Cícero, eighty-two years old in 1926, was a sincere friend of the poor backlanders. He had guided them in organizing a thriving agricultural community at Joàzeiro after the disastrous drought of 1877 and had led them in successfully resisting the big landowners who claimed the ground upon which they built their "New Jerusalem." His reputation was enhanced by a miracle: In the mouth of one of his female parishioners, during communion, the host bled with the blood of Christ (detractors said the poor woman was tubercular). His fame spread to every state of the North and Northeast and pilgrims flocked to the Cairiri valley to worship at the shrine of Padre Cícero, the "Saint of Joàzeiro." The pilgrims included no small number of bandits, who were welcomed and protected as long as they did not disturb the decorum of the Holy City. Floro Bartolomeu, a medical doctor from Bahia, recognized the great political potential of Padre Cícero and formed a partnership with him. Together they overthrew the state government in 1914—with some moral and material support from Senator Pinheiro Machado, the strong man of the federal government, who did not like the regime in Fortaleza. Thereafter, Rio recognized Padre Cícero as virtually sovereign in the Cairiri valley, and Floro, his spokesman, as a power on the national scene.[37]

In Joàzeiro, Floro raised a force of some five hundred jagunços and marched them off to the town of Campos Sales near the Piauí border. Floro hoped to intercept the Prestes Column in this area, but he did not employ his troops well. He was a sick man, near death from a degenerative bone disease. Suffering from frequent and severe headaches, he was irritable and quarreled constantly with allies and subordinates. While Floro's Patriotic Battalion was immobilized at Campos Sales by confused leadership and internal dissension, the Prestes Col-

umn crossed into Ceará fifty kilometers to the north, marching
rapidly to the east.[38]

Before he withdrew from Campos Sales, Floro wrote a letter
to Virgulino Ferreira da Silva, the most notorious bandit in the
Northeast. Virgulino—better known as "Lampião," because he
fired shots from his Winchester in such rapid succession that its
muzzle gave off the light of a street lamp—was invited to come
to Joàzeiro and join Floro's Patriotic Battalion. The invitation
was typed on Patriotic Battalion stationery, signed by Floro, and
sent to Joàzeiro where it was countersigned by Padre Cícero and
handed over to a messenger for delivery to Lampião. It took the
messenger some time to locate the famous *cangaceiro,* or bandit,
who was camped in Pernambuco. By the time Lampião and his
forty-nine men reached Joàzeiro, on March 4, 1926, Floro Bartolomeu was in Rio on his deathbed. Padre Cícero, however,
honored his expiring partner's commitment and pressured a
federal official in Joàzeiro, a Ministry of Agriculture inspector,
to sign a document commissioning Lampião as a captain in the
army reserve. Captain Virgulino, as he henceforth called himself, traded in his old Winchesters for new army Mausers, and
on March 7 he and his men rode out of Joàzeiro supposedly to
fight the revolutionaries. If the cangaceiros had any intentions
of combating the Prestes Column, they soon gave them up and
resumed their normal bandit activities.[39]

The commissioning of Lampião, seized upon by the opposition in the federal Congress, embarrassed the administration in
Rio and upset the governments of four northeastern states that
had signed a treaty committing their armed forces to pursue
him without letup. Lampião was no common jagunço—no part-
time gunman who led a settled and peaceful life except when
called to arms by his patron—but an extraordinary cangaceiro, a
full-time roving bandit. Cold-blooded and cruel, Lampião had
few professed admirers in 1926, though he did have class; brave,
dashing, always well-dressed, he was also an accomplished har-
monica player whose lilting theme song, "Mulher Rendeira,"
became a perennial Brazilian favorite and would even make the

Hit Parade in the United States as "The Bandit." Lampião had all the requisites of a folk hero and would be celebrated as one after his death; in the 1920's, however, he seemed to be the very embodiment of evil.[40]

General João Gomes, commander in chief of all government forces in operations against the rebels in the North and Northeast, was not happy to have Lampião under his "command"— even if only theoretically. In fact, the general exercised no control over Lampião's cangaceiros and very little over the bands of jagunços that operated in his theater as Patriotic Battalions. João Gomes found this situation extremely distasteful and went so far as to denigrate the military qualities of the Patriotic Battalions in a newspaper interview. Considering the general's great prestige in the federal army, the Bernardes administration chose to ignore him. The army was useless in the campaign against the rebels in the Northeast, but the federal government could not risk alienating any more of its officers and driving them and their troops into the arms of the revolution. That this remained a danger was demonstrated in the northeastern state of Sergipe on January 19, 1926, when the federal garrison in the state capital rose in revolt. Four hundred soldiers from the Twenty-eighth Light Infantry Battalion—led by a lieutenant whom they had freed from the unit stockade, where he had been confined for subversive activity—attacked the governor's mansion in Aracajú. But the Sergipe state militia rallied to the cause of the government and, within five hours, routed the federals and captured the leaders of the mutiny.[41]

Shortly after the incident at Aracajú, the federal government appointed an officer of unquestioned loyalty to take command of its troops in Bahia and Sergipe. At the end of January 1926 General Álvaro Mariante arrived at the military district headquarters in Salvador. Seven years earlier Mariante, then a major, had journeyed from Salvador to Dianópolis, Goiás, where he made peace between the federal government and Abílio Wolney. In 1922, as a lieutenant colonel stationed in Rio de Janeiro, he played a decisive role in frustrating the coup planned for July 5 by arresting the chief conspirators at Vila Militar the night before. In 1924–1925, as a colonel, he served with distinction in the campaign against the rebels in Paraná. He did not share the distaste of his superior, General João Gomes, for the Patriotic Battalions and he got along very well with their leaders. When João Gomes finally resigned his command in disgust, in April 1926, Álvaro Mariante succeeded him as commander in chief of all government forces operating against the rebels in the North and Northeast.[42]

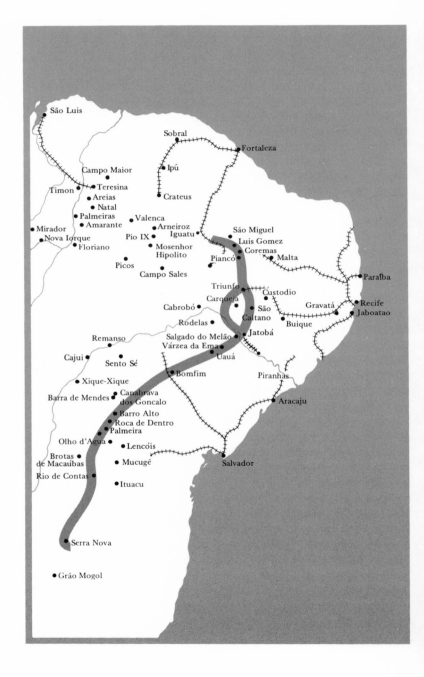

Defeat in the Sertão

VIII Luís Carlos Prestes promised the revolutionary conspirators in Recife that his rebel column would arrive in Triunfo, Pernambuco, between February 12 and 15, 1926. Fugitive federal army Lieutenant Cleto Campelo, the head of the conspiracy, would personally lead the revolt in Recife, while three of his associates would attempt to subvert the federal garrison in the capital of the neighboring state of Paraíba. Waldemar Lima was sent to inform the Recife underground of the column's route of march, which would take the rebels from Natal, Piauí, through southern Ceará, across the southwestern corner of Rio Grande do Norte, and through western Paraíba to Triunfo, Pernambuco. The march from Natal to Valença, Piauí, was uneventful, but on the morning of January 14, as the rebels were marching southeast from Valença, they learned that an enemy force was moving in the opposite direction on another trail toward that town, where the column rearguard, Siqueira's detachment, was still camped. A messenger was immediately dispatched to Valença to tell Siqueira to hold his position, while the column's main body swung around to strike the enemy from the rear. But the loyalists, one hundred thirty Pernambuco state militiamen, chased

Siqueira out of the town, capturing three of his men, before the rebel main force arrived on the scene. The subsequent appearance of so many rebels around Valença dissuaded the Pernambucans from attempting to pursue the enemy.[1]

Cordeiro's detachment occupied Picos on January 16, meeting resistance only from the town's mayor and police chief, who were easily overpowered. Other prominent townspeople welcomed the rebels and invited Prestes to a banquet in his honor. While Cordeiro and the chief-of-staff were dining with the local dignitaries, their forces were attacked by part of a battalion of the Bahia state militia, which had moved into Piauí from the São Francisco valley. Prestes and Cordeiro left the banquet early and withdrew to Monsenhor Hipólito, where the column's main body was located. There, another honor awaited Luís Carlos Prestes: Miguel Costa, at the insistence of other high rebel officers, promoted him to brigadier general. Although the number of rebel soldiers was dwindling—as dozens of Piauiense volunteers deserted, some to devote themselves to looting in the column's wake—officer rank continued to rise. Directing a force of fewer than thirteen hundred men were one major general, one brigadier general, two colonels (Siqueira and João Alberto), two lieutenant colonels (Cordeiro and Dutra), and one honorary colonel (Manuel Bernardino). General Prestes gave evidence that he was worthy of his new rank by successfully evading the enemy from Bahia and leading the column to Pio IX and into Ceará, on the night of January 22, avoiding Floro Bartolomeu's concentration around Campos Sales.[2]

In Ceará desertions from the column continued, as Manuel Bernardino slipped away with his brother and twelve comrades. Even more damaging was the desertion of Batista Santos, a political refugee from Goiás who had joined the column in Floriano, Piauí. Santos, a state legislator in Goiás, apparently broke with Totó Caiado after the senator had forced him to serve in his Patriotic Battalion. He followed the rebels to Piauí and, in Floriano, helped Moreira Lima edit *O Libertador*. Santos won the confidence of the column headquarters and learned about the plans for uprisings in Recife and Paraíba. In Ceará he went to the authorities and informed on the conspirators.[3]

Government forces in Pernambuco and Paraíba were immediately alerted and a dragnet was put out for the fugitive officers. Two of them were spotted when they took a train from Recife to Paraíba City (now João Pessoa) on February 4. They were followed to a house in Paraíba City where some accomplices and a large cache of arms were hidden. The place was raided at 2:30 A.M. on February 5, and after a brief shoot-out, the two rebel officers and their accomplices surrendered. The prisoners were transferred that night to Recife, where the authorities intensified their search for Cleto Campelo and the remaining conspirators. Some alleged subversives were arrested and a quantity of bombs confiscated in a predawn police raid in Recife on February 9, but Cleto remained at large. The government was jittery, anticipating a revolt during the pre-Lenten carnival period, when the streets of the city would be filled with uncontrollable mobs of revelers. Troops patrolled the streets and rumors swept Recife that the Prestes Column was about to attack the city and, worse yet, that the government was going to ban all carnival celebrations.[4]

It was in this supercharged atmosphere that delegates from five northeastern states assembled in Recife for a Congress on Regionalism. The congress was unofficial and its delegates were mostly artists and intellectuals, but it had important political implications. Paradoxically, a conference whose theme was regionalism turned out to be a manifestation of nationalism. The delegates, meeting in the former Dutch city of Recife, deplored the lowly status of their region in the decentralized Brazilian republic. They called not for the secession of the Northeast from Brazil, as some of their forefathers had done in previous centuries, but for the strengthening of the nation—for the elimination of the pseudo-federal system that, under the cloak of states' rights, allowed the partnership of São Paulo and Minas Gerais to oppress the rest of the country.[5]

While the economic and political power of the Northeast had been generally declining since Dutch rule ended in 1654, the depths to which the region had sunk under the republic raised the ire of its artists and intellectuals, if not that of its politicians, most of whom had sold out to the power brokers of the South.

Only one northeasterner, Epitácio Pessoa of Paraíba, had been elected president of the republic, and he was chosen to fill out the last three years of the term of deceased President Rodrigues Alves of São Paulo, to warm the presidential seat until Artur Bernardes of Minas Gerais took over for a full four-year term. Epitácio Pessoa, during his brief administration, had not forgotten his region: He had committed the federal government to a program of building reservoirs to provide water for cattle and crops during the Northeast's periodic droughts. But when Bernardes took over in Rio he canceled Epitácio's drought-relief program. Now, in 1926, Bernardes was preparing to turn over the presidency to São Paulo's Washington Luís, who was scheduled to be elected, without opposition, on March 1.

No specific plan of action was agreed to at the Recife conference of February 7–11, 1926, but some truly revolutionary ideas were broached there. Perhaps the strongest voice at the conference was that of Gilberto Freyre, a young social historian from Recife. Freyre believed that solutions for many of the problems that beset Brazil could be found through the study of regional history. But he was entirely opposed "to all traditionalism which is a mere digging up of the past, to all regionalism which is purely political in nature, to all exaltation of individual states." [6] What made Brazil a nation, Freyre maintained, was miscegenation, which best could be studied where it began and developed to its fullest: in the sugar plantation area along the northeast coast. Miscegenation was a positive good, he insisted, to the horror of many of those who read about the conference in the newspapers of the South, and the black man's contribution to the nation and to Brazilian culture was of the highest order. Freyre's findings delighted some aspiring young novelists at the conference, who seized his miscegenation theme and went on to develop a "regional" literature that, in reality, was national and popular and went far beyond the chic "modernism" of São Paulo. "From the midst of acquiescense arose a wave of writers in rebellion—the great novelists of the Northeast," noted Josué de Castro of Recife. "They were called proletarian writers because they ferreted out the dark holes and hidden places known only to the poor. Around their writing was a strong odor of life, a smell nauseating to people who lived in cleaner places." [7]

As the conference adjourned on February 11 and the rhetoric of their literary champions died away, the people of Recife were warming up their samba bands for carnival. The government refused to permit the usual pre-carnival processions and, for a while, it seemed that carnival itself would be banned. But the authorities eventually decided that such a drastic measure would be counterproductive, and carnival was held on schedule; the crowds were smaller than usual, however, and the atmosphere was uncharacteristically tense. The worst fears of the government did not materialize: Ash Wednesday came and went without serious incident. But on Thursday, February 18, Cleto Campelo, Waldemar Lima, and about twenty-five armed followers seized the police station in the suburb of Jaboatão at two o'clock in the morning. They freed the prisoners at the jail, locked up the police, and cut the telegraph line to Recife. Then the revolutionaries went to the Jaboatão railroad station, seized a shipment of arms and commandeered a passenger train. It was after sunrise before they pulled out of Jaboatão, heading west, toward Triunfo and their rendezvous with the Prestes Column. Despite the cutting of the telegraph line, word of the assault on Jaboatão spread rapidly among the government forces that had gathered in eastern Pernambuco to protect Recife from the Prestes Column. A unit of the Alagoas militia intercepted the rebel train at the town of Gravatá, seventy kilometers west of the Pernambucan capital. In the fight that ensued, Cleto Campelo was mortally wounded and command of the revolutionary group passed to Waldemar Lima. Waldemar got the train under way again at Gravatá, but it was derailed a few kilometers down the track. Most of the revolutionaries surrendered near the wreck, including Waldemar Lima, who died in the hands of his captors, his throat cut. [8]

João Alberto crossed the Serra da Ibiapaba from Piauí into Ceará ten days ahead of the column main body. On the morning of January 13, after a night march down the serra, he seized Ipú, a small city of a few thousand on the railroad between

Fortaleza and Crateus. His troops moved in on the city suddenly and met no resistance. The merchants of Ipú furnished
the rebels three thousand Winchester cartridges and 9,000
milreis as "voluntary" contributions; the local branch of the
Bank of Brazil gave up 16,000 milreis. This was the largest cash
confiscation that the rebels had made since leaving Mato
Grosso. The week before he made this haul, João Alberto had
taken nearly 4,000 milreis from the tax collector's office in the
town of Campo Maior, Piauí, which also had been occupied
without resistance. With all this money in his possession, João
Alberto decided to pay for the animals, food, and supplies that
his soldiers requisitioned from the people of Ipú. He paid out
6,000 milreis in this generous but irregular gesture for a
member of the rebel high command, whose policy was to hoard
money—for the purchase of arms, for emergencies, perhaps
for life in exile, which Prestes had foreseen as a possibility
before the column left Mato Grosso.[9] João Alberto, a compas-
sionate son of the Northeast, had the instincts of a social revolutionary, which were in disharmony with Prestes' perpetual-
motion campaign scheme. Prestes loved the people no less than
João Alberto, but he was more willing to sacrifice their immediate interests for dimly perceived goals.

For all the time he had spent in the army and in Rio Grande
do Sul, João Alberto was still identifiable as a northeasterner. To
Moreira Lima, João Alberto on horseback presented a perfect
image of the northeastern cowboy described in *Os sertões*, Eu-
clides da Cunha's classic account of backcountry warfare in the
1890's. Loose jointed and lethargic, the northeastern *vaqueiro*
would hunch forward, his legs glued to the belly of his scrawny,
slow-moving, head-down horse, plodding behind a herd of
equally indolent cattle on some backlands trail. Then, as da
Cunha tells it, the vaqueiro noticed a steer straying off into the
catinga. In a flash, horse and rider were transformed and took
off like a dart after the wayward steer. They tore through the
thorny thicket at top speed, jumping gullies and dodging boul-
ders, huge cacti, and joàzeiro trees, the sturdy rider lending
vigor to the frail pony. Once the steer was dominated and returned to the herd, the vaqueiro "is again slumped over in the

saddle, once more ungainly and inert, swinging with the slow gait, with the dreary appearance of a hopeless invalid." [10]

The vaqueiro of the northeastern backlands, the *sertão,* was the antithesis of the gaúcho of the southern pampas. He had no use for the gaúcho's fancy clothes, which would have been ripped to shreds in the catinga; the vaqueiro dressed in leather from head to toe and draped leather sheets about his horse to protect his mount from the cruel thorns. The gaúcho, who loved to gallop over the boundless plains, was "conditioned to a kind environment that delighted him," according to da Cunha, and was "more chivalrous and attractive" than the vaqueiro of the northeastern sertão. But the gaúcho did not know "the horrors of the drought and the raw struggles with the dry and parched earth." [11] The vaqueiro saved his energy for the crises that were sure to lie ahead. The harsh environment of the sertão required men to band together in order to survive. The vaqueiro was no individualist; his sense of community was far stronger than that of the gaúcho and his loyalty to his chief was virtually unshakable. When called to arms by his patron, the peaceful vaqueiro became the fearsome jagunço.

Unlike the gaúcho warrior, the jagunço was not theatrically heroic: He seldom assumed a romantic or vainglorious pose. More tenacious than the gaúcho, "he is more resistant, more dangerous, stronger, tougher." He "seeks out his adversary with the firm purpose of destroying him by whatever means he may." Unlike the gaúcho, the vaqueiro was a good marksman. Coldly calculating his enemy, he would place his shots with great care, at times seeming to fall asleep at the sights of his rifle. The ambush, not the cavalry charge, was his preferred mode of combat. Patient and cunning in retreat, he was a demon in leading his enemy on. The intruder in the sertão, the invader who threatened to appropriate the vaqueiro's meager property or that entrusted to his care by his patron was likely to have before him, "looking at him down a rifle barrel," a man who hated him with "an unextinguishable hatred" lurking hidden in the shadows of some thicket. [12] The Prestes Column was ill prepared to deal with the jagunços of the northeastern sertão.

"Beginning in Ceará," João Alberto would recall, "we felt the

effects of obstinate resistance to our march on the part of the
people." He noted that "the civilian population, hospitable and
sympathetic in the states we had traversed as far as Piauí, now
confronted our men ferociously." João Alberto was saddened to
see the poor people "who would have benefited by the victory of
revolutionary ideas, throw themselves bravely against the men
of the Column in unequal combat." While João Alberto blamed
government propaganda for the hostility of his fellow northeasterners, his colleagues from the South were little interested in
excuses for the savagery of the jagunços and tended to regard
them, and the society that produced them, with loathing. To
Moreira Lima, the people of the sertão, the *sertanejos,* were almost subhuman.[13] No punishment seemed too harsh for the
murderous brutes whose small-scale but almost daily attacks
took a steadily mounting toll in lives of high-minded revolutionaries as the column marched across the Northeast.

But this was hardly foreseen at the outset of the rebels'
northeastern campaign, which got off to a good start with João
Alberto's seizure of Ipú, Ceará. In the local telegraph office the
revolutionaries sent wires to Sobral and Fortaleza calling upon
the people of those cities to prepare to welcome their liberators.
The ruse worked: Many government troops were pulled out of
southern Ceará and deployed around the state capital, while
João Alberto marched in the opposite direction, toward Arneiroz, and as Prestes approached that town from the west. On
his way to Arneiroz, João Alberto entered the town of Crateus,
where he encountered strong resistance from local forces holed
up in a church. After two of his men were killed in an unsuccessful attack on the church, on the afternoon of January 16, João
Alberto withdrew his forces from Crateus under cover of darkness. On January 26 he reached Arneiroz and linked up with the
main body of the Prestes Column, which had occupied the town
the day before. At Arneiroz the rebels were greeted by an opposition chief from a neighboring village, who joined the column with a few followers. Contrary to rebel expectations, this
turned out to be a rare occurrence in Ceará, where a total of
only twenty volunteers were added to the column. The conser-

vative Feitosa family, which dominated Arneiroz and the surrounding area, rejected an invitation to join the revolution.[14]

To avoid the jagunço concentrations around Joàzeiro, the revolutionaries marched rapidly eastward from Arneiroz, toward the southwestern corner of Rio Grande do Norte, where they would pivot to the south and proceed directly from there across western Paraíba to Triunfo, Pernambuco. The column crossed the Fortaleza-Joàzeiro railroad near Iguatu on January 29, and on February 3 they reached the Rio Grande do Norte border near São Miguel. The skies were clear and the days were hot and dry during the column's passage through Ceará. The landscape was hard and diamond-bright, with ancient, jagged mountains rising from sandy, rock-strewn plains covered with cacti and patches of thorn bushes. The catinga was almost barren of leaves, for the rainy season had not yet arrived in Ceará. A few splashes of green among the lifeless thickets were provided by hardy joàzeiro trees, and along the dry stream beds there were stands of slender, deep-rooted carnaúba palms, whose young leaves secreted a wax that was valuable to the makers of floor polish and phonograph records. The revolutionaries, like the cattle and goats that roamed the area, found bitter-tasting water in holes dug into the dry creek beds or in the little reservoirs maintained by the more affluent ranchers. The change from rain-drenched Piauí was drastic and not altogether unwelcome: Malarial symptoms disappeared quickly in the new climate. Malaria contracted in Maranhão and Piauí took the lives of six revolutionaries, more than had been lost there to enemy bullets. In the northeastern sertão, the jagunços were the greatest menace to rebel health.[15]

Shortly after the rebels crossed the railroad near Iguatu, Ceará, the governor of the neighboring state of Rio Grande do Norte received a telegram from Rio notifying him of the event. The federal high command believed that the next rebel objective was São Miguel, Rio Grande do Norte, and suggested that the governor send out a force to meet the revolutionaries, who, he was assured, numbered only about seventy poorly armed men. There were only four policemen in the little mountaintop town of São Miguel, so the governor telegraphed the local political boss and requested that he mobilize his jagunços. But he had rounded up only twenty-eight gunmen—four Cearenses and the rest Potiguares, men of Rio Grande do Norte—by the time the rebel column was spotted in the area on February 3. On their way to lay an ambush west of the town, the loyalists ran into João Alberto's vanguard. In a fire fight that lasted from four o'clock in the afternoon until sundown, one rebel was killed and two loyalists wounded. One of the latter, a Cearense jagunço, fell into enemy hands as his outnumbered comrades, fearing encirclement, withdrew under cover of darkness; he died with his throat cut. During the night a band of a dozen Potiguares, sent out to reinforce the twenty-eight-man contingent, had a brief encounter with the rebels and captured one of them, whom they sent back to São Miguel in the custody of three jagunços. Under interrogation the prisoner confirmed the worse fears of the people of São Miguel—that more than a thousand revolutionaries were converging on their town of thirteen hundred.[16]

There was a mass flight of civilians from São Miguel at dawn on February 4 when the three jagunços who had brought the prisoner back fired a few shots at the troops of Djalma Dutra, who suddenly appeared in the town, having spent the night climbing up a steep mountain trail that the loyalists had left unguarded. With João Alberto's detachment pressing forward on another trail, the undermanned and outmaneuvered government forces abandoned the town to the revolutionaries, who proceeded to sack it. Enraged by the resistance they had encountered, the rebel soldiers broke into homes and stores, smashing furniture and destroying property that they could not use or carry, while their officers sat at a table in the local inn studying maps of the region. The total loss of private property in the town of São Miguel would be officially set at 307,303.50 milreis. The revolutionaries departed São Miguel on the same day they arrived, after burning the registry of deeds and all other documents in the public records office. From São Miguel they marched on Luís Gomes, a town of about the same size, near the Paraíba border. By this time the word had spread among the Potiguares that the government was wrong: The rebels "are not seventy, they are seven hundred, they are fourteen hundred, they are many more." The town of Luís Gomes was almost deserted when the Prestes Column passed through on February 5. The few merchants and homeowners who remained in the town suffered less property loss than those who fled, whose holdings were subject to unrestricted looting; as in São Miguel, the files of the public records office in Luís Gomes were destroyed. The rebel headquarters camped that night in the state of Paraíba.[17]

While the column main body marched south through Paraíba, on its way to Triunfo, Pernambuco, via Piancó, João Alberto's detachment swung to the east to distract the enemy and also to try to establish contact with the revolutionaries who were supposed to start an uprising in the state capital. João Alberto got at least as far east as the town of Malta, on the railroad to Paraíba city, where he put to flight a small force from the state militia. On a ranch near Malta the rebel colonel seized a shipment of forty Mauser rifles, a case of 7-mm. ammunition, and two thousand Winchester cartridges—all bound for a Patriotic Battalion that was being raised in the Paraibano sertão. In his incursion along the railroad João Alberto learned of the capture of the conspirators in the state capital, the details of which appeared in the Paraíba city press on February 6. From the vicinity of Malta, João Alberto withdrew to the southwest, toward Piancó, where he expected to rejoin the column.[18]

The master of Piancó was Padre Aristides Ferreira da Cruz. Padre Aristides, a native of another part of the Paraíbano sertão, had served Piancó as its parish priest for ten years—until he got involved in politics and his bishop removed him from his pastorate. Despite the loss of his benefice, Padre Aristides remained in Piancó and pursued his political struggle against the local oligarchy. The bishop then suspended him from the priesthood for fornication. Aristides stoutly declared his innocence, but since he would have to suffer the penalty anyway—and since he wanted to relieve the bishop of the burden of sin for maintaining an unjust sentence—he moved his favorite choir girl off a nearby farm and into his town house, where she bore him four children. In the meantime, Padre Aristides had risen to power in Piancó by hitching his wagon to the ascending star of Epitácio

Pessoa, whose allies were swept into office all over Paraíba in the state and local elections of 1915 and 1916.[19]

Later, after Epitácio went to Rio as president of Brazil, presumably no longer interested in the politics of Piancó, local enemies of Padre Aristides instigated a revolt. The uprising was set off by charges that the suspended priest had stolen his neighbor's prize bull; the animal was discovered on Padre Aristides' ranch with the priest's brand superimposed over the owner's. In a twenty-six-hour-long gunfight, Padre Aristides and his partisans were forced out of Piancó. President Epitácio Pessoa, however, came to the aid of his backcountry protégé: He ordered the Paraíba milita to escort Padre Aristides to Piancó and restore him to power—and if the militia could not do the job, he would send in the federal army. The state troops proved sufficient for the task. Shortly after his restoration, Padre Aristides was able to prove that his ranch foreman had bought the bull in good faith from a relative of the owner, who had stolen it. Popular feeling swung strongly to Padre Aristides' side and allowed him to banish his enemies from Piancó. His position seemed secure until the Prestes Column arrived on the scene in February 1926.[20]

When he first learned that the rebels were marching toward Piancó, Padre Aristides seemed inclined to offer them no resistance, perhaps even to abandon the town. His own family joined a mass flight that left Piancó practically deserted by February 8. Among the few citizens who remained were an old lady who owned a bakery, the state tax collector—an educated man who believed that the revolutionaries would respect his property if he stayed, an idea he might have gotten from reading Batista Luzardo's speeches in the *Diário do Congresso*—and the town's telegraph operator. While the exodus was under way, Padre Aristides received a telegram from the governor urging him to rally his gunmen to the defense of the town. The rebels, according to the governor, numbered only about two hundred and were poorly armed; Padre Aristides was asked to hold Piancó until a force from the state milita, which was already on its way, could reach the town. With twelve state militiamen already in Piancó, the number of defenders reached forty-four after Padre Aristides committed himself and his armed followers to resist the rebels on February 8.[21]

Earlier that day the revolutionaries had passed through the village of Coremas, wounding one of the three militamen on duty there who tried to stop them. The column headquarters and the detachments of Cordeiro and Dutra camped within six kilometers of Piancó that night; Siqueira's detachment, the rebel rearguard, was near Coremas, about twenty-five kilometers from Piancó. João Alberto's men were more than a day's march away, to the northeast. General Prestes had no reason to wait for João Alberto before moving in on Piancó; area residents questioned by the rebels had indicated that the town was undefended and practically deserted.[22]

At about eight o'clock on the morning of February 9 a captain and a few soldiers from Cordeiro's detachment rode down a slope into the valley of the nearly dry Piancó River and onto the empty streets of the town on its banks. The rebels penetrated only a few blocks before they were fired upon and forced to retreat, with several men killed or wounded. The rest of Cordeiro's detachment moved quickly into the valley and pressed into the town, receiving fire from small, mobile groups of loyalists. By shifting their positions the two dozen or so loyalists at the entrance to the town appeared, to the rebels, to be a much larger force. Nevertheless, the revolutionaries were determined to avenge their dead and wounded, and Dutra's detachment was brought up and thrown into the fight for Piancó.[23]

The rebels, now some five hundred strong, pushed into the center of town where the resistance was localized at the jail and at the nearby house of Padre Aristides. At another house a white flag went up: Manuel Cândido, the tax collector, wanted to get himself and his family out of the line of fire. The firing on both sides, which had already slackened, halted with the appearance of the white flag. Most of the surviving state militiamen and about half of the armed civilians took advantage of the truce to flee the town. The jail was abandoned and Piancó's defenders were reduced to fourteen men, holed up in the house of Padre Aristides. When the firing resumed, it was not intense, as both sides were trying to save ammunition. Dutra's men found some gasoline in a mechanic's shop and used it to make a fire bomb; one of them was shot and killed trying to throw it through a window in Padre Aristides' house. Surrounded, probably out of ammunition, and threatened with incineration, Padre Aristides and his men gave up at two o'clock in the afternoon; only one of the fourteen escaped, through a window in the house.[24]

Manuel Cândido, the tax collector, and Dona Antônia César, the elderly bakery owner, claimed to have witnessed the events that followed.[25] The fifty-four-year-old Padre Aristides, dressed in a white shirt and trousers of dark sackcloth with suspenders, and his twelve comrades were taken from the house to the brink of a flooded clay pit near the jail. There Padre Aristides addressed the commander of the troops that had captured him.

"I know that I am going to die; I only ask that the force commander give me a brief respite, only while I pray a small prayer. . . . An act of contrition. . . . I am a priest and I must not die without asking God to forgive my great sins."

"What kind of respite!" the troops grunted, "What a priest! What a nothing! . . . Cut the throat of this murderer of our comrades . . . and all these bandits with him."

The order was given by the officer in charge and the knife-wielding soldiers set upon the prisoners, cutting their throats and throwing them into the clay pit. When the thirteen bodies were recovered the next day by loyalist troops, Padre Aristides was found with his carotid arteries severed, evidence of a strong blow on one cheek, and a stab wound in the left shoulder. Colonels Cordeiro and Dutra, the rebel high command would claim, had left the prisoners in the care of two lesser officers before the massacre occurred. The headquarters group arrived in Piancó about an hour after the slaughter—in time for Captain Moreira Lima, a native Paraibano, to prevent another captain from killing a captured seventeen-year-old state militiaman. Other loyalists taken prisoner outside the town were not so lucky: Five jagunços, a father and his sons, one of whom was dragged to death behind a horse, were murdered and left for the vultures on the road south of Piancó.[26]

In the next few days, as loyalist troops, including contingents of Padre Cícero's devotees from Ceará, passed through Piancó, there was ample evidence to suggest that the revolutionaries were waging a war of extermination against the backlanders. After the atrocities at Piancó, the rebels would receive no quarter from the warriors of the northeastern sertão. The sertanejos would be fighting not just to protect their meager property but, they believed, for their very lives. A people never noted for their mercy, they would show none toward the revolutionaries. "They treated us with cruelty," Captain Landucci would complain; "in inhabited places, in the catinga, on the march and at rest, at every bend in the road, there were ambushes waiting, which took a daily toll of our comrades." The revolutionaries were "brutally hunted, not combated." [27] Under these circumstances, most rebel officers were unlikely to object if their troops continued to wreak vengeance on the jagunços who fell into their hands. Colonal Siqueira Campos, who had no part in the Piancó massacre, admitted that "when I began to be violently combated by mercenary battalions who lay in ambush to assassinate my boys, I gave a general and impersonal order that characters of that type not be brought into my presence any more, and that those who captured them could decide their fate." [28]

The wave of hatred that swept the sertão did not please Padre Cícero Romão Batista, the "Saint of Joàzeiro." He wrote a letter to Luís Carlos Prestes on February 20 and gave it to one of his most dedicated followers, with orders to run the length of Brazil, if necessary, to deliver it. Padre Cícero said his heart was anguished and his soul tormented by the spectacle of Brazilians locked in a "fratricidal and exterminating struggle." While he praised the patriotic ideals of the revolutionaries, he urged them "to reflect on the widows and orphans that are appearing everywhere in painful abundance; on the hunger and misery that accompany your steps, calling down on you the curses of your countrymen, who cannot understand the reasons for your stormy passage through our great hinterland." If Prestes and his men would agree to surrender, Padre Cícero would act as their advocate before the constituted authorities of the republic and make sure that they would receive full legal guarantees. Padre

Cícero's "principal desire," he wrote, was to save the revolutionaries "from the moral ruin into which you are unconsciously falling with the grim acts and revolutionary excesses that, certainly, will carry you to an inevitable material ruin." More than two months passed before the letter was delivered; the rebels did not accept Padre Cícero's offer.[29]

Five revolutionaries and about the same number of loyalists were killed in combat at Piancó; fourteen rebels were wounded, one mortally. The Paraíba state troops who were supposedly marching to the relief of Padre Aristides reached Piancó on the morning following the massacre, after firing a few shots at the rebel rearguard, Siqueira's detachment, as it withdrew from the area. Later in the day, February 10, João Alberto's detachment approached Piancó and, finding it occupied by the enemy, moved off to the south after a brief exchange of fire. João Alberto caught up with the column headquarters across the border in Pernambuco, just east of the town of Triunfo. The rebel main body reached the Triunfo area on February 12, thus fulfilling the promise made to Cleto Campelo. For ten days the Prestes Column maneuvered about in central Pernambuco, fighting off the state militia, Floro Bartolomeu's jagunços from Ceará, and various other government forces, while waiting for word from Cleto.[30]

On February 16 part of Dutra's detachment was sent east from the village of São Caitano to try to make contact with Cleto. This force, led by Major Ary Salgado Freire, turned back on February 18, short of the town of Buique. Later that day, some one hundred and eighty kilometers farther east, Cleto was shot to death in a fight with government troops and Waldemar Lima suffered the fate of Padre Aristides. But when Ary returned to the rebel headquarters on February 22, he brought no news of Cleto and his associates. The revolutionaries could wait no longer; they had to get out of Pernambuco. While small bands of jagunços constantly harassed the rebels, hundreds of government troops were moving in for the kill over Pernambuco's motor roads, which, despite the onset of heavy rains, were still passable for trucks. Eighteen kilometers west of Custódio, on February 14, the detachments of Dutra and João Alberto had put to flight a motorized force of more than one hundred Pernambuco militiamen, destroying six enemy vehicles and capturing a large quantity of ammunition. But on February 22 another motorized force attacked the column as it was crossing a road near the village of Carqueja, inflicting heavy losses on the detachments of Siqueira, Cordeiro, and Dutra before the rebels were able to break contact and withdraw into the Serra Negra. The Prestes Column, in the Serra Negra, was being hemmed in on three sides by government troops; on the fourth side was a stretch of lowlands, a swamp now that the rainy season was under way, and, beyond that, the São Francisco River.[31]

The revolutionary chiefs in the Serra Negra seemed to have only two choices, other than attempting to surrender. They could try to break through the government semicircle and head for Piauí, where, presumably, they would be free of jagunço attacks and in a good position to countermarch through Goiás and Mato Grosso to exile in Paraguay or Bolivia; or they could try to cross the São Francisco River and continue the struggle in the state of Bahia. Despite the heavy losses they had suffered in the Northeast—perhaps one hundred veterans of the southern campaign killed or disabled since leaving Piauí, most in Pernambuco—the rebel leaders were not yet ready to call off the crusade and run for exile.[32] They would cross the São Francisco and invade Bahia.

The leaders of the Prestes Column still hoped that Isidoro would send them in Bahia the munitions they had requested, and they expected the people of the Bahian sertão to be more congenial than the sertanejos the rebels had encountered in the states to the north. The year before, "Colonel" Horácio de Matos of Bahia's Chapada Diamantina, an immense plateau in the center of the state, had won national fame by defeating the state militia, thus successfully defending his unofficial title of "Governor of the Sertão." The revolutionaries would try to make a deal with Colonel Horácio. With Isidoro's arms and the goodwill of the people of the Bahian sertão, the Prestes Column expected to be able to hold out at least until November 15, when Artur Bernardes' presidential term would expire. The new president, Washington Luís of São Paulo, might be persuaded to offer the rebels amnesty, perhaps even some political concessions, in order to begin his term on a note of national concord. In Bahia, a major seaboard state, the revolutionaries could not be ignored; they would still be the "unvanquished column," spreading the revolution to new areas of Brazil, not a dispirited band of adventurers, fleeing in the direction from whence they had come, toward the borders of a foreign country.

Crossing the São Francisco River from Pernambuco into Bahia was no easy matter, and the loyalists did not expect the rebels to try it. The São Francisco, the "highway of the sertão," was, at its narrowest points, almost a kilometer wide during the rainy season. The great river, originating in central Minas Gerais, was navigable as it flowed through the semi-arid interior of Bahia—sustained by streams descending from the well-watered Goiás plateau—and along the Pernambuco border to the mighty Paulo Afonso falls, two hundred and fifty kilometers from the ocean, on Bahia's boundary with the state of Alagoas. The falls were skirted by a one-hundred-and-fifteen-kilometer railroad from Piranhas, Alagoas, to Jatobá, Bahia—now known as Petrolândia. After his colleagues agreed to the invasion of Bahia, Prestes presented them with a plan to seize Jatobá, where he expected to find the boats necessary to take the revolutionary forces across the river.[33]

Leaving the Serra Negra on February 23, the Prestes Column made a diversionary march of fifty kilometers to the northwest and then, on February 24, wheeled to the southeast. Marching day and night, through catinga and mudflats, drenched by torrential rains, the rebels reached the São Francisco near Jatobá on the morning of February 25. Siqueira's detachment, sent to occupy Jatobá, was stoutly resisted by the town's forty-man garrison, and the boats that had been there were put beyond the rebels' grasp. While Siqueira kept the loyalists at Jatobá under siege, the revolutionaries searched the river upstream for boats, and at first finding none, prepared some of their best swimmers for a plunge into the muddy, turbulent waters to cross the nine hundred meters to the Bahia side to capture some of the vessels that were moored there. But then a small canoe was found hidden in the bushes on the Pernambuco side. Two men crossed the river in this canoe and brought back a larger one, capable of carrying eight men. A squad of heavily armed rebels crossed to Bahia in the larger canoe and returned to Pernambuco with two small cargo boats rigged with jib-headed sails. These vessels, plus several canoes found on the Bahia side, transported the twelve hundred revolutionaries, including scores of wounded, across the São Francisco during the afternoon and night of February 25. Very few of their horses were able to swim the river; most were abandoned on the Pernambuco side. The crossing of the São Francisco, Captain Landucci would recall, "was a calamity." [34]

In Bahia the Prestes Column struck out southwest, toward the Chapada Diamantina. Except for a few of the wounded, the column was on foot as it began to march through the Bahian catinga, now green with the rainy season and displaying clusters of tiny pink and gold flowers. After three days the rebels reached the village of Salgado do Melão, which they occupied without resistance. In this area, they found few horses and cattle, but an abundance of donkeys and goats. The sertanejo's *bode assado,* or roast goat, was often substituted for the gaúcho's churrasco, as the revolutionaries plodded across northern Bahia, many of them mounted on donkeys. Not until March 5, a week after they had crossed the São Francisco, did the rebels begin to find significant numbers of horses. [35]

In the meantime the column had begun to encounter armed resistance in Bahia: At least two of a handful of jagunços gave up their lives trying to stop the column from entering the village of Várzea da Ema. On a trail through the catinga, the rebel vanguard was challenged by a single sertanejo, about sixty years old, wielding an ax. He prostrated one rebel with a chop in the shoulder and held several others at bay, shouting, "You bandits! Through here you will not pass!" Fortunately for the aged jagunço, his adversaries were from the detachment of the northeasterner João Alberto, who had taught them compassion for the people of the sertão. On direct orders from the detachment commander, the sertanejo was not shot but overpowered and tied to a tree—and guarded by one of João Alberto's men until the last soldier of the rearguard detachment had passed the spot. The result of the incident was one rebel wounded, one jagunço captured and released. "Thus we crossed the northeast of Bahia, without news of any regular troops whatever, but always suffering casualties in analogous incidents." [36]

As the revolutionaries approached the East of Brazil Railroad they had their first encounter in Bahia with regular troops, soldiers of the São Paulo state militia, when a rebel patrol was forced back from the town of Uauá. Two days later, on March 11, a squadron from Dutra's detachment captured a packtrain en route from the railroad to the Paulista outpost at Uauá; coffee, sugar, cakes, and cigarettes were appropriated, in addition to a number of large sacks of rice and beans, in which several thousand 7-mm. rifle cartridges were mixed with the grain. On the night of March 13 the column crossed the railroad about fifty kilometers north of Bonfim, where more than a thousand federal and state troops were concentrated. After rounding up hundreds of horses and cattle west of the railroad on March 14, the column swung to the south and for nearly two weeks encountered no resistance as it ascended into the Chapada Diamantina, the domain of Horácio de Matos. On March 25 the rebel high command wrote a letter to Colonel Horácio inviting him to join the revolution.[37]

The Chapada Diamantina, a plateau of eight hundred meters or more in elevation, extends for about three hundred kilometers from north to south in the center of the state of Bahia. Rising abruptly from the chapada's broad plains are three quartzite ridges that eons of erosion have cut up into innumerable flat-topped mountains, thirteen hundred to two thousand one hundred meters in altitude. Although the high plains have most of the characteristics of the semi-arid sertão, including catinga, they also have streams, originating in the quartzite mountains, that flow year round toward the Atlantic Ocean. It was in the beds of these streams that diamonds were discovered around 1820. A succession of new finds brought a rush of garimpeiros into the chapada and sustained the mining boom past mid-century. By 1870, however, most surface deposits of marketable gems had been exhausted and the economy of the area was in full decline. Then industrial uses were discovered for the formerly valueless carbonado, or black diamond, that was found in abundance in the chapada. A French firm set up shop in Lençóis, at the foot of the chapada, and began buying carbonados, reviving the economy of the area in the 1870's. By the beginning of the twentieth century the carbonado boom was over, although industrial diamonds, as well as gem stones, would still be produced by those who had the capital to divert rivers and mine subsurface deposits. But the returns steadily diminished and in the 1920's even large-scale operations were becoming unprofitable. The new diamond fields of Mato Grosso, where the Bahian José Morbeck held sway, lured away many miners from the Chapada Diamantina, including Arquimedes de Matos, brother of Colonel Horácio.[38]

Horácio de Matos was the nephew of Colonel Clementino de Matos, who established the Matos clan as a major power in the Chapada Diamantina by defeating the armed forces of rival families and repelling an expedition of three hundred state troops, whose artillery piece he kept as a souvenir. Clementino, on his deathbed in 1912, summoned the men of the clan to his home to witness the investiture of their new chief. Surprisingly, Clementino entrusted the destinies of the clan not to a noted warrior, but to a man of peace, a thirty-year-old storekeeper and diamond buyer, Horácio de Matos. In a trembling voice the old man spoke from his bed, holding Horácio by the hand, to the assemblage of nephews, cousins, and godsons. He recounted the history of the clan, paid tribute to its fallen heroes, and recited its code of honor:

"Do not humiliate anyone—but also never let yourself be humiliated by any man, no matter who he may be.

"Do not steal, ever, no matter what the circumstances—nor permit anyone to steal and go unpunished.

"Be loyal to friends and relatives, protecting them always.

"Be faithful in dealing with enemies, respecting them in time of peace and confronting them in time of war.

"Do not provoke anyone or commit aggression—but if you are offended, put honor above everything, and react in the full meaning of the word, for life without dignity is worthless." [39]

After Clementino finished speaking, each male relative received six blows from a ferule wielded by Horácio, symbolizing his submission to the new chief. As head of the Matos clan, Horácio strove to keep the peace in the Chapada Diamantina. He did not react violently when rival families took over some municipal governments in the area, and when his own brother was killed (not without justification, for he was the black sheep of the family), Horácio declared that he was leaving the case to the courts of law, a novel attitude in the sertão. Horácio's pacific principles were mistaken for weakness within the clan and among its enemies. Dona Casimira de Matos, Horácio's aunt, called the jagunços to arms in 1915 and sent them out against the clan's rivals, who were becoming increasingly insolent and aggressive.[40]

Horácio was forced to choose between abdicating his chieftainship and leading the clan in war. Reluctantly, he chose the latter and became the most celebrated warlord of the Brazilian backlands. Time and again, circumstances beyond his control would compel him to take up arms against rival clans and against the state government to safeguard interests entrusted to him. As his enemies fell back before him, Horácio acquired power he had not sought and, perhaps, did not want. In 1919 he joined other backland chiefs in an armed movement against the state government, which left him in charge of Lençóis, the "capital" of the mining district. The 1919 revolt in Bahia was ended by federal intervention and the "Treaty of Lençóis" of 1920, which recognized Horácio's authority over twelve municípios in the sertão.[41]

Horácio, who was strongly fatalistic, seemed to have a complete disregard for his personal safety in battle, which gave rise to rumors that he had a corpo fechado, an impenetrable body. An enemy bullet that creased the top of the wooden shoulderstock of his Mauser automatic, about a centimeter from his nose, left him unshaken. He could sleep soundly in a house under siege, with bullets crashing through the windows. Genuinely religious, he would reply to cries of "Viva Horácio!" with "Viva God, who is our protector!" But he was no ascetic; he enjoyed playing cards and dancing and was especially proficient in the exhausting jaguar dance, a kind of quadrille performed by one gentleman and ten young ladies. Usually soft-spoken, he was nevertheless frank and open with those he trusted and could become quite animated in discussions with friends. He considered Governor Francisco de Góis Calmon, whom he had supported in the election of 1923, to be his *amigo,* and once grabbed him by the arm and shook him during a friendly argument in the state capital. The governor apparently did not appreciate being jostled by this jagunço in city clothes, who, when he visited Salvador, sported a diamond-headed walking cane with a sword inside. For whatever reason, Góis Calmon embarked on a campaign to crush Horácio de Matos at the end of 1924.[42]

Governor Góis Calmon named one of Horácio's sworn enemies to be police commissioner in Lençóis and in January 1925 sent an expedition of five hundred state troops marching on the mining area to install his appointee in office. Colonel Horácio sent telegrams to the governor, assuring him of his continued loyalty and asking him to withdraw the appointment and call back the troops, and to President Bernardes, urging him to do something to stop the invasion. But he got no satisfaction from either. President Bernardes was perhaps influenced by rumors spread by Horácio's enemies, one of whom was a member of his cabinet, that the backlands chief sympathized with Isidoro's revolutionaries. At any rate, the president was at first inclined to let the governor handle the situation in his state as he saw fit. The forces of the state of Bahia, however, were no match for the jagunços of Horácio de Matos, who rallied to the defense of Lençóis. After a month of fighting and maneuvering around Lençóis, the government commander was dead and his badly mauled troops were in full retreat to Salvador. About this time Horácio's friends in Rio, including Congressman Francisco Rocha, persuaded the president to call a halt to the governor's persecution of the backlands chief and to try to make peace between Salvador and the Chapada Diamantina.[43]

In March 1925 Congressman Rocha arrived in the chapada with a peace mission that was empowered by the president and the governor to arrange a settlement with Horácio. The peace delegation found Horácio amenable. All parties agreed that the whole affair resulted from misunderstandings caused by a perfidious telegraph operator who changed the texts of Horácio's wires to the governor and to the president. Horácio emphatically denied that he had any sympathy for the revolution. While it was later revealed that a young man claiming to be an emissary from Isidoro had been in Lençóis, Horácio had turned down his invitation to join the Tenente revolution. In April 1925 Governor Góis Calmon officially withdrew the appointment that Horácio had objected to and there was a return to the status quo ante in the Chapada Diamantina.[44]

With the settlement of 1925 the Bernardes government acquired an ally in Horácio de Matos, who hoped that the president would care to strengthen their ties by providing the colonel's constituents with the federal economic aid that his predecessor had denied them. Colonel Horácio was no traditional backcountry political boss, who preferred his people in poverty, ignorance, and isolation, so that he could better control them and market their votes. Horácio wanted to revive agriculture in the war-torn and depressed mining region, to open up the area by building roads and railways and by dredging the Paraguaçu River to make it navigable as far as Lençóis. A man of limited education himself, he wanted his people to have more schools and looked forward to the day when competitive sports would replace clan warfare as their principal diversion.[45] Colonel Horácio was awakened from his dream of peace by the intrusion of the Prestes Column.

After the rebels invaded Bahia, General Álvaro Mariante sent a telegram to Colonel Horácio de Matos asking him to organize a Patriotic Battalion. On March 14, 1926, Horácio read the telegram to a gathering of his principal supporters in Lençóis, and, with their unanimous consent, decreed the formation of the Diamond Mines Battalion, with Horácio as commander and Franklin de Queiroz, his cousin, as adjutant. That same day Captain Queiroz was sent to the north of the chapada to set up observation posts and organize the defense of the area immediately threatened by the rebels. Ten days later the adjutant reported back to Horácio that the rebels had entered the chapada and committed some depredations. However, neither Captain

Queiroz nor any other Horacista had resisted the revolutionaries; the jagunços seemed to be holding their fire, hoping that the rebels would go away. In organizing the Diamond Mines Battalion, Horácio had committed himself only to the defense of the Chapada Diamantina. He would never join the revolutionaries, but if they would leave his people and their property alone, he would not fight them.[46]

There were some members of the Matos clan who sought to promote an understanding between Horácio and Prestes, to spare the Chapada Diamantina the torments of renewed warfare or, perhaps, even to further the cause of the revolution. Manuel Querino de Matos, Horácio's cousin, disapproved of the organization of the Diamond Mines Battalion (he had not attended the Lençóis meeting) and was known for his revolutionary sympathies. Another cousin of Horácio appeared with a friend at the rebel headquarters near Barro Alto on March 25 and volunteered their services as mediators. The column high command accepted their offer and gave them a letter to deliver to Horácio, urging him to come over to the revolution or, at least, promise to stay neutral, in which case the rebels would not attack him. But the logistical demands of the revolutionaries made neutrality impossible. Manuel Querino, the revolution's best friend in the high councils of the Matos clan, turned suddenly and violently against the rebels when they sacked his ranch. On March 27 Manuel Querino, without consulting Horácio, led a handful of jagunços in an attack on the column's vanguard; the sertanejo force inflicted a number of casualties on the rebels before withdrawing after an hour of fighting, leaving two of its number dead on the field.[47]

Believing that Horácio had broken the tacit truce, the rebels launched an assault on the town of Barra de Mendes on March 28 and easily overcame its few defenders. Thereafter, Horacista resistance stiffened as jagunço ambushes took a daily toll in rebel lives. Rebel foraging parties were especially hard hit: "The jagunços lay in wait for them, firm and terrible," Moreira Lima wrote, "hitting them with well-placed shots, retreating from one bend in the road to the next, but always fighting." On a road near Alagadiço, men from Siqueira's detachment killed a cousin and a nephew of Horácio, who were carrying correspondence to the colonel from his aunt, the formidable Dona Casimira. The killing of Horácio's two kinsmen, on April 2, 1926, transformed a defensive struggle for the protection of property into a blood feud. Horácio de Matos would cross the breadth of Brazil in his vendetta against the Prestes Column.[48]

After the Horacista attacks began, the column marched rapidly for the southern exit of the Chapada Diamantina "to escape from that inferno of ambushes and torments of every kind." They occupied Rio de Contas, the southernmost town of the plateau on April 6 and the next day descended into the valley of the Brumado River. For two more weeks they continued on their southward course, now free of jagunço attacks, across southern Bahia and into Minas Gerais. Broad fields covered with flowers opened before them. The only resistance they encountered was passive: Most of the inhabitants of the towns, villages, and farms of the area abandoned their homes and fled as the column approached. Still, there was enough livestock around to sustain the revolutionaries, and the column's sad caravan of stretcher-borne wounded was not being added to. During this period the column lost only a few stray foragers and Padre Manuel de Macedo, who deserted after an argument with Prestes and a headquarters cook, in Rio de Contas. So the revolutionaries wandered southward until April 22 when the column's rearguard was attacked in Serra Nova, Minas Gerais, by the Bahian jagunços of Horácio de Matos and Abílio Wolney.[49]

The resumption of jagunço attacks made the rebel high command face up to an unavoidable decision. The column could not go on indefinitely fighting off these small-scale attacks, suffering daily casualties. Rather than keep the revolution alive, the column would itself be nibbled to death. In Minas Gerais, João Alberto would recall, "we turned our backs completely on our hopes of victory in order to proceed exclusively with a struggle for existence, not letting ourselves be beaten." The column's principal leaders resolved to march immediately, by the most direct route possible, to the most accessible foreign border. The decision to emigrate was made in secret and accepted by Prestes "with repugnance." [50]

Nevertheless, the resourceful chief-of-staff came up with an acceptable plan to achieve the goal so desired by his colleagues. The rebels could not march directly west toward Goiás, because General Mariante had anticipated such a move and was concentrating thousands of state and federal troops along the São Francisco River in Minas Gerais. But with so many jagunços from the Middle São Francisco and the Chapada Diamantina pouring into Minas Gerais, those areas were now virtually defenseless. The column would wheel around, strike out to the northeast toward Salvador, and then, as their pursuers raced off toward the Bahian capital, swing rapidly to the west, through the Chapada Diamantina, and cross the São Francisco between Xique Xique and Remanso. From there it would be only a short march to Piauí, where no one was likely to bother them as they crossed the state en route to Goiás, Mato Grosso, and the border of Bolivia or Paraguay.

Manaus

Obidos

Belém

São Luis

Sobral

Fortaleza

Campo Maior   Ipú
Timon   Teresina   Crateus
Grajaú   Arcias
Colinas   Natal
Palmeiras   Valença
Mirador   Amarante   São Miguel
Loreto   Nova Iorque   Pio IX   Arneiro   Luis Gomez
Carolina   Floriano   Monsenhor   Iguatú   Coremas
    Hipolito Pianco   Malta
Balsas   Uruçui   Picos
    Campos Sales   Joazeiro   Paraíba
Pedro Afónso   Triunfo   Custodio   Gravatá   Recife
    Cabrobo   Carqueja   São   Tabostao
Tocantínia   Rodelas   Caitaba   Buique
    Remanso   Salgado do Mel   Jatobá
    Cajuí   Várzea da Ema   Uaua   Piranhas
Porto Nacional   Xique Xique   Senhor   Bonfim
Natividade   Canabrava
Dianópolis   Barra de Mendes   dos Gonçal   Aracajú
Taguatinga   Alagadico   Barro Alto
    Barreiras   Boca de Dentro
Formosa   Olho d'Agua   Palmeira
Arraias   Tiririca dos Bodes   Lençóis
São Domingos   Brotas   Agua
    de Macaubas Rega   Muçuge   Salvador
Neuclándia   Rio de Contas   Ituaçu
Posse
Aranguaiana   Mambai
Cuiabá   Goiás   Planaltina
Presidente   Inhumas   Anápolis   Luziánia
Murtinho   Caiapónia   Bela Vista   Silvania   Serra Nova
San Matias   Zeca   Chatanapolis   São Francisco
Alto Araguaia   Lopes   Silvania   São Romão   Grão Mogol
    Mineiros   Rio Verde   Pirapora
Cabecera Alta   Jata
Goiaz   Itumbiara

Corumbá

Camapuá

Jaraguari
Ribeirão Claro
Campo Grande   Riba   Tres Lagoas
    do Rio   Presidente
Porto Murtinho   Parado   Epitacio
Cabeceira do Apa   Presidente
Bela Vista   Pedro Juan Caballero   Baura
Ponta Porã   Campanaró
    Amambai   Panchita
    Jacarei
    Guaira
Puerto Adela   Porto Mendes   São Paulo
Santa Helena   Santa Cruz   Santos
Asunción   Benjamim   Catanduvas   Formigas   Ponta Grossa   Rio de Janeiro
Foz do Iguaçu   Belarmino
Puerto Aguirre   Laranjeiras
    Santo António   Campo Erê   Porto União
    Barracão   Porto Feliz   Clevelândia
Monteguado   Alto Uruguai   Palmeira
    Pósadas
    Comandai
    Santo Angelo   Iui
Santo Tome   São Luis   São Borja   Cruz Alta
Itaqui   Tupanciretã
Paso de Los Libres   Alegrete
Uraguaiana   Saicá   São Simão   Porto Alegre
Monte Caseros   Rosario
    Artigas   Livramento

    Rio Grande

Buenos Aires

The Road to Exile

LX In southern Bahia, Horácio de Matos' forces from the Chapada Diamantina, about six hundred men, were joined by two smaller bands of jagunços from the Middle São Francisco, commanded by José Honório Granja, formerly of southern Piauí, and Abílio Wolney, formerly of Dianópolis, Goiás. The three "colonels" followed the Prestes Column into northern Minas Gerais, where advance elements of Horácio's and Wolney's outfits fell on the rebel rear at Serra Nova on April 22. But the revolutionaries soon managed to break contact with their pursuers and throw them off the trail. While the jagunços were searching for them in Minas Gerais, the rebels suddenly appeared at the Bahian town of Ituaçu and occupied it, on May 4, 1926, before its inhabitants had a chance to flee. From Ituaçu the column set a course along the watershed of the Chapada Diamantina to avoid streams swollen by that year's unusually long rainy season; the rains, which normally would have begun to taper off in March, continued with little letup through April and into May.[1]

The second rebel invasion of the Chapada Diamantina caught Horácio and his best jagunços some four hundred kilometers to the south, in the vicinity of Grão Mogol, Minas Gerais. As the column reentered the chapada some residents armed

themselves and prepared to resist, while others fled into the catinga with no thought other than to escape from the revolutionaries who, they believed, were out to exterminate them. Anatolino Medrado, brother-in-law of Colonel Horácio and son of
Colonel Douca Medrado, political boss of Muçugê, was captured
by the rebels south of that town. He was brought to the rebel
headquarters where it was decided to use him as a hostage to
force an entrance into Muçugê, where the rebels hoped to pick
up some arms and ammunition. When Douca Medrado learned
of the capture of his son, he left for his ranch and urged his
fellow townspeople not to resist the rebels. But a handful of determined citizens ignored their chief and ambushed Dutra's detachment as it approached the town through a rocky canyon on
the morning of May 7. It took the rebels the rest of the day to
fight their way out of the trap, in which they lost at least eight
men killed. Fortunately for young Anatolino, he remained
under the protection of General Prestes, who took a liking to
him and decided that he and his father were not responsible for
the resistance. The chief-of-staff set Anatolino free six weeks
later.[2]

Prestes' magnanimity was not shared by many of his comrades, and other chapada towns did not have Muçugê's excellent
defensive setting. Bent on revenge, the revolutionaries assaulted
a succession of towns and villages in the Chapada Diamantina,
overpowering their determined but hopelessly outnumbered
defenders. Agua Rega, Tiririca dos Bodes, Olho d'Agua,
Roça de Dentro, and Canabrava dos Gonçalo were seized, looted,
and put to the torch; the last was only a village, but seventy-three
houses went up in flames there. "Our forces," Moreira Lima admitted, "were forced to take certain extreme measures in the
way of reprisals, but only in those localities whose inhabitants
armed themselves and received us with bullets." As Horácio de
Matos and his men raced homeward from Minas Gerais, the
Prestes Column cut a swath of death and destruction through
the Chapada Diamantina. By the time Horácio's troops reached
Brotas de Macaúbas, on the northwestern edge of the chapada,
on May 25, the revolutionaries were two hundred thirty kilometers to the north at the São Francisco River near Cajuí.[3]

While Horácio was marching overland to the Chapada Diamantina, General Mariante sent Wolney's jagunços down the São Francisco in steamboats. At Xique Xique, Wolney joined forces with "Colonel" Franklin Lins de Albuquerque, the coronelíssimo of the Middle São Francisco, and together they intercepted the rebels when they appeared at the river near Cajuí. After a fight on May 26 the revolutionaries pulled back from the river and disappeared into the catinga. The rebels had worn out most of their horses in the forced march from the chapada to the river; when they returned to the bush, almost all were on foot. Nevertheless, they moved rapidly through a waterless stretch of catinga and reemerged five days later around a bend in the river at Sento Sé. But the riverine jagunços were there waiting for them. To attempt a crossing there and at that time would be to risk annihilation. Even if the jagunços could be held off, and a few canoes captured, the river itself would claim many lives: It was wide and wild, near flood stage. But the rains had finally ended and the water was receding; the longer they could delay the crossing, the easier it would be, especially if they could lure the government troops away from the river. So the Prestes Column undertook a thirty-two-day campaign in northeastern Bahia to disorient the enemy while the water in the river fell to a safer level.[4]

While government forces concentrated along the São Francisco, the rebels moved to the southeast, meeting practically no resistance as they replenished their cavalhada. Then they struck out boldly across the East of Brazil Railroad and by June 20 were within one hundred seventy kilometers of Salvador. They still met little resistance and in one town were mistaken for government troops and welcomed with a brass band. General Mariante was dazzled by these maneuvers and the politicians in Salvador demanded protection. The alert on the river was relaxed as government troops were shifted by rail to Salvador. The Prestes Column, after marching parallel to the coast for about a week, collecting tens of thousands of milreis in tribute from local merchants, turned inland on June 26. Less than a week later the rebels appeared at the village of Rodelas, on the São Francisco, less than sixty kilometers from where they had crossed into

Bahia. The village was occupied without a fight and several small canoes were found there. A platoon from João Alberto's detachment crossed the river in the canoes and captured four sail-rigged cattle boats. In these vessels the nine hundred revolutionaries and almost all of their horses crossed to Pernambuco on July 2 and 3, 1926. José Honório Granja's jagunços arrived on the scene in time to wound one rebel and shoot some holes in the sails of the last boats to cross. The second crossing of the São Francisco was the most successful operation of the rebels' four-month Bahian campaign, in which they lost some three hundred men.[5]

The rebels marched rapidly across western Pernambuco, exchanged a few shots with local forces, and entered Piauí, near Simões, on July 11. That same day, Abílio Wolney and his one hundred and thirty-seven jagunços, who were at Cabrobó on the São Francisco, were put on the column's trail. Horácio de Matos and his five-hundred-and-seventy-man battalion—which was on its way from the Chapada Diamantina to the river, reorganized and equipped with government arms—was ordered to ascend the Rio Prêto, west of the São Francisco, to try to intercept the rebels as they marched south from Piauí. The revolutionaries, however, did not immediately turn south in Piauí; they marched directly west and, on July 23, seized the city of Floriano, where they put out the last issue of *O Libertador*. They turned south on July 24 and Wolney caught up with them a week later, at Uruçuí. Wolney's jagunços harassed the rebels' rear as the column drove south toward the Rio Prêto. There, near Formosa, Bahia, on August 18, the revolutionaries clashed with Horácio's jagunços. The column maneuvered around Horácio's battalion without much difficulty and entered the state of Goiás on August 20.[6]

Abílio Wolney followed the rebels into his home state of Goiás, where he and his jagunços were incorporated into Colonel Franklin's "Geraldo Rocha" Battalion to minimize problems with Senator Totó Caiado. With the addition of Wolney's contingent, Franklin's battalion was about the same size as Horácio's, numbering nearly six hundred men. In addition to these two units, General Mariante's command in Goiás included two small jagunço battalions, commanded by José Honório Granja of Piauí and Rotílio Mendonça of Bahia, and contingents of the state militias of Bahia, Pernambuco, Alagoas, and Minas Gerais. The movements of these forces, somewhat more than two thousand men in all, were coordinated by General Mariante's chief-of-staff, federal army Major Pedro Aurélio de Góis Monteiro. The pursuit forces were officially designated *grupos de caça*, or hunter groups, and were expected to live off the land. So the poor people of Goiás not only had to endure a second passage of the Prestes Column but had to provide sustenance for the two thousand jagunços and militiamen who were chasing them. The government commanders, however, were legally empowered to commit federal funds for the reimbursement of those whose property they requisitioned for official use, and Horácio de Matos, at least, made a conscientious effort to see that the receipts given by his officers were redeemed at full value.[7]

Since the horse population of northern Goiás had not increased significantly since the Prestes Column first passed through the area in 1925, rebels and their pursuers were sometimes forced to proceed on foot. The pace, however, was rapid, especially after August 27, 1926, when a patrol from Wolney's outfit made a surprise attack on Siqueira's detachment when the rebels stopped to lay an ambush for their pursuers. The jagunços were led by a rebel deserter, a former federal army sergeant who had slipped away from the column in Bahia. Outmaneuvering the would-be ambushers, the ex-sergeant and his jagunços penetrated the security of Siqueira's headquarters area, where Miguel Costa happened to be at the time. At least five revolutionaries were killed by the raiders and a greater number were wounded, including General Miguel, who was hit above the heart and would have to spend several days in a stretcher. The traitor who led the assault was killed, along with several of his jagunços, in a counterattack by the men of Siqueira Campos.[8]

The Hero of Copacabana acquired a healthy respect for the fighting qualities of the jagunços. "In the battalions of Franklin de Albuquerque, Abílio Wolney, Horácio de Matos, Floro Bartolomeu, Geraldo Rocha, and others, there was more disorder

than there was in the rebel forces," Colonel Siqueira Campos
noted, "but in them there was solidarity, a need for mutual cooperation, an instinct that brought them all together in a common
awareness." The Patriotic Battalions were "commanded by cau-
dillos without the slightest knowledge of combat theory," but
they were more effective than regular units in fighting the revolutionaries. In fact, Siqueira admitted, the jagunços "employ
revolutionary methods. In truth, they are revolutionaries in the
service of legality." [9] Captain Moreira Lima, however, would not
concede that the men of the sertão were in any way "revolutionary." The backlanders, according to the column's secretary,
were "an amorphous mass that has no idea of liberty, a veritable
herd of brutes. . . . a simple collection of pariahs, guided by the
unconscious impulses of inferior instincts. It is this moral state
that permits the easy domination of the chiefs of the interior
over the sertanejos. . . . The sertanejo, evidently, came to a stop
on the lower rungs of the ascending ladder of civilization." Captain Landucci, a veteran of the Italian front in World War I,
deplored the backlanders' disregard for the rules of civilized
warfare. The jagunços, in violation of the Hague Convention of
1899, hollowed out the noses of their bullets so that they would
splatter on impact, causing severe wounds.[10]

The jagunços kept the Prestes Column on the run but were
unable to overtake it and wipe it out. President Bernardes' desire to prevent the rebels from escaping into exile was shared by
President-elect Washington Luís, who advocated a plan to intercept and crush the revolutionaries on the high plateau of Goiás.
The plan was devised by Colonel Pedro Dias de Campos, who
commanded the militia of Washington Luís' state of São Paulo.
Dias de Campos proposed setting up an east-west line across the
central plateau of Goiás, a distance of four hundred kilometers,
manned by fewer than three thousand Paulista troops, to block
the rebels' route south. The plan was accepted by the federal
government, over the objections of General Mariante, and by
the beginning of September 1926 the Paulistas were moving into
position. Colonel Horácio's adjutant, Captain Franklin de
Queiroz, marched rapidly forward on his battalion's left flank to
make contact with the São Paulo forces and coordinate their

operations on the plateau. Queiroz was appalled by the situation he found in São Domingos, Goiás, where the Paulistas were driving away the local population with their unreasonable requisitions and their arrogant and menacing behavior. He was afraid that the Diamond Mines Battalion would have a hard time advancing beyond this point, because the troops from São Paulo were stripping the land of all its resources. Also, there was the danger that the Paulistas would mistake the jagunços for rebels and open fire on them. This fear was realized on October 2, when São Paulo troops fired on the jagunços by mistake, killing an officer and two soldiers of the Diamond Mines Battalion near Niquelândia, Goiás.[11]

In the meantime, the revolutionaries were maneuvering through the loyalist "line." They passed west of Arraias on September 7 and three weeks later reached the Anápolis-Goiás city motor road, having suffered only a few casualties in rearguard actions and forager fights in the month since the encounter near Dianópolis. As they crossed the motor road, some twenty kilometers west of Anápolis, the rebels were approached by an old man who said that he had been searching for them to tell them that Santa Dica had predicted that they would win. Santa Dica apparently wanted an alliance with the Prestes Column. She was a young voodoo priestess—"plump, congenial, appetizing," a "luscious mulatto"—who had a sizable following among the country people in the Anápolis-Goiás city area. Her popularity disturbed Totó Caiado, who in 1925 had sent the Goiás militia against her. The militiamen shot down a number of believers in a massacre on the Peixe River and arrested Santa Dica. She was free after nine months in prison in Goiás city when the Prestes Column reappeared in the area. Although the revolutionaries ignored her overtures in September 1926, her continuing subversive activities were brought to the attention of the Caiado dynasty, which expelled her from the state four months later.[12]

After the rebels crossed the Anápolis–Goiás city road, João Alberto and part of his detachment continued south to divert the enemy as the rest of the column swung to the southwest. Colonel Franklin's jagunços got on João Alberto's trail, while other loyalist forces, moving about on the numerous motor roads of

southern Goiás, occasionally intercepted other rebel units. Nine
men from Dutra's detachment were killed and nine captured in
a surprise attack on the rebel rearguard as the column entered
the state of Mato Grosso near the headwaters of the Araguaia
River. Other actions took their toll and by October 22, 1926,
when the four detachments were reunited, about eighty kilometers west of Coxim, the column had been reduced to eight
hundred men, of whom only six hundred were physically fit—
and these were dangerously low on ammunition.[13] But the
border of Bolivia was now only four hundred kilometers away,
across the Pantanal, the vast floodplain of the Paraguay River,
which was still fairly dry as the rainy season was just beginning.
General Prestes, however, was reluctant to embark on the final
leg of the odyssey; he persuaded his colleagues to delay the trek
across the Pantanal for a few more weeks.

The state militia of Mato Grosso defeated the forces of Dr.
José Morbeck early in 1926 and occupied the key border towns
of Alto Araguaia and Araguaiana. Although Morbeck fled to
Goiás and organized resistance to the government of Mato
Grosso ended in the Garças-Araguaia area, the state was still unable to extend its authority over the numerous *garimpos,* or diamond mining camps, which remained havens for smugglers and
all kinds of criminals. A large percentage of the garimpeiros
were virtual prisoners in the mining district: Because of their
criminal records they could not venture out of the area even to
enjoy the proceeds of big strikes, which were not rare. So fancy
clothes, beer, wines, liquors, and other luxuries were brought
into the mining camps for sale to the lucky garimpeiros, who
also were enticed by troupes of comely prostitutes. Truly a state
within a state, the mining district was served by lines of supply
and communication, slightly rerouted with the departure of
Morbeck, that reached all the way to the diamond houses of
Europe. The society was generous and ambulatory—most of its
ten thousand souls lived in lean-tos and were not interested in
accumulating wealth—and excluded only lawmen. The men of
the Prestes Column, like any fugitives, would be welcome as long

as they obeyed the code of the garimpeiros and refrained from trespassing on the claims of others.[14]

General Prestes wanted to break down the revolutionary column into autonomous bands and scatter them through the mining district. Instead of marching off to a foreign country, to wait in exile for an appropriate time to renew the struggle, the rebels could remain in Brazil, building a regional base of support. "We would create a nucleus of resistance from which the government would not be able to dislodge us." But General Miguel Costa was adamantly opposed to the idea; the column, he insisted, should not disappear that way, "ending a glorious journey across Brazil to scatter in armed bands of dubious idealism." Prestes had come up with a truly revolutionary plan, but he could not convince his colleagues, who were prisoners of the concepts he had previously sold them—the armed protest demonstration and the "war of movement." To Miguel and the detachment commanders, "it seemed impractical to stack arms in that region and await the government's attack." Besides, they had no confidence in the garimpeiros. Everywhere they had gone, except Maranhão and Piauí, the people had turned against them. It was likely to be the same in the garimpos, if they stuck to their principles, for the aspirations of the revolutionaries were quite different from those of the people upon whom they fed. Most of the rebel leaders found it difficult to imagine themselves and the backlanders as partners in revolution. The column could not disperse among the garimpeiros "without seriously compromising its objective." [15]

While rejecting Prestes' proposal, the detachment commanders did not insist on marching immediately to Bolivia in October 1926; they were willing to remain in Brazil for a few weeks longer, while they made one last effort to get in touch with Marshal Isidoro. The column's leaders believed that Isidoro was planning an uprising in Rio Grande do Sul, where there had been one every year since 1923. The 1926 gaúcho revolt, like the two previous ones, would probably be launched in the southern spring, they felt, at least before November 15, when Artur Bernardes was scheduled to turn over the presidency to Washington

Luís. Should that year's gaúcho rising set off a nationwide wave of revolution, the Prestes Column, intact in Mato Grosso, would be in a position to strike a decisive blow against the government. It was a slim hope, but it prompted the column leaders to try to find out from Isidoro what was going on in the south before they made the final move across the border into Bolivia.[16]

Djalma Dutra was chosen by his colleagues as their emissary to Isidoro; he would leave for the Paraguayan border on October 25, with Moreira Lima as his alternate and a guard of eleven men. Dutra and his party would be escorted part of the way south by Siqueira Campos and eighty picked men from his detachment, who were to try to lead the pursuing jagunços off toward Campo Grande, while the rest of the column withdrew north into the diamond mining district. Siquerira was supposed to rejoin the column in the valley of the Garças River, after which the four detachments (Dutra's now commanded by Ary Salgado Freire, promoted to lieutenant colonel on October 25) were to march together toward San Matías, Bolivia. They would remain on the Brazilian side of the border until the end of January 1927; should they receive no word from Dutra, they would cross into Bolivia at the beginning of February.[17]

The plan was imperfectly executed. Dutra and Moreira Lima had to go to Libres, Argentina, to find Isidoro. On November 23 Moreira Lima left Libres with a letter from Isidoro to Prestes and Miguel Costa, asking them to remain in the field for two more months, as a revolt was already under way in Rio Grande do Sul. It was two months, however, before Moreira Lima found the Prestes Column in Bolivia on February 3, 1927. But it did not matter; by that time the Chimangos had crushed the revolt in Rio Grande do Sul—there was no "revolutionary situation" in Brazil that the Prestes Column could have exploited. The column crossed into Bolivia on February 3, but without Siqueira and his men.[18]

The jagunços of Colonel Franklin de Albuquerque were not led astray by Siqueira's feint toward Campo Grande at the end of October 1926; they followed the column main body into the mining district. There the rebels were put under intense pressure by Franklin's men and by the Bahian Diamond Mines Battalion, which now included a contingent of local garimpeiros, led by Horácio's brother, Arquimedes de Matos, who knew the area well. Arquimedes took command of the battalion on December 20, when Horácio left for Rio to undergo surgery for an inflamed appendix. By this time the jagunços were no longer obstructed by the São Paulo militia under Colonel Pedro Dias de Campos. Dias de Campos had been recalled; General Mariante was back in full command of the campaign against the rebels; and the jagunço chiefs had a free hand to pursue the struggle as they saw fit. They kept the rebels on the run, attacking them almost daily, chasing them back and forth across the Goiás–Mato Grosso border. Siqueira Campos moved in and out of the mining area in November, marched far to the west, circling Cuiabá, but was unable to reestablish contact with the column main body, which left the Garças valley for the Bolivian border in late December. When his comrades entered the Mato Grosso Pantanal, Siqueira was looking for them seven hundred kilometers to the east in southern Goiás. Siqueira was at Cristianópolis, Goiás, on February 8 when he learned at the local telegraph office that the column had entered Bolivia. With thousands of government troops concentrated along the Bolivian border, Siqueira decided to head for Paraguay. He crossed the border at Bella Vista, Paraguay with sixty-five men on March 23, 1926.[19]

As the column main body was leaving the mining district, on December 24, 1926, it ran into a force of Mato Grosso militiamen coming from Cuiabá. Perhaps as many as four hundred, mostly green recruits, the militiamen took up defensive positions on the motor road near Presidente Murtinho. After several hours of firing, they were dislodged and put to flight by a flank attack conducted by João Alberto and Ary Salgado Freire. In this engagement, which cost the rebels but one man killed, the only sizable loyalist force between the column and the Bolivian border at San Matías was shattered and rendered useless to the government. The Bahian jagunços of Franklin de Albuquerque and Arquimedes de Matos, however, continued to press in on the column's rear, as the rebels maneuvered to the north of Cuiabá, crossed the Paraguay River near its headwaters, and then swung south into the Pantanal. The rebels lost almost all of their horses in the Pantanal and at times marched in water up to their chests. Revolutionary soldiers spent some nights perched on top of huge anthills, the only dry ground available, where they were relentlessly tormented by thick clouds of mosquitoes. Cattle virtually disappeared as the column approached the Bolivian border, and the rebels were reduced to eating hearts of palm. On February 3 the column crossed the unmarked frontier and camped north of San Matías. That same day, Ary Salgado Freire went to the Bolivian town to arrange for the surrender of the rebels to the commandant of its garrison. In San Matías, Ary was delighted to encounter Lourenço Moreira Lima, who had arrived there from Argentina a few days earlier.[20]

On February 4, 1926, the six hundred twenty Brazilian revolutionaries handed over to the San Matías garrison their military arms—ninety Mauser rifles, four machine guns, two automatic rifles, and eight thousand rounds of ammunition—and formally placed themselves under the protection of the Bolivian government. By this time Bahian jagunços were pouring over the Bolivian border in pursuit of the revolutionaries. The jagunços withdrew from foreign soil after the government of Bolivia protested to Rio, and after the Bolivians turned over the arms they had taken from the Prestes Column to Colonel Franklin de Albuquerque. The revolt that had begun in São Paulo on July 5, 1924, definitely came to an end on March 24, 1927, when Siqueira Campos and sixty-five rebels crossed into Paraguay and surrendered twenty Mauser rifles and one thousand cartridges. Not counting Siqueira's meanderings, which covered some nine thousand kilometers, or any of the various excursions on the main body's flanks, the Prestes Column marched about twenty-five thousand kilometers in twenty-five months, from São Luís Gonzaga, Rio Grande do Sul, to San Matías, Bolivia.[21]

The march of the Prestes Column was an amazing feat, and after it was over, it captured the imagination of the Brazilian bourgeoisie. People who had ignored the column's call to revolutionary action when the rebels were in the field showered them with the most extravagant praise once they were in exile. In 1927 Brazil wanted heroes but not a revolution. Three years later, with the country in the grips of the world depression, everyone seemed to want to overthrow the government of President Washington Luís and prevent the inauguration of his designated successor, another Paulista. Among the "revolutionaries" of 1930 were Epitácio Pessoa, Borges de Medeiros and the Chimangos of Rio Grande do Sul, Artur Bernardes and the oligarchy of Minas Gerais, and, with one notable exception, the leaders of the Prestes Column. The revolution of 1930 was like the coup of 1889 that overthrew the monarchy, though it was acted out on a larger stage (the whole country rather than only Rio de Janeiro) and took longer (days instead of hours). Troops began to move against the government; other troops joined them; the army high command decided that the revolutionary movement was irresistible and put the chief of state on a ship and sent him into exile—all with scarcely a shot being fired.

Brazil's great national revolutions have all been bloodless or nearly so; substantial losses of life are characteristic of regional uprisings and unsuccessful national revolts. Brazil's rulers have shown remarkable judgment in times of national crisis. Emperors, regents, and presidents alike have unfailingly abdicated when confronted by the vital forces of the nation. Yet they have consistently and stubbornly resisted well-armed but narrowly based movements that threatened to plunge the nation into disorder. Historically, a Brazilian revolution that is fired upon is lost, a fact most of the Tenentes of 1922 seemed to comprehend. Only Siqueira Campos and his comrades at Fort Copacabana refused to accept the armed resistance at Vila Militar as evidence of an irresistible counterrevolutionary tide. Siqueira apparently believed that he could rebuild revolutionary momentum by parading his courage and determination before the government troops drawn up along Copacabana Beach. The young lieutenant did not sally forth with his handful of followers to fight the loyalists but to inspire them—to convince them by his example that the revolutionary course was the honorable one, to induce them to join his march on the presidential palace and overthrow the government. Siqueira's plan was undone when some government soldier took a shot at one of his men.

Like Siqueira's walk along Copacabana Beach, the march of the Prestes Column was undertaken for inspirational purposes. The operation was not military—not designed to seize or hold terrain or to destroy the enemy or his will to fight by combat. Military operations, however, were conducted against the revolutionaries and they had to fight for their survival. The fortitude and skill of a few dedicated officers—Luís Carlos Prestes above all—enabled the column to survive for two years in a hostile countryside. Their success in resisting the pressures of internal disintegration is more impressive than their escapes from annihilation by outside forces. Those who have little conception of the immensity of Brazil and the nature of its interior terrain are apt to overvalue the column's evasive maneuvers. With no air reconnaissance and no radio communications, the government troops in the catinga and the campo cerrado were at a decided disadvantage in pursuing an enemy who had no objectives other than survival. If achievement were to be measured solely in terms of survival, the Prestes Column would have to be rated far below the band of Lampião, which was not overcome until 1938. Nevertheless, the people of Brazil's urban centers were quite correct in paying high tribute to these educated young men who forsook the comforts of civilization to demonstrate for the causes of military honor and liberal democracy in a harsh and unsympathetic environment.

It was natural that the organizers of the 1930 revolution, which proclaimed liberal ideals, would try to recruit the heroes of the Prestes Column. Of the column's high command, only Luís Carlos Prestes, who was studying Marxism-Leninism in Argentina, rejected the call to arms in 1930. Two former detachment commanders lost their lives that year: Siqueira Campos died in an airplane crash and Djalma Dutra was mistakenly shot by a revolutionary sentry. Miguel Costa, João Alberto, Juarez Távora, and Cordeiro de Farias all held important posts in the revolutionary government headed by Getúlio Vargas, an ex-Chimango, Borges de Medeiros' successor as governor of Rio Grande do Sul. João Alberto, as provisional governor of São Paulo, and Miguel Costa, as commander of the state militia, committed themselves to social revolution and discarded the liberal-democratic principles they had espoused as members of the Prestes Column. They helped provoke São Paulo's "Constitutionalist" reaction of 1932, in which their former commander in chief, Isidoro Dias Lopes, and old antagonist, Bertoldo Klinger, lined up with the counterrevolutionaries.

João Alberto, Távora, and Cordeiro remained faithful to the Vargas regime as it turned to the right after the defeat of the Constitutionalists in 1932. Miguel Costa, however, joined Prestes in a leftist uprising in 1935. Prestes had slipped into Brazil from Moscow earlier that year and had taken over the leadership of the Brazilian Communist Party. The revolt of the National Liberation Alliance failed and Prestes was tracked down and arrested in 1936, along with his wife, Olga, a German-Jewish woman whom he had met in Moscow. The Vargas regime kept Prestes in prison in Brazil for nine years and turned Olga over to the Gestapo; she died in a Nazi gas chamber. Miguel Costa was jailed for a short time and then released. The other former leaders of the column put aside their "minimum aspirations" for press freedom and the secret ballot and served a fascistic government that held no elections for eight years and rigorously censored the press.

After some early flirtations with the Axis, the Vargas dictatorship joined the Allies in World War II. Cordeiro de Farias went to Italy as artillery commander in the Brazilian division that served with General Mark Clark's Fifth Army. The experience of fighting fascism abroad helped transform the Brazilian army into a champion of democracy at home. Under military pressure Vargas restored political liberty in Brazil early in 1945 and released Prestes from jail. Later in the year, when Vargas seemed about to renege on his promises to hold free elections and step down from the presidency, Cordeiro delivered to him a military demand for his immediate resignation.

Vargas gave in to the ultimatum and the elections were held on schedule in December 1945. Marshal Eurico Gaspar Dutra, who had been minister of war during the dictatorship, won the presidency, and Prestes was elected senator from Rio de Janeiro. Prestes, however, lost his office when the Dutra government outlawed the Communist Party in 1947. Vargas returned to the presidency after winning the elections of 1950 and Prestes struck up an informal alliance with his labor minister and "political heir," João Goulart. Prestes would play an important role in Brazilian politics in the 1950's and early 1960's. Miguel Costa and his small Socialist Party were shunned by the bigwigs and the gallant old revolutionary's death in 1959 went virtually unnoticed. João Alberto, a power during the dictatorship, held only minor posts during the second Vargas administration. He died in 1955 without a penny to his name.

An attempt by Vargas partisans on the life of an opposition journalist—in which the intended victim's bodyguard, an air force major, was killed—led the military to hand Vargas another ultimatum in 1954. Vargas answered it with his suicide. In the elections of 1955 Prestes and the devotees of the martyred Getúlio supported the presidential candidacy of Juscelino Kubitschek. The other major candidate—backed by conservative, anti-Communist, Catholic, and anti-Vargas forces—was Juarez Távora. Kubitschek and his vice presidential running mate, João Goulart, won handily. Kubitschek's chosen successor lost the next election, but Goulart was reelected vice president.

When President Jânio Quadros resigned in 1960, Goulart became president of Brazil, but with the powers of his office greatly reduced by a hostile Congress. Prestes was one of the leaders in the struggle to restore full powers to the presidency, which was accomplished by a plebiscite in 1963. The influence of the Communist Party chief reached its zenith during the presidency of João Goulart. When Goulart was overthrown by a military coup in 1964, Prestes was forced into hiding. The two other surviving members of the Prestes Column high command were given jobs in the new military government: Cordeiro de Farias was named minister for regional agencies and Juarez Távora became minister of transportation.

Notes

Chapter i

1. The turbulent course of Brazil's "Old Republic," 1889–1930, is traced in several general histories. The one written closest to the events, and found most useful for this study, is Sertório de Castro, *A república que a revolução destruiu* (Rio de Janeiro, 1932).

2. General Isidoro Dias Lopes to General Abílio de Noronha, July 17, 1924, in Abílio de Noronha, *Narrando a verdade: Contribuição para a história da revolta em S. Paulo* (São Paulo, 1924), pp. 86–88. Isidoro's service record is in Ficha de referência: Isidoro Dias Lopes, IV-16-119, Ministério da Guerra, Arquivo do Exército, now in Brasília.

3. Tenente Alfredo Augusto Ribeiro Júnior, "Manifesto," in Edgard Carone, *A primeira república, 1889–1930: Texto e contexto* (São Paulo, 1969), pp. 259–262.

4. *Correio da Manhã* (Rio de Janeiro), October 9, 1921. A second, somewhat less offensive letter appeared a few days later. Two individuals of unsavory reputation confessed to forging the letters in March 1922. Afonso Arinos de Melo Franco, *Um estadista da república,* II (Rio de Janeiro, 1955), pp. 1042–1043.

5. Virgílio de Melo Franco, *Outubro, 1930* (Rio de Janeiro, 1930), pp. 121–124; Paulo Amora, *Bernardes: O estadista de Minas na república* (São Paulo, 1964), pp. 11–12, 25–37.

6. Marshal Fernando Setembrino de Carvalho to Dr. Joaquim Francisco de Assis Brasil, December 7, 1923, and Ato da pacificação do Rio Grande do Sul, in Flores da Cunha, *A campanha de 1923* (Rio de Janeiro, n.d.), pp. 257–262, 269–273.

7. João Lyra, *Cifras e notas (Economia e finanças do Brasil)* (Rio de Janeiro, 1925), pp. 44–45.

8. Brazil, Census Bureau, *Recenseamento geral do Brasil realizado em 1 de setembro de 1920,* IV, part 1 (Rio de Janeiro, 1924), p. 545.

9. Leoncio Basbaum, *História sincera da república, de 1889 a 1930* (São Paulo, 1962), p. 303.

10. A. B. Gama [Affonso Ruy de Souza], *Columna Prestes (2 annos de revolução)* (Salvador, Bahia, 1927), p. 29; *The Times* (London), June 30, 1924, pp. 15, 22.

11. Cyro Costa and Eurico de Góes, *Sob a metralha (histórica da revolta em São Paulo, de 5 de julho de 1924)* (São Paulo, 1924), p. 132.

12. Juarez Távora, *Á guisa de depoimento sobre a revolução brasileira de 1924,* I (São Paulo, 1927), pp. 178–186; Costa and Góes, *op. cit.,* p. 2.

13. Noronha, *op. cit.,* pp. 58–67; Távora, I, *op. cit.,* pp. 192–195; Costa and Góes, *op. cit.,* pp. 2–3; U.S. Consul in São Paulo (Haberle) to Secretary of State, August 18, 1924, U.S. Department of State, Decimal File, 832.00/417.

14. Távora, I, *op. cit.,* pp. 186–187, 196–226; Costa and Góes, *op. cit.,* p. 8.

15. Távora, I, *op. cit.,* pp. 228–229; J. Nunes de Carvalho, *A revolução no Brasil, 1924–1925,* 2 ed. (Rio de Janeiro, 1930), p. 75; Carlos Castilho Cabral, *Batalhões patrióticas na revolução de 1924* (São Paulo, 1927), pp. 28–30.

16. Maurício de Lacerda, *Entre duas revoluções* (Rio de Janeiro, 1927), pp. 150–152; Fichas de referéncia; Isidoro Dias Lopes, IV-16-119, Arquivo do Exército.

17. Nunes de Carvalho, *op. cit.,* pp. 77–78; Lourenço Moreira Lima, *A coluna Prestes (marchas e combates),* 2 ed. (São Paulo, 1945), pp. 36, 59–60; José Carlos de Macedo Soares, *Justiça: A revolta militar em São Paulo* (Paris, 1925), p. 37.

18. Távora, I, *op. cit.,* pp. 229–231.

19. *Ibid.,* pp. 232–233; Moreira Lima, *op. cit.,* p. 46.

20. "Um communicado dos chefes do movimento," in Costa and Góes, *op. cit.,* pp. 56–60.

21. In Costa and Góes, *op. cit.*, pp. 131–134.

22. Polícia de São Paulo, *Movimento subvesivo de julho,* 2 ed. (São Paulo, 1925), pp. 39–40, 61–77; Nelson Tabajara de Oliveira, *1924: A revolução de Isidoro* (São Paulo, 1956), p. 102; Távora, I, *op. cit.*, pp. 246–247, 253–254; Macedo Soares, *op. cit.*, pp. 32, 44–45, 229; Costa and Góes, *op. cit.*, pp. 65–66; Moreira Lima, *op. cit.*, p. 41; Aureliano Leite, *Dias de pavor* (São Paulo, 1924), p. 141; U.S. Consul in São Paulo (Haberle) to Secretary of State, August 3, 1924, USDS, 832.00/409; Távora, III, *op. cit.*, pp. 249–257.

23. Távora, I, *op. cit.*, p. 274; João Nepomuceno da Costa, *A circumscripção militar de Matto Grosso e o levante sedicioso de São Paulo* (São Paulo, 1924), pp. 41–58.

24. Richard M. Morse, *From Community to Metropolis: A Biography of São Paulo, Brazil* (Gainesville, 1958), p. 242.

25. Noronha, *op. cit.*, pp. 126–131, 133.

26. Aroldo de Azevedo, *Arnolfo Azevedo: Parlamentar da primeira república* (São Paulo, 1968), pp. 363–365; Macedo Soares, *op. cit.*, pp. 117, 389–390; Paulo Duarte, *Agora nós* (São Paulo, 1927), pp. 81–83, 87–89; Oscar de Barros Falcão, *A revolução de 5 de julho de 1924 (a componente militar)* (Rio de Janeiro, 1962), pp. 11–17.

27. Noronha, *op. cit.*, pp. 137–140; Macedo Soares, *op. cit.*, p. 105; Távora, I, *op. cit.*, pp. 272–273; Polícia de São Paulo, *op. cit.*, pp. 53–57.

28. Noronha, *op. cit.*, pp. 86–88.

29. Nunes de Carvalho, *op. cit.*, pp. 99–100; Abílio de Noronha, *O resto da verdade* (São Paulo, 1925), pp. 75–77; Távora, I, *op. cit.*, pp. 277–278; Macedo Soares, *op. cit.*, pp. 124–126.

30. Falcão, *op. cit.*, p. 19.

31. *Ibid.*, pp. 19–20, 30.

32. *Ibid.*, pp. 19–25, 30; Nunes de Carvalho, *op. cit.*, pp. 105–107; João Cabanas, *A columna da morte* (Rio de Janeiro, 1927), pp. 123–194; Ayres de Camargo, *Patiotas paulistas na columna sul* (São Paulo, 1925), pp. 93–178.

33. Falcão, *op. cit.*, pp. 31–32; Nepomuceno da Costa, *op. cit.*, pp. 114–118.

34. S. Dias Ferreira [and Sady Valle Machado], *A marcha da Columna Prestes* (Pelotas, Rio Grande do Sul, 1928), p. 155; Gama, *op. cit.*, pp. 109–110. Juarez Távora discusses his family and his early years in *Uma vida e muitas lutas* (Rio de Janeiro, 1973), pp. 7–108.

35. Hélio Silva, *1922: Sangue na areia de Copacabana* (Rio de Janeiro, 1964), pp. 189–193, 198–202; Távora, *Uma vida*, pp. 116–119.

36. Távora, I, *op. cit.*, pp. 66–68, 108–109.

37. *Ibid.*, pp. 109–154; Nunes de Carvalho, *op. cit.*, pp. 90–94; João Alberto Lins de Barros, *Memórias de um revolucionário* (Rio de Janeiro, 1954), pp. 21–24.

38. Italo Landucci, *Cenas e episódios da revolução de 1924 e da coluna Prestes* (São Paulo, 1952), pp. 11–12; Falcão, *op. cit.*, pp. 32, 35; Távora, *Uma vida*, pp. 148–150.

39. Landucci, *op. cit.*, p. 12; Falcão, *op. cit.*, pp. 32, 35; Távora, III, *op. cit.*, pp. 257–258.

40. Landucci, *op. cit.*, pp. 12–13.

41. *Ibid.*, pp. 13–15; Falcão, *op. cit.*, pp. 33–34.

42. Távora, *Uma vida*, pp. 150–151. Landucci (*op. cit.*, pp. 15–16) claims the battalion "lost" 400 men. The government commander reported having found 24 rebel dead by August 20; the next day he noted that rebel bodies were still being found. 90 rebels, including 23 wounded, were taken prisoner. Although government forces lost only four killed and 28 wounded, they made no attempt to pursue the fleeing revolutionaries. Nepomuceno da Costa, *op. cit.*, pp. 127–132. *Cf.* Falcão, *op. cit.*, pp. 34, 36, 39.

43. This is the opinion of Italo Landucci (*op. cit.*, pp. 9–10) of the Italian company, who has published the most vivid account of the battle. Juarez Távora deals briefly with this action in *A guisa de depoimento*, III, pp. 257–258, and in somewhat more detail in *Uma vida*, pp. 147–151; he blames his defeat on the "inexpertness or bad faith" of a guide.

44. Joseph L. Love, *Rio Grande do Sul and Brazilian Regionalism, 1882–1930* (Stanford, 1971), pp. 81–82; Francisco de Assis Cinta, *Os escandalos da primeira república* (São Paulo, 1936), pp. 113–126.

45. Landucci, *op. cit.*, pp. 19–26; João de Talma (pseud. of Reis Perdigão), *Da fornalha de Nabucodonosor* (Buenos Aires, 1926), pp. 53–88; Dilermando Cândido de Assis, *Das barrancas do alto Paraná* (Rio de Janeiro, 1926), pp. 63–262; Falcão, *op. cit.*, pp. 42–48; Gama, *op. cit.*, pp. 188–189.

46. Talma, *op. cit.*, p. 89; Jorge Americano, *A lição dos factos—revolta de 5 de julho de 1924* (São Paulo, 1924), p. 229; Nunes de Carvalho, *op. cit.*, pp. 121–123.

47. F. L. Whitley, Report of Reconnaissance of Southern Brazil, June 13, 1922, USDS, 832.00/248; interview with William O'Day, Pôrto Alegre, April 29, 1966.

48. Cabanas, *op. cit.*, pp. 207–227; Landucci, *op. cit.*, pp. 25–27; Dilermando, *op. cit.*, pp. 279–282, 304; Falcão, *op. cit.*, pp. 48–52; Arlindo de Oliveira, Depoimento, in Hélio Silva, *1926: A grande marcha* (Rio de Janeiro, 1965), pp. 40–42; Nepomuceno da Costa, *op. cit.*, pp. 151–152; Távora, *Uma vida*, pp. 154–157.

49. Tabajara de Oliveira, *op. cit.*, p. 115; Nunes de Carvalho, *op. cit.*, p. 124; Gama, *op. cit.*, p. 24; Távora, *Uma vida*, p. 158.

50. Glauco Carneiro, *O revolucionário Siqueira Campos*, I (Rio de Janeiro, 1966), pp. 39–62; João Alberto, *op. cit.*, p. 127; Tabajara de Oliveira, *op. cit.*, p. 158; Osvaldo Cordeiro de Faria, "Siqueira Campos," in Carlos Chevalier, ed., *Os 18 do forte* (Rio de Janeiro, n.d.), pp. 57–70.

51. This account of the Copacabana episode is based primarily on the conscientious reconstruction of events in Carneiro, *op. cit.*, I, pp. 173–268. Some details regarding the setting were supplied by William O'Day, who arrived on the scene fifteen minutes after the last shots were fired (interviews with William O'Day, Pôrto Alegre, April 28–29, 1966).

52. Carneiro, I, *op. cit.*, pp. 262, 267–268. On September 2, 1923, the Rio opposition newspaper *Correio da Manhã* published an anonymous poem entitled *Os 18 do forte*. The number refers to those who made the last stand on the beach, generally believed at the time to have been eighteen. The poem permanently fixed this number to the legend.

53. Carneiro, I, *op. cit.*, pp. 276–277, 282–286; Távora, I, *op. cit.*, pp. 66–68, 108–109.

54. Carneiro, I, *op. cit.*, pp. 287–299.

55. *Ibid.*, pp. 54, 315–316; Távora, I, *op. cit.*, pp. 111–112; U.S. Consul in Pôrto Alegre (Hoffman) to Secretary of State, November 8 and December 3, 1924, USDS, 832.00/470,477; Flores da Cunha, *op. cit.*, p. 82.

56. Juarez Távora to Luís Carlos Prestes, October 12, 1924, in Moreira Lima, *op. cit.*, pp. 524–525; Nunes de Carvalho, *op. cit.*, p. 124; Gama, *op. cit.*, p. 24; Carneiro, I, *op. cit.*, p. 317.

57. Juarez Távora to Luís Carlos Prestes, October 12, 1924, in Moreira Lima, *op. cit.*, 524–525.

58. *Ibid.*

Chapter ii

1. Jorge Amado, *O cavaleiro da esperança* (*vida de Luís Carlos Prestes*), 10 ed. (Rio de Janeiro, 1956), pp. 37–56.

2. *Ibid.*, pp. 56–63.

3. Umberto Peregrino, *História e projeção das instituções culturais do exército* (Rio de Janeiro, 1967), pp. 20–21; Estevão Leitão de Carvalho, *Dever militar e política partidaria* (São Paulo, 1959), p. 54; Amado, *op. cit.*, p. 63.

4. Amado, *op. cit.*, pp. 73–74.

5. Basbaum, *op. cit.*, pp. 285–286, 309–310.

6. Amado, *op. cit.*, p. 94.

7. J. B. Magalhães, *A evolução militar do Brasil* (Rio de Janeiro, 1958), p. 350.

8. Amado, *op. cit.*, pp. 66–78. *Cf.* Wilson Martins, *O modernismo (1916–1945)* (São Paulo, 1965), pp. 44–72, 279–280.

9. Silva, *1922*, pp. 196–197; Carvalho, *Dever*, p. 54; Egydio Moreira de Castro e Silva, *A margem do ministério Calógeras* (Rio de Janeiro, n.d.), pp. 66–86.

10. Silva, *1922*, p. 197.

11. Miguel de Castro Ayres, *O exército que eu vi* (Rio de Janeiro, 1965), p. 63; Silva, *1922*, pp. 197–198.

12. Castro Ayres, *op. cit.*, pp. 63–65; Silva, *1922*, p. 198.

13. Távora, I, *op. cit.*, p. 111–112; Amado, *op. cit.*, p. 108.

14. Távora, I, *op. cit.*, pp. 144–148; Amado, *op. cit.*, p. 108.

15. Gama, *op. cit.*, pp. 54–58.

16. U.S. Vice-Consul in Manaus (Roth) to Secretary of State, September 1, 1924, USDS 832.00/429; U.S. Consul in Pará (Potts) to Secretary of State, August 18, 1924, USDS 832.00/423.

17. Távora, I, *op. cit.*, pp. 62–63.

18. The radio station at Puerto Aguirre, Argentina, across from Foz do Iguaçú, relayed much information on rebel activities in Brazil. Landucci, *op. cit.*, pp. 28–29.

19. Carneiro, *op. cit.*, pp. 315–316.

20. Herman G. James, *Brazil after a Century of Independence* (New York, 1925), pp. 246–247; Amado, *op. cit.*, p. 109.

21. Dias Ferreira, *op. cit.,* p. 15; Amado, *op. cit.,* p. 109.

22. Amado, *op. cit.,* pp. 109–110; Moreira Lima, *op. cit.,* pp. 526–528.

23. Gama, *op. cit.,* pp. 24–25; Dias Ferreira, *op. cit.,* pp. 19–20.

24. Dias Ferreira, *op. cit.,* pp. 20–23.

25. Luiz Carlos Prestes, "Boletim ao Povo de Santo Ângelo," in Dias Ferreira, *op. cit.,* pp. 23–27. Two passages are omitted from the bulletin as printed in Gama, *op. cit.,* pp. 27–30.

26. Dias Ferreira, *op. cit.,* pp. 27–29; Falcão, *op. cit.,* pp. 76–78.

27. Dias Ferreira, *op. cit.,* pp. 30–34; Carneiro, *op. cit.,* pp. 318–321.

28. Isidoro Dias Lopes, *et al.* "A revolução," in Dias Ferreira, *op. cit.,* pp. 32–34.

29. Dias Ferreira, *op. cit.,* pp. 36–38; Távora, *Uma vida,* p. 160.

30. Dias Ferreira, *op. cit.,* p. 38; João Alberto, *op. cit.,* pp. 24–28.

31. João Alberto, *op. cit.,* pp. 28–29. João Alberto's account of the Alegrete attack differs substantially from that of Juarez Távora (*Uma vida,* pp. 159–161). The following narrative of the battle at Alegrete and the retreat to Uruguaiana relies primarily on João Alberto's memoir (*op. cit.,* pp. 29–36), which is more complete and less self-serving than Távora's recollections, and is supported by Euclydes de Castro Carvalho, *Revolução 1924* (Prata, Rio Grande do Sul [1926]), pp. 75–77. Clearly written, unpretentious, transparently honest, João Alberto's book is felicitously devoid of personal rancor and, to a large degree, of political rhetoric. It is an extraordinary achievement.

32. João Alberto, *op. cit.,* pp. 37–39. Cf. Távora, *Uma vida,* p. 161.

33. This description of Honório Lemes (sometimes written Honório Lemos or Honório de Lemos) and his campaigns through November 9, 1924, is drawn mainly from João Alberto, *op. cit.,* pp. 37–45. A few details have been contributed by other sources, including Távora, *Uma vida,* pp. 161–165, and Dean Ivan Lamb, *The Incurable Filibuster: Adventures of Colonel Dean Ivan Lamb* (New York, 1934), *passim.* This last book, like most of its genre, has a high hokum content.

34. João Alberto, *op. cit.,* pp. 45–47.

35. Dias Ferreira, *op. cit.,* pp. 44–45; Carneiro, I, *op. cit.,* pp. 328–330.

36. Carneiro, I, *op. cit.,* pp. 330–333; Dias Ferreira, *op. cit.,* pp. 45–47.

37. Carneiro, I, *op. cit.*, pp. 333–338, 342; Falcão, *op. cit.*, pp. 77–78.

38. Dias Ferreira, *op. cit.*, pp. 42–43; Falcão, *op. cit.*, pp. 74–75; João Alberto, *op. cit.*, pp. 46–49; Távora, *Uma vida*, pp. 165–170.

39. Gama, *op. cit.*, pp. 32–33, 58–66; Heraclito Fontoura Sobral Pinto, *A conspiração Protogenes Pereira Guimarães: Razões de recurso offerecidas pelo procurador criminal da Republica, interino, ao juiz da 1° vara federal do Distrito Federal* (Rio de Janeiro, 1926).

40. Távora, *Uma vida*, pp. 166–167; Falcão, *op. cit.*, pp. 72–73.

41. Távora, *Uma vida*, pp. 167–173; Falcão, *op. cit.*, p. 73.

42. Landucci, *op. cit.*, pp. 29–31; Luís Carlos Prestes to Leonel Rocha, November 29, 1924, in Gama, *op. cit.*, pp. 31–32. Dias Ferreira (*op. cit.*, pp. 54–55) implies that João Francisco personally met with Prestes in São Borja on November 15, 1924, but Landucci, who accompanied the general on his trip, does not mention such a meeting—or even any crossing by João Francisco into Rio Grande do Sul.

43. Isidoro Dias Lopes to Luís Carlos Prestes, December 23, 1924, in Moreira Lima, *op. cit.*, pp. 529–534; Dias Ferreira, *op. cit.*, p. 30; Falcão, *op. cit.*, p. 78.

44. Arthur Ferreira Filho, *História geral do Rio Grande do Sul, 1503–1960* (Pôrto Alegre, 1960), pp. 167–168; Falcão, *op. cit.*, pp. 78–79; Dias Ferreira, *op. cit.*, pp. 57–63; João Alberto, *op. cit.*, pp. 57–58.

45. Isidoro Dias Lopes to Luís Carlos Prestes, December 23, 1924, in Moreira Lima, *op. cit.*, pp. 529–534 (this is the reply to Prestes' letter of December 8); João Alberto, *op. cit.*, pp. 57–58.

46. Luís Carlos Prestes to Isidoro Dias Lopes (ca. February 8, 1925) and Oswaldo Cordeiro de Farias, "Marcha da Coluna Prestes de S. Luiz, no Rio Grande do Sul, até Porto Mendes," in Moreira Lima, *op. cit.*, pp. 107–111, 594–597; Dias Ferreira, *op. cit.*, pp. 64–90; João Alberto, *op. cit.*, pp. 59–74.

Chapter iii

1. Rondon claimed descent from three tribes: the Terena and the Guaná, Guaicuru peoples from the Chaco, and the Borôro, an unrelated tribe indigenous to Mato Grosso. Esther de Viveiros, *Rondon conta sua vida* (Rio de Janeiro, 1958), p. 18. See also Kalervo Oberg, *The Terena and the Caduveo of Southern Mato Grosso, Brazil* (Washington, 1949), pp. 1–5.

2. Viveiros, *op. cit.*, pp. 28–44.

3. Tristão de Alencar Araripe, *Tasso Fragoso: Um pouco de história do nosso exército* (Rio de Janeiro, 1960), pp. 119–134, 143–150; Viveiros, *op. cit.*, pp. 46–58.

4. Viveiros, *op. cit.*, pp. 61–342 *passim.*

5. *Ibid.*, p. 470.

6. *Ibid.*, pp. 341–351.

7. *Ibid.*, pp. 376–423; Theodore Roosevelt, *Through the Brazilian Wilderness* (New York, 1920), *passim.*

8. Viveiros, *op. cit.*, pp. 426–460, 486–491.

9. Cândido Mariano da Silva Rondon to Raul Soares, October 23, 1921, in Viveiros, *op. cit.*, p. 475.

10. Viveiros, *op. cit.*, p. 477.

11. *Ibid.*, pp. 476–478.

12. Jackson de Figueiredo, *A columna de fogo* (Rio de Janeiro, 1925), pp. 14, 45.

13. *Ibid.*, pp. 85–86.

14. The minister of war (Setembrino de Carvalho) to the army chief-of-staff, September 25, 1924, livro 534, número 82, Ministério da Guerra, Arquivo do Exército. Bernardes appointed Figueiredo censor of the press in Rio. Amora, *op. cit.*, p. 62.

15. Viveiros, *op. cit.*, p. 493.

16. *Ibid.*, pp. 493–495.

17. Moreira Lima, *op. cit.*, pp. 101, 103; Adaucto Castello Branco, *Catanduvas* (São Paulo, 1927), pp. 5–15; Cabanas, *op. cit.*, pp. 252–253.

18. Rondon leaflet, in Viveiros, *op. cit.*, p. 495; Castello Branco, *op. cit.*, pp. 16–31. Laranjeiras was also known as Mallet.

19. The minister of war (Setembrino de Carvalho) to the commanding general, Third Military Region, November 5, 1924, livro 530, número 32, Ministério da Guerra, Arquivo do Exército.

20. Castello Branco, *op. cit.*, pp. 32–35.

21. *Ibid.*, pp. 22, 37–54; Cabanas, *op. cit.*, pp. 276–277.

22. Cabanas, *op. cit.*, pp. 262–277, 281; Viveiros, *op. cit.*, p. 496.

23. Cabanas, *op. cit.*, pp. 277–289; Castello Branco, *op. cit.*, pp. 54–90.

24. João Alberto (*op. cit.*, pp. 66–67) confuses Alto Uruguai with Barracão. Prestes, in a letter to Isidoro, undated, written between February 7 and 22, 1925 (in Moreira Lima, *op. cit.*, pp. 107–111), says that two hundred deserted at Alto Uruguai and claims that only fifteen hundred men (and more than four thousand horses) began the march in São Luís. An undated report by Cordeiro de Farias (in Moreira Lima, *op. cit.*, p. 595) agrees with João Alberto that the column started out with some two thousand men. All sources agree that after the desertions at Alto Uruguai, Prestes had no more than thirteen hundred men. For conditions on the march through the forests on the left bank of the Uruguay, see the above and Mário Portela Fagundes to Luís Carlos Prestes, January 14, 1925, in Dias Ferreira, *op. cit.*, pp. 101–103.

25. João Alberto, *op. cit.*, pp. 67–70; Prestes to Antônio de Siqueira Campos, January 26, 1925, in Dias Ferreira, *op. cit.*, p. 104; Cordeiro de Farias, "A marcha," in Moreira Lima, *op. cit.*, p. 596.

26. João Alberto, *op. cit.*, pp. 70–71; Cordeiro de Farias, "A marcha," in Moreira Lima, *op. cit.*, p. 596.

27. Dias Ferreira, *op. cit.*, pp. 90–93; Cordeiro de Farias, "A marcha," in Moreira Lima, *op. cit.*, p. 596; João Alberto, *op. cit.*, p. 72.

28. Moreira Lima, *op. cit.*, p. 130; Prestes to Siqueira Campos, January 26, 1925, in Dias Ferreira, *op. cit.*, p. 104; Cordeiro de Farias, "A marcha," in Moreira Lima, *op. cit.*, p. 597.

29. Cordeiro de Farias, "A marcha," in Moreira Lima, *op. cit.*, p. 597.

30. Moreira Lima, *op. cit.*, p. 147; João Alberto, *op. cit.*, pp. 62, 69.

31. João Alberto, *op. cit.*, pp. 74–75.

32. Prestes to Isidoro, undated, and Cordeiro de Farias, "A marcha," in Moreira Lima, *op. cit.*, pp. 109, 597; João Alberto, *op. cit.*, p. 75.

33. Isidoro to Prestes, December 23, 1924, in Moreira Lima, *op. cit.*, p. 530.

34. João Alberto, *op. cit.*, p. 49.

35. Cordeiro de Farias, "A marcha," in Moreira Lima, *op. cit.*, p. 597; João Alberto, *op. cit.*, p. 75; Dias Ferreira, *op. cit.*, p. 36.

36. Cordeiro de Farias, "A marcha," and Prestes to Isidoro, undated, in Moreira Lima, *op. cit.*, pp. 109, 597.

37. Mendes Teixeira to Fidêncio de Melo, February 2, 1925, in Dias Ferreira, *op. cit.*, pp. 113–114; Cabanas, *op. cit.*, p. 297; Hélio Silva, *1926*, p. 68.

38. Prestes to Isidoro, undated, in Moreira Lima, *op. cit.*, p.109.

39. *Ibid.*, pp. 109–111.

40. João Alberto, *op. cit.*, pp. 76–78; João Alberto to Prestes, February 20, 1925, Cordeiro de Farias to Prestes, undated and February 24, 1925, in Dias Ferreira, *op. cit.*, pp. 105–112; Cordeiro de Farias, "A marcha," in Moreira Lima, *op. cit.*, pp. 597–598.

41. Falcão, *op. cit.*, p. 106.

42. João Alberto to Prestes, February 20, 1925, in Dias Ferreira, *op. cit.*, pp. 105–107.

43. Landucci, *op. cit.*, p. 37.

44. Isidoro to Prestes, February 22, 1925, in Moreira Lima, *op. cit.*, pp. 536–537.

45. *Ibid.*, p. 537.

46. Landucci, *op. cit.*, pp. 38, 57; Cordeiro de Farias, "A marcha," in Moreira Lima, *op. cit.*, p. 598.

47. Falcão, *op. cit.*, pp. 137–141.

48. João Francisco P. de Souza, Manifesto, September 2, 1925, in Dilermando, *op. cit.*, pp. lv–lxi; Isidoro to Prestes, December 23, 1924, in Moreira Lima, *op. cit.*, p. 533.

49. Castello Branco, *op. cit.*, pp. 121–130; Falcão, *op. cit.*, pp. 111–116; Viveiros, *op. cit.*, pp. 496–497.

50. Cabanas, *op. cit.*, pp. 324–325.

51. *Ibid.*, pp. 326–327; Falcão, *op. cit.*, 119–122; Moreira Lima, *op. cit.*, p. 113.

52. Dialogue in Tabajara de Oliveira, *op. cit.*, p. 134; see also Moreira Lima, *op. cit.*, pp. 114–115, 117–118; Távora, III, *op. cit.*, pp. 12–13.

53. Tabajara de Oliveira, *op. cit.*, pp. 134–135, 172; Moreira Lima, *op. cit.*, pp. 114–115, 117–118; João Alberto, *op. cit.*, p. 170.

54. Moreira Lima, *op. cit.*, pp. 114–115, 117–118; Dias Ferreira, *op. cit.*, pp. 98–99; Cabanas, *op. cit.*, pp. 330–331.

55. Comando da Iª Divisão Revolucionária, Boletim, April 14, 1924, in Moreira Lima, *op. cit.*, pp. 540–544; Landucci, *op. cit.*, pp. 57, 60–61; Moreira Lima, *op. cit.*, pp. 113–114, 598; Gama, *op. cit.*, p. 44; Cabanas, *op. cit.*, pp. 332–342.

56. Cabanas, *op. cit.*, p. 297; Isidoro to Prestes, December 23, 1924,

in Moreira Lima, *op. cit.*, p. 533; Távora, *Uma vida*, pp. 170–175.

57. Cabanas, *op. cit.*, pp. 338–339; Moreira Lima, *op. cit.*, pp. 123–124.

58. Moreira Lima, *op. cit.*, pp. 120–134; João Alberto, *op. cit.*, pp. 86–80; Chevalier, *op. cit.*, pp. 72–80.

59. Viveiros, *op. cit.*, p. 497.

60. Henry H. Keith, *Soldiers as Saviors: The Brazilian Military Revolts of 1922 and 1924 in Historical Perspective* (Doctoral dissertation, University of California, Berkeley, 1970), p. 319.

61. Xavier de Oliveira, *O exército e o sertão* (Rio de Janeiro, 1932), pp. 39–43, 60, 174; Licínio dos Santos, *O meu Paiz*, (Rio de Janeiro, 1927), pp. 74–77; Leitão de Carvalho, *Dever militar*, pp. 50–51; Theodorico Lopes Gentil Torres, *Ministros da Guerra do Brasil, 1808–1946* (Rio de Janeiro, 1947), pp. 176–178.

62. Eurico Gaspar Dutra, interview, Rio de Janeiro, June 27, 1965; Viveiros, *op. cit.*, p. 496.

Chapter iv

1. Cabanas, *op. cit.*, pp. 342–344; Távora, III, *op. cit.*, pp. 16–17; Moreira Lima, *op. cit.*, pp. 124–127; interview with Durval Soares, Rio de Janeiro, December 13, 1965.

2. Primeira Divisão Revolucionária, Boletim no. 10, May 14, 1925, in Moreira Lima, *op. cit.*, pp. 546–548; Moreira Lima, *op. cit.*, pp. 91–95; Nepomuceno da Costa, *op. cit.*, p. 19.

3. Virgílio Corrêa Filho, *Pedro Celestino* (Rio de Janeiro, 1945), pp. 136–139, 191, 202.

4. Távora, III, *op. cit.*, pp. 18–21; Primeira Divisão Revolucionária, Boletim no. 11, June 2, 1925, in Moreira Lima, *op. cit.*, pp. 551–552; Moreira Lima, *op. cit.*, pp. 134–135; interview with Durval Soares, Rio de Janeiro, December 13, 1965.

5. José Maria Bello, *História da República (1889–1954)* (São Paulo, 1964), p. 198; Corrêa Filho, *op. cit.*, pp. 102–103.

6. Corrêa Filho, *op. cit.*, pp. 102–103; Jorge Americano, *op. cit.*, p. 229.

7. Corrêa Filho, *op. cit.*, pp. 103–104; Manuel J. Murtinho to Generoso Ponce, October 25, 1907, in Carone, *op. cit.*, pp. 165–167.

8. Corrêa Filho, *op. cit.*, pp. 104–111, 123–133; Virgílio Corrêa Filho, *Matto Grosso* (Rio de Janeiro, 1922), p. 336.

9. *Correio do Sul* (Campo Grande, Mato Grosso), November 12, 1926; Corrêa Filho, *Pedro Celestino*, pp. 133–137.

10. Cabanas, *op. cit.*, pp. 233–244, 250–252; Nunes de Carvalho, *op. cit.*, p. 122.

11. Távora, III, *op. cit.*, p. 261.

12. João Alberto to Prestes, May 7, 1925, in Dias Ferreira, *op. cit.*, pp. 132–134; Corrêa Filho, *Pedro Celestino*, pp. 182–183; Bertoldo Klinger, *Narrativas aotobiograficas, IV: 380 léguas de campanha em 3 mezes* (Rio de Janeiro, 1949), p. 16; Primeira Divisão Revolucionária, Boletim no. 10, May 14, 1925, in Moreira Lima, *op. cit.*, p. 546; Moreira Lima, *op. cit.*, p. 135; João Alberto, *op. cit.*, p. 89; Távora, III, *op. cit.*, p. 20.

13. Eul Soo Pang, *The Politics of Coronelismo in Brazil: The Case of Bahia, 1889–1930* (Doctoral dissertation, University of California, Berkeley, 1970), pp. 41–42; Magalhães, *op. cit.*, p. 344.

14. Primeira Divisão Revolucionária, Boletim no. 10, May 14, 1925, in Moreira Lima, *op. cit.*, p. 547; Nepomuceno da Costa to Mário Gonçalves, July 12, 1925, in Nepomuceno da Costa, *op. cit.*, p. 46; Nepomuceno da Costa, *op. cit.*, p. 159; Corrêa Filho, *Pedro Celestino*, pp. 180–181.

15. Primeira Divisão Revolucionário, Boletim no. 10, May 14, 1925, in Moreira Lima, *op. cit.*, p. 547; João Alberto to Prestes (May 7, 1925), in Dias Ferreira, *op. cit.*, pp. 132–134; Corrêa Filho, *Pedro Celestino*, p. 183.

16. Klinger, IV, *op. cit.*, pp. 17–22; Primeira Divisão Revolucionária, Boletim no. 10, May 14, 1925, in Moreira Lima, *op. cit.*, p. 547; Landucci, *op. cit.*, p. 63.

17. Primeira Divisão Revolucionária, Boletim no. 10, May 14, 1925, in Moreira Lima, *op. cit.*, p. 547; Moreira Lima, *op. cit.*, pp. 141–142; Klinger, IV, *op. cit.*, pp. 18–19.

18. Klinger, IV, *op. cit.*, pp. 20–32.

19. João Alberto, *op. cit.*, p. 91; Moreira Lima, *op. cit.*, pp. 141–142.

20. João Alberto, *op. cit.*, pp. 90–92.

21. *Ibid.*, p. 92; Primeira Divisão Revolucionária, Boletim no. 10, May 14, 1925, in Moreira Lima, *op. cit.*, pp. 545–546.

22. João Alberto, *op. cit.*, pp. 92–93; Klinger, IV, *op. cit.*, pp. 33–34; Moreira Lima, *op. cit.*, p. 142.

23. Landucci, *op. cit.*, p. 64; João Alberto to Prestes, May 14, 1925, in Moreira Lima, *op. cit.*, pp. 550–551; Klinger, IV, *op. cit.*, pp. 34–36; João Alberto, *op. cit.*, pp. 92–96; Moreira Lima, *op. cit.*, pp. 142–143.

24. Moreira Lima, *op. cit.*, pp. 134, 142–143, 149; João Alberto to Prestes, May 14, 1925, in Moreira Lima, *op. cit.*, pp. 550–551; João Alberto, *op. cit.*, pp. 96–99.

25. Moreira Lima, *op. cit.*, pp. 142–143.

26. Távora, III, *op. cit.*, p. 27; Moreira Lima, *op. cit.*, p. 144; Klinger, IV, *op. cit.*, pp. 37–55.

27. In Landucci, *op. cit.*, pp. 73–75. The version in Moreira Lima (*op. cit.*, p. 144) omits the date. The date is confirmed in Klinger, IV, *op. cit.*, p. 63.

28. This account of Klinger's career prior to May 12, 1925, is based on Bertoldo Klinger, *Parada e desfile duma vida de voluntário do Brazil na primeira metade do século* (Rio de Janeiro, 1958), pp. 11–217. This volume, like others by Klinger, uses the author's eccentric Portuguese orthography.

29. *Correio do Sul* (Campo Grande), April 15, 1926.

30. Klinger, *Narrativas*, IV, pp. 55, 66–67.

31. *Ibid.*, pp. 49–63.

32. *Ibid.*, p. 63.

33. Leopoldo Nery Fonseca Júnior, *declaracões*, in Gama, *op. cit.*, pp. 209–214; Hélio Silva, *1922*, pp. 424–428.

34. Nery in Gama, *op. cit.*, pp. 213–214; Hélio Silva, *1922*, pp. 429–430.

35. Moreira Lima, *op. cit.*, pp. 136, 142–144, 146; Távora, III, *op. cit.*, pp. 23–25; João Alberto, *op. cit.*, pp. 99–100.

36. Moreira Lima, *op. cit.*, pp. 143, 146–147; João Alberto, *op. cit.*, pp. 100–101.

37. João Alberto, *op. cit.*, p. 99.

38. Moreira Lima, *op. cit.*, pp. 135–137. Moreira Lima's book, first published in 1928, is by far the most valuable firsthand account of the march of the Prestes Column. The author, who joined the column in April 1925, became its secretary and, for much of the march, kept its "official" log as well as a personal diary. Moreira Lima's book is based on these and many other documents, a large number of which appear in the volume's 107 pages of appendices. Although he wrote with revolu-

tionary fervor, Moreira Lima also made a conscientious effort to produce a complete and accurate record of the march. His framework of events is factual, his observations are sometimes acute and often revealing, and his interpretations always open to question.

39. Moreira Lima, *op. cit.*, pp. 131, 136–137, 154; Távora, III, *op. cit.*, pp. 278–279.

40. *Ibid.*, pp. 147–149; Távora, III, *op. cit.*, pp. 29–30.

41. Moreira Lima, *op. cit.*, p. 149; João Alberto, *op. cit.*, pp. 92, 98–99.

42. Moreira Lima, *op. cit.*, pp. 149–150; Primeira Divisão Revolucionária, Boletim no. 14, June 10, 1925, in Moreira Lima, *op. cit.*, p. 543; Tabajara de Oliveira, *op. cit.*, p. 112.

43. Moreira Lima, *op. cit.*, 149–151; Dias Ferreira, *op. cit.*, p. 143; interview with Durval Soares, December 13, 1965.

44. Prestes to Isidoro, undated, in Moreira Lima, *op. cit.*, pp. 110–111.

45. Forty-three years later Prestes reaffirmed that the objective of the column was not to strike the decisive blow against the Bernardes government, a task that was to fall to other revolutionaries. The mission of the column, Prestes claimed in 1968, was diversionary, to distract the government's attention from the activities of revolutionaries in Brazilian cities. If this was in fact the rebel intention, the march of the column was counterproductive: It kept the government on a war footing and prompted it to maintain a high level of vigilance everywhere. After May 1925 city revolts occurred only in areas in which the column was operating, and to which it had drawn the government's attention. Paulo Patarra, "Este é o camarada Prestes," *Realidade*, III, 33 (December 1968), p. 50. For an earlier (1928) view of the objectives of the column, attributed to Prestes, see Amado, *op. cit.*, p. 133.

46. Prestes to Isidoro, undated in Moreira Lima, *op. cit.*, p. 111.

47. Moreira Lima, *op. cit.*, p. 347.

48. Klinger, *Narrativas*, IV, pp. 86–88.

Chapter v

1. Corrêa Filho, *Pedro Celestino*, pp. 184–195.

2. *Ibid.*, pp. 189–195, 220.

3. *Ibid.*, pp. 192–204. Alto Araguaia was then known as Santa Rita

do Araguaia, the name now used only for the settlement on the Goiás side of the Araguaia River.

4. *Ibid.*, pp. 202–214.

5. Félix Pacheco to Estevão Alves Corrêa, June 6, 1925, in Corrêa Filho, *Pedro Celestino*, p. 203; Klinger, *Parada e desfile*, pp. 235, 245.

6. Klinger, *Narrativas*, IV, pp. 86–88, 97–98.

7. *Ibid.*, pp. 89–90, 97–105; Miguel Costa, "Relatório oficial dos combates travados nos dias 18, 19, 20 de junho do corrente ano," in Moreira Lima, *op. cit.*, pp. 559–563.

8. Moreira Lima, *op. cit.*, p. 155; Miguel Costa, "Relatório," in Moreira Lima, *op. cit.*, pp. 561–562; Landucci, *op. cit.*, p. 70; Klinger, *Narrativas*, IV, pp. 89–92, 104–108.

9. Miguel Costa, "Relatório," in Moreira Lima, *op. cit.*, p. 563. Juarez Távora (*op. cit.*, III, pp. 32–33) cites the same reasons for not pressing the attack, and adds: "The purposes of the campaign did not include crushing the government forces by violence."

10. Moreira Lima, *op. cit.*, p. 155.

11. *Ibid.*, p. 156; Távora, *op. cit.*, p. 36; Corrêa Filho, *Pedro Celestino*, pp. 214–221; João Alberto, *op. cit.*, pp. 167–168.

12. Moreira Lima, *op. cit.*, pp. 165–166; João Alberto, *op. cit.*, pp. 105–106; Klinger, *Narrativas*, IV, pp. 115, 135.

13. Klinger, *Narrativas*, IV, pp. 109–113, 123–131; Moreira Lima, *op. cit.*, p. 166.

14. Klinger, *Narrativas*, IV, pp. 113, 131; Comando das forças revolucionárias, Boletim no. 16, August 7, 1925, in Moreira Lima, *op. cit.*, p. 555; Távora, III, *op. cit.*, p. 37.

15. Klinger, *Narrativas*, IV, pp. 114–115, 135.

16. *Ibid.*, pp. 115, 135–136; Távora, III, *op. cit.*, p. 37.

17. Klinger, *Narrativas*, IV, pp. 115–116; Landucci, *op. cit.*, p. 72; Moreira Lima, *op. cit.*, p. 167.

18. Moreira Lima, *op. cit.*, p. 166; Távora, III, *op. cit.*, pp. 38–39; Landucci, *op. cit.*, p. 71; Klinger to Chefes das Forças Revolucionárias, June 29, 1925, in Moreira Lima, *op. cit.*, p. 554.

19. Távora, III, *op. cit.*, p. 39. Landucci (*op. cit.*, pp. 68–70) best describes the demoralizing effect Klinger's operations had on the column.

20. Landucci, *op. cit.*, p. 71; Juarez Távora to Modesto Lafayette

(June 30, 1925), in Klinger, *Narrativas,* IV, p. 136; Távora, III, *op. cit.,* p. 39.

21. Klinger, *Narrativas,* IV, pp. 117–118, 136, 148; Távora, III, *op. cit.,* pp. 39–41; Távora to Modesto (June 30, 1925), in Klinger, *Narrativas,* IV, p. 136; interview with Durval Soares, Rio de Janeiro, December 13, 1965. Over the years João Alberto (*op. cit.,* pp. 109–110) forgot that Modesto was acting on Távora's orders; Durval Soares, a soldier in Siqueira's detachment during the attack, did not forget.

22. Dias Ferreira, *op. cit.,* p. 140.

23. João Alberto, *op. cit.,* p. 110.

24. Klinger, *Narrativas,* IV, p. 118.

25. Landucci, *op. cit.,* pp. 72–73; Dias Ferreira, *op. cit.,* pp. 152–153.

26. Moreira Lima, *op. cit.,* p. 168; Távora, III, *op. cit.,* p. 41; Comando das forças revolucionárias Boletim no. 16, August 7, 1925, in Moreira Lima, *op. cit.,* p. 556.

27. Miguel Costa to Bertoldo Klinger, June 30, 1925, and Klinger to Chefes das Forças Revolucionárias em Goiás, in Moreira Lima, *op. cit.,* pp. 554–555; Klinger, *Narrativas,* IV, pp. 419, 421, 423.

28. Moreira Lima, *op. cit.,* pp. 168, 441; Comando das forças revolucionárias, Boletim no. 16, August 7, 1925, in Moreira Lima, *op. cit.,* p. 556; Klinger, *Narrativas,* IV, pp. 139–140.

29. Zoroastro Artiaga, *História de Goiás,* 2 ed. (Goiânia, 1959), p. 262.

30. José M. Audrin, *Entre sertanejos e indios do norte* (Rio de Janeiro, 1947), pp. 244–245; Artiaga, *op. cit.,* pp. 261–272; Pang, *op. cit.,* pp. 165–169.

31. Artiaga, *op. cit.,* p. 267; James, *op. cit.,* pp. 454, 458, 461, 464.

32. Távora, III, *op. cit.,* pp. 46–47; Klinger, *Narrativas,* IV, pp. 176, 196; Moreira Lima, *op. cit.,* pp. 168–169.

33. Klinger, *Narrativas,* IV, pp. 174–175, 196, 243; Moreira Lima, *op. cit.,* pp. 176, 437.

34. Bertoldo Klinger to Antônio Ramos Caiado, July 25, 1925, in Klinger, *Narrativas,* IV, pp. 242–243.

35. Klinger, *Narrativas,* IV, pp. 155–177.

36. *Ibid.,* pp. 187–188, 200–207, 209–222.

37. Moreira Lima, *op. cit.,* p. 177; Dias Ferreira, *op. cit.,* p. 143; Klinger, *Narrativas,* IV, pp. 244–245.

38. Comando das forças revolucionárias, Boletim no. 16, August 7, 1925, and Prestes, *et al.* to Isidoro (ca. September 13, 1925) in Moreira Lima, *op. cit.*, pp. 556, 566; Távora, III, *op. cit.*, pp. 47–48; Moreira Lima, *op. cit.*, p. 177; Klinger, *Narrativas,* IV, pp. 224–234.

39. João Alberto, *op. cit.*, pp. 112–113; Klinger, *Narrativas,* IV, pp. 234–235.

40. João Alberto, *op. cit.*, p. 113; Moreira Lima, *op. cit.*, pp. 177–178; Klinger, *Narrativas,* IV, pp. 234–245.

41. Klinger, *Narrativas,* IV, pp. 246–262; Comando das forças revolucionárias, Boletim no. 16, August 7, 1925, in Moreira Lima, *op. cit.*, pp. 556–557.

42. Klinger, *Narrativas,* IV, pp. 262–284.

43. *Ibid.*, pp. 286–301.

44. *Ibid.*, pp. 301–308, 339–390; Moreira Lima, *op. cit.*, p. 179.

45. Moreira Lima, *op. cit.*, p. 169. Moreira Lima says that the messenger was dispatched "two or three days after our leaving Rio Bonito" (Caiapônia), which the column evacuated on July 6. Moreira does not reproduce this letter, but he does publish most of an "open letter" to Isidoro, supporting him in his quarrel with João Francisco, dated July 11, 1925 (in *op. cit.*, pp. 563–565). It seems likely that the public and private letters went with the same messenger. There is no documentary evidence that the revolutionaries had decided to invade the Northeast before the Zeca Lopes encounter. The column was marching southeasterly when it abruptly turned north after the Zeca Lopes fight.

The northern half of Bahia is geographically part of the Northeast; the southern half is closer culturally and topographically to Minas Gerais and the Center-East of Brazil.

46. Moreira Lima, *op. cit.*, pp. 169–170. In the book's preface (p. 19), written in 1928, the author's brother mentions an "established plan . . . to carry the war to the Northeast, where adherences were expected, and, with the column reinforced with the contingents that would join it, march to the coast in quest of a victorious solution." Should the "established plan" fail, the column would seek to prolong the struggle in the backlands "with the objective of maintaining the armed protest against the tyranny."

47. Moreira Lima, *op. cit.*, p. 181; João Alberto, *op. cit.*, p. 115.

48. *Ibid.*, pp. 180, 182; Távora, III, *op. cit.*, pp. 50–51; Prestes, *et al.* to Isidoro, undated, in Moreira Lima, *op. cit.*, p. 566.

Chapter vi

1. Landucci, *op. cit.*, pp. 150, 157–158; Moreira Lima, *op. cit.*, pp. 161, 164–165, 187, 227, 448.

2. Hélio Silva, *1926*, p. 87; Landucci, *op. cit.*, p. 150; Moreira Lima, *op. cit.*, pp. 165, 187; João Alberto, *op. cit.*, p. 127.

3. João Alberto, *op. cit.*, p. 127; Moreira Lima, *op. cit.*, p. 150; Landucci, *op. cit.*, pp. 160–161.

4. Moreira Lima, *op. cit.*, pp. 151–152, 162; Landucci, *op. cit.*, p. 153.

5. Moreira Lima, *op. cit.*, pp. 152–153, 160–161, 185; Landucci, *op. cit.*, pp. 78–79.

6. Moreira Lima, *op. cit.*, pp. 164, 274, 331, 380; João Alberto, *op. cit.*, pp. 1–13, 132.

7. Landucci, *op. cit.*, p. 164.

8. João Alberto, *op. cit.*, pp. 127, 130; Távora, III, *op. cit.*, pp. 163–245; Landucci, *op. cit.*, p. 164. Juarez Távora apparently was strongly influenced by the writings of Alberto Torres, a nationalist intellectual of the early republican period. Távora, *uma vida*, p. 122.

9. Moreira Lima, *op. cit.*, p. 152.

10. João Alberto, *op. cit.*, pp. 75, 127.

11. Moreira Lima, *op. cit.*, pp. 318–319.

12. Dias Ferreira, *op. cit.*, pp. 262–263; Moreira Lima, *op. cit.*, p. 319.

13. Dias Ferreira, *op. cit.*, pp. 259–261; Moreira Lima, *op. cit.*, pp. 163–164, 417; João Alberto, *op. cit.*, p. 129.

14. Moreira Lima, *op. cit.*, pp. 160, 187–188; João Alberto, *op. cit.*, p. 114.

15. Moreira Lima, *op. cit.*, pp. 130–131; João Alberto, *op. cit.*, p. 92.

16. Carneiro, *Siqueira Campos*, I, pp. 40–43; Moreira Lima, *op. cit.*, pp. 130–131.

17. João Alberto, *op. cit.*, pp. 118–122, 171–173; Moreira Lima, *op. cit.*, pp. 131, 172, 261, 411; Landucci, *op. cit.*, pp. 168–170.

18. Moreira Lima, *op. cit.*, pp. 132, 237, 272–273; Landucci, *op. cit.*, pp. 169–170.

19. Gama, *op. cit.*, pp. 166–168.

20. Landucci, *op. cit.*, pp. 110, 120, 203–209; Dias Ferreira, *op. cit.*, pp. 249–252.

21. Moreira Lima, *op. cit.*, pp. 178–179; Landucci, *op. cit.*, pp. 135, 169–173; João Alberto, *op. cit.*, pp. 111–112.

22. Landucci, *op. cit.*, pp. 136–137; João Alberto, *op. cit.*, pp. 71–72, 128; Moreira Lima, *op. cit.*, p. 148.

23. Landucci, *op. cit.*, pp. 136–138; Moreira Lima, *op. cit.*, pp. 133, 433; Dias Ferreira, *op. cit.*, pp. 264–266; João Alberto, *op. cit.*, p. 55. Nogueira's Elixir was widely advertised as both a prophylactic and a cure for syphilis.

24. Interview with Durval Soares, Rio de Janeiro, December 13, 1965; Landucci, *op. cit.*, pp. 158–160.

25. Hélio Silva, *1926*, p. 87; Comando das forças revolucionárias, Boletim no. 16, August 7, 1925, in Moreira Lima, *op. cit.*, p. 87; interview with Durval Soares, Rio de Janeiro, December 13, 1965.

26. Dias Ferreira, *op. cit.*, pp. 255–256; João Alberto, *op. cit.*, p. 163; Landucci, *op. cit.*, p. 151; Moreira Lima, *op. cit.*, p. 194; Audrin, *op. cit.*, pp. 249–250.

27. Moreira Lima, *op. cit.*, p. 221; interview with Durval Soares, Rio de Janeiro, December 13, 1965; João Alberto, *op. cit.*, p. 125; Audrin, *op. cit.*, p. 250.

28. Moreira Lima, *op. cit.*, pp. 170–171, 317; Landucci, *op. cit.*, pp. 160–161.

29. Moreira Lima, *op. cit.*, pp. 171, 195–196.

30. Távora, III, *op. cit.*, pp. 261, 287; Klinger, *Narrativas*, IV, p. 63; interview with Durval Soares, Rio de Janeiro, December 13, 1965; Moreira Lima, *op. cit.*, pp. 268–269; Comando das forças revolucionárias, Boletim no. 16, August 7, 1925, in Moreira Lima, *op. cit.*, pp. 557–558; Dias Ferreira, *op. cit.*, p. 264; Rossini Maranhão, *Carolina, meu mundo perdido* (Rio de Janeiro, 1971), pp. 85–86.

31. Moreira Lima, *op. cit.*, p. 184; Dias Ferreira, *op. cit.*, pp. 222, 264–266, 279–284.

32. Távora, III, *op. cit.*, pp. 50–53; Prestes, *et al.*, to Isidoro (ca. September 13, 1925), in Moreira Lima, *op. cit.*, p. 566; Moreira Lima, *op. cit.*, pp. 179–183. In his memoirs (*op. cit.*), João Alberto has little to say about these events on the São Francisco River. The accounts of Moreira Lima and Távora vary considerably; the latter's is more credible.

33. Távora, III, *op. cit.*, pp. 52–54.

34. *Ibid.;* João Alberto, *op. cit.,* pp. 125–126; Prestes, *et al.,* to Isidoro, undated, in Moreira Lima, *op. cit.,* p. 566.

35. Moreira Lima, *op. cit.,* p. 184; Prestes to João Alberto, August 22, 1925, and Prestes, *et al.* to Isidoro, undated, in Moreira Lima, *op. cit.,* pp. 565–567; Távora, III, *op. cit.,* p. 55.

36. Távora, III, *op. cit.,* pp. 55–56; Moreira Lima, *op. cit.,* pp. 184–186.

37. Moreira Lima, *op. cit.,* pp. 188–189; Távora, III, *op. cit.,* p. 257.

38. Moreira Lima, *op. cit.,* pp. 186–187, 190; Távora, III, *op. cit.,* pp. 56–57.

39. Flores da Cunha, *op. cit.,* pp. 89–90, 115.

40. Miguel Costa, Prestes, and Távora to Batista Luzardo (ca. September 13, 1925) in Moreira Lima, *op. cit.,* pp. 190–193; photographs in Hélio Silva, *1926,* opposite p. 42, and Landucci, *op. cit.,* following p. 32. Dr. Ataíde's mission apparently included more than delivering a letter to Luzardo; it is possible that he was supposed to arrange for a shipment of arms. *Cf.* Moreira Lima, *op. cit.,* p. 177; Landucci, *op. cit.,* p. 135.

41. Miguel Costa, Prestes, and Távora to Batista Luzardo, undated, in Moreira Lima, *op. cit.,* pp. 192–193.

42. Amora, *op. cit.,* pp. 77–81; Falcão, *op. cit.,* p. 137; U.S. Vice-Consul in Pôrto Alegre (Farrand) to the Secretary of State, November 5, 1925, USDS, 832.00/542.

43. Moreira Lima, *op. cit.,* p. 193; Távora, III, *op. cit.,* pp. 57–58; João Alberto, *op. cit.,* pp. 126–127; Artiaga, *op. cit.,* p. 216.

44. Audrin, *op. cit.,* p. 244; Gelmires Reis, "Efemérides goianas," *Revista do Instituto Histórico e Geográfico de Goiaz,* I (1940), p. 40.

45. João de Minas (pseud. of Ariosto Palombo), *Jantando um defunto (a mais horripilante e verdadeira descrição dos crimes da revolução)* (Rio de Janeiro, 1928), pp. 58–59; Audrin, *op. cit.,* p. 244; Távora, III, *op. cit.,* pp. 267–268.

46. Audrin, *op. cit.,* pp. 244–245; Pang, *op. cit.,* pp. 166–168.

47. Audrin, *op. cit.,* p. 245; Artiaga, *op. cit.,* p. 271; Pang, *op. cit.,* pp. 168–169, 256; Moreira Lima, *op. cit.,* pp. 186–187.

48. Antonio César de Siqueira to Delegado de Polícia do Porto Nacional, October 6, 1925, and Miguel Costa, *et al.,* to Batista Luzardo, October 22, 1925, in Moreira Lima, *op. cit.,* pp. 568–570.

49. Miguel Costa, *et al.* to José M. Audrin, in Audrin, *op. cit.*, pp. 251–252; Távora, III, *op. cit.*, pp. 57–58; Moreira Lima, *op. cit.*, p. 197; Miguel Costa, *et al.*, to Luzardo, October 22, 1925, in Moreira Lima, *op. cit.*, p. 570; Dias Ferreira, *op. cit.*, p. 148.

50. Moreira Lima, *op. cit.*, p. 198.

51. *Ibid.*, p. 199; Audrin, *op. cit.*, pp. 252–253.

52. Moreira Lima, *op. cit.*, pp. 198–199; Dias Ferreira, *op. cit.*, pp. 149–150.

53. Audrin to Miguel Costa, October 21, 1925, in Moreira Lima, *op. cit.*, pp. 575–577.

54. Miguel Costa, *et al.*, to Audrin, October 22, 1925, in Moreira Lima, *op. cit.*, pp. 577–579.

55. Audrin, *op. cit.*, pp. 258–259.

56. *Ibid.*, pp. 260–261.

Chapter vii

1. Moreira Lima, *op. cit.*, pp. 199–201, 275; Dias Ferreira, *op. cit.*, pp. 150–151. Tocantínia was then called "Piabanha," the name of a large, exceptionally tasty fish, or "Ipiabanha"—"i" being Guarani for "water" or "water of."

2. Miguel Costa, Prestes, and Távora, *Circular aos homens de responsibilidade da cidade de Carolina,* October 22, 1925, in Moreira Lima, *op. cit.*, pp. 574–575; Moreira Lima, *op. cit.*, pp. 200, 202, 212–213; Távora, III, *op. cit.*, pp. 58–63; Dias Ferreira, *op. cit.*, p. 151.

3. Moreira Lima, *op. cit.*, p. 200. It is highly unlikely that the Indians were Xavantes or Javaés, as Moreira Lima and Dias Ferreira (*op. cit.*, p. 151) contend. These tribes, though related to the Xerentes, were located far away in the Araguaia valley at this time. José M. Audrin, *Os sertanejos que eu conheci* (Rio de Janeiro, 1963), pp. 181–186.

4. Moreira Lima, *op. cit.*, pp. 200–201; Dias Ferreira, *op. cit.*, pp. 151–152.

5. Moreira Lima, *op. cit.*, pp. 205–208, facsimile op. p. 226; Dias Ferreira, *op. cit.*, pp. 154–155; Diogenes Gonçalves, *et al.*, to Comando Geral das Forças Revolucionárias, November 8, 1925, in Moreira Lima, *op. cit.*, pp. 205–206. The musical proclivities of the people of Carolina have amazed other visitors. *Cf.* Francisco de Barros Júnior, *Caçando e*

pescando por todo o Brazil (São Paulo, n.d.), III, p. 169; Maranhão, *op. cit.,* pp. 33–37.

6. João Alberto, *op. cit.,* pp. 128–129; Felipe Moreira Lima, preface, in Moreira Lima, *op. cit.,* pp. 21–23.

7. Moreira Lima, *op. cit.,* pp. 199, 207.

8. *Ibid.,* p. 208; *Diário do Congresso Nacional,* May 26, 1926, p. 319. A total of "about 20,000 milreis" was collected from the businesses of Carolina, Balsas, and Colinas (Távora, III, *op. cit.,* pp. 287–288); since Carolina was the largest of the three, its levy was probably the greatest. *Cf.* Maranhão, *op. cit.,* pp. 75–86.

9. Moreira Lima, *op. cit.,* p. 212.

10. Juarez Távora to Dioclides Mourão and to Tarquínio Lopes Filho, November 21, 1925, in Moreira Lima, *op. cit.,* pp. 579–581; Dias Ferreira, *op. cit.,* p. 155; Távora, III, *op. cit.,* pp. 62–63.

11. Moreira Lima, *op. cit.,* p. 213; interview with Fernandes Távora, Fortaleza, November 16, 1965.

12. Landucci, *op. cit.,* p. 85; Moreira Lima, *op. cit.,* pp. 202–203; Távora, III, *op. cit.,* pp. 63–64. João Alberto (*op. cit.,* p. 102) says that there was "a wave of adherences in Goiás" and states (*op. cit.,* p. 128) that before the column reached Maranhão it included a total of "more than 200" volunteers from Goiás, Minas Gerais, and Mato Grosso. Moreira Lima (*op. cit.,* p. 181), writing twenty-five years closer to the events, says that "only in Maranhão and Piauí were there serious adherences to the column."

13. Moreira Lima, *op. cit.,* pp. 210–211.

14. Interview with Durval Soares, Rio de Janeiro, December 13, 1965; Távora, III, *op. cit.,* pp. 67–68; Moreira Lima, *op. cit.,* p. 218. Colinas was then known as Picos.

15. Juarez Távora to Batista Luzardo, undated, in Gama, *op. cit.,* pp. 111–114; 1° Tenente Jacob Manuel Gayoso e Almedra to Commandante do Destacamento do Piauhy, December 23, 1925, in Mathias Olympio de Mello, *A incursão dos rebeldes no Piauhy* (Teresina, 1926), pp. 16–21; Moreira Lima, *op. cit.,* pp. 215–216; Hygínio Cunha, *Os revolucionários do sul através dos sertões nordestinos do Brasil* (Teresina, 1926), pp. 22–24, 37–41; interview with "Lieutenant X," Teresina, November 18, 1965. This retired officer, who participated in the events at Uruçui and the defense of Teresina as a corporal in the federal twenty-fifth Light Infantry Battalion, consented to the interview on the condition that I

not reveal his name. However, he has supplied little information that cannot be found elsewhere; the value of his testimony lies in corroborating other sources, especially Hygínio Cunha's impressive book. For this account of the Benedito Leite/Uruçui episode, he contributed the estimate of Dutra's numerical strength, which could be inferred from various other sources.

16. Távora, III, *op. cit.*, pp. 69–76; Moreira Lima, *op. cit.*, pp. 215, 218–222.

17. Raimundo Lustosa Nogueira, *E assim veio o banditismo no estado do Piauhy* (Salvador, Bahia, 1942), pp. 7–29; Mathias Olympio, *op. cit.*, pp. 25–28; João Gomes Ribeiro Filho to Mathias Olympio, December 26, 1925, in Mathias Olympio, *op. cit.*, pp. 27–28; Gama, *op. cit.*, pp. 152–153; Távora, III, *op. cit.*, pp. 73–75; Moreira Lima, *op. cit.*, pp. 221, 275; *O Piauhy* (Teresina), January 12, 1926.

18. James, *op. cit.*, pp. 486–487.

19. Juarez Távora to Batista Luzardo, undated, in Gama, *op. cit.*, pp. 132–134; *Diário do Congresso Nacional*, May 25, 1926, p. 310; Távora, III, *op. cit.*, pp. 69–71; Moreira Lima, *op. cit.*, pp. 215–216, 219–220; Hygínio Cunha, *op. cit.*, pp. 40–41, 50; Gayoso to Commandante, December 23, 1925, in Mathias Olympio, *op. cit.*, p. 21.

20. Hygínio Cunha, *op. cit.*, p. 81; Moreira Lima, *op. cit.*, pp. 217–218; Gama, *op. cit.*, p. 79 (facsimile of *O Libertador*, December 26, 1925).

21. Távora, III, *op. cit.*, pp. 72–73; Hygínio Cunha, *op. cit.*, pp. 51–54.

22. Gayoso to Commandante, December 23, 1925, in Mathias Olympio, *op. cit.*, p. 21; *O Piauhy*, December 20, 1925; Hygínio Cunha, *op. cit.*, pp. 54–55; Távora, III, *op. cit.*, pp. 73–75; Moreira Lima, *op. cit.*, pp. 215, 219. One rebel was captured near Benedito Leite on December 7. The eyeglasses did not belong to Prestes, who did not own a pair, and, in any case, was in Floriano at the time of the fighting near Palmeiras. *Cf.* Gama, *op. cit.*, pp. 114–115.

23. Moreira Lima, *op. cit.*, pp. 219, 223, 275; Dias Ferreira, *op. cit.*, p. 166; Hygínio Cunha, *op. cit.*, p. 59; Távora, III, *op. cit.*, pp. 76–79. Timon was then known as Flores.

24. F. Pires de Castro, *Acção do governador—o cerco de Theresina—o plano do General João Gomes contra a rebellião—as causas determinantes de seu malogro—estado geral do espírito das tropas e dos seus chefes—remédios contra a rebellião—notas posteriores* (Teresina, 1926), pp. 3–18; João Gomes to

Mathias Olympio, December 26, 1925, in Mathias Olympio, *op. cit.*, pp. 27–28; *O Piauhy*, December 16, 1925; Hygínio Cunha, *op. cit.*, pp. 48–49, 81.

25. Távora, III, *op. cit.*, pp. 80–81; Távora to Prestes, December 30, 1925, in Moreira Lima, *op. cit.*, pp. 224–225; Hygínio Cunha, *op. cit.*, pp. 62, 77; João Alberto, *op. cit.*, p. 133; Landucci, *op. cit.*, pp. 107–110.

26. Moreira Lima, *op. cit.*, pp. 151, 220, 235; Dias Ferreira, *op. cit.*, p. 161; Gama, *op. cit.*, p. 108; interview with Fernandes Távora, Fortaleza, November 16, 1965. The mission of Waldemar Lima was a mystery to Miguel Costa, who did not remember him when he appeared in the Parnaíba valley on December 27. Miguel to Prestes, December 27, 1925, in Moreira Lima, *op. cit.*, pp. 581–582.

27. Távora to Prestes, December 30, 1925, in Moreira Lima, *op. cit.*, pp. 224–225; João Alberto, *op. cit.*, p. 133; Dias Ferreira, *op. cit.*, p. 163; Moreira Lima, *op. cit.*, pp. 179, 240.

28. Hygínio Cunha, *op. cit.*, p. 91; Távora, III, *op. cit.*, pp. 81–83; Távora, to Batista Luzardo, undated, in Gama, *op. cit.*, pp. 129–130.

29. *"Sou Juarez Távora e entrego-me prisioneiro."* Major Antônio da Costa Araújo Filho, Parte de combate, in Hygínio Cunha, *op. cit.*, pp. 84–89. Távora says his words upon surrendering were *"Não e preciso atirar; sou official do Exercito e me entrego"* (It is not necessary to shoot; I am an officer of the army and I surrender), Távora to Batista Luzardo, undated, in Gama, *op. cit.*, p. 130. See also Hygínio Cunha, *op. cit.*, pp. 83–84; Távora, *uma vida*, pp. 195–196.

30. Távora, III, *op. cit.*, pp. 83–85; Hygínio Cunha, *op. cit.*, p. 91; Costa Araújo, Parte de combate, in Hygínio Cunha, *op. cit.*, p. 86.

31. Hygínio Cunha, *op. cit.*, pp. 91–92.

32. Moreira Lima, *op. cit.*, pp. 225, 228, 230, 235.

33. Prestes to Távora, January 4, 1926, and Távora to Prestes, January 1, 1926, in Moreira Lima, *op. cit.*, pp. 229–230, 234–235.

34. Moreira Lima, *op. cit.*, pp. 232–233; Hygínio Cunha, *op. cit.*, pp. 94–95, 103–107; Pires de Castro, *op. cit.*, p. 17; João Alberto to Miguel Costa, January 26, 1926, in Moreira Lima, *op. cit.*, pp. 590–591.

35. Nogueira, *op. cit.*, pp. 33–34, 113–114; *O Sertão* (Lencóis, Bahia), September 7, 1925; Wilson Lins, *O médio São Francisco: uma sociedade de pastores e guerreiros*, 2 ed. (Salvador, Bahia, n.d.), pp. 94–95; Pires de Castro, *op. cit.*, pp. 11–13. The term "warlord" is borrowed from Eul Soo Pang, whose perceptive doctoral dissertation (*op. cit.*) defines the

relationships between the coronéis and the federal and state governments. Colonel Franklin's outfit was called the "Geraldo Rocha Battalion," in honor of Francisco Rocha's brother-in-law, a journalist and strong supporter of President Bernardes. This Patriotic Battalion was the successor of one with the same name that had fought against the rebels in Paraná. Franklin did not serve in the Paraná campaign, but took command of the revived battalion after the rebels reached the banks of the São Francisco. Wilson Lins, *op. cit.*, pp. 94–95; Castello Branco, *op. cit.*, p. 16; interview with Wilson Lins (Colonel Franklin's son), Salvador, Bahia, June 17, 1965.

36. Otacílio Anselmo, *Padre Cícero: Mito e realidade* (Rio de Janeiro, 1968), p. 528.

37. The literature on Padre Cícero is truly voluminous. Two of the best books are Anselmo, *op. cit.*, and Ralph della Cava, *Miracle at Joàseiro* (New York, 1970).

38. Anselmo, *op. cit.*, pp. 528–529; Waldemar Lima to Miguel Costa, January 24, 1926, in Moreira Lima, *op. cit.*, pp. 589–590.

39. Anselmo, *op. cit.*, pp. 529, 532–537; Leonardo Mota, *No tempo de Lampião*, 2 ed. (Fortaleza, 1967), pp. 30–35. Apparently, this document was handwritten and given to Lampião. The inspector's signature later appeared on a typewritten commission dated April 12, 1926. In those days, with Lampião around, the federal employee admitted that he would have signed a paper firing President Bernardes had Padre Cícero requested it. Optato Gueiros, *Lampeão: Memórias de um oficial ex-comandante de forças volantes*, 4 ed. (Salvador, Bahia, 1956), pp. 75–77.

Before Lampião was "commissioned," his men apparently traded shots on two occasions with members of the Prestes Column who intruded into the cangaceiros' camping grounds in Pernambuco (Moreira Lima, *op. cit.*, p. 271). Aside from these encounters in February 1926, Lampião's band probably had no contact with the rebels. *Cf.* Dias Ferreira, *op. cit.*, pp. 183–184.

40. *Diário do Congresso Nacional*, May 26, 1926, p. 321; Gama, *op. cit.*, pp. 218–220; Edmar Morel, *Padre Cícero: O Santo do Joàzeiro* (Rio de Janeiro, 1946), pp. 134–136.

41. Gama, *op. cit.*, pp. 68, 152–153; U.S. Consul in Bahia (Donovan) to the Secretary of State, January 21, 1926, USDS, 832.00/553.

42. Lourival Coutinho, *O General Góes depõe*, 3 ed. (Rio de Janeiro, 1956), pp. 17–27, 33–37; Hélio Silva, *1922*, p. 193.

Chapter viii

1. Hygínio Cunha, *op. cit.*, p. 126; Martins Napoleão, *O discurso Baptista Luzardo e os acontecimentos do Piauhy* (Teresina, 1926), pp. 41–42; Dutra to Prestes, January 14, 1926, in Moreira Lima, *op. cit.*, p. 607. *Cf.* Moreira Lima, *op. cit.*, pp. 237–238, 607–608.

2. Moreira Lima, *op. cit.*, pp. 238–240, 275; Comando da Primeira Divisão Revolucionária, Boletim no. 21, January 20, 1926, in Moreira Lima, *op. cit.*, pp. 586–587; Landucci, *op. cit.*, p. 163; Hygínio Cunha, *op. cit.*, p. 126. Monsenhor Hipólito was then known as Riachão.

3. Moreira Lima, *op. cit.*, pp. 203, 220.

4. U.S. Consul in Recife (Davis) to the Secretary of State, February 10 and February 20, 1926, USDS, 832.00/560–561; *A União* (João Pessoa), February 6, 1926.

5. Nathaniel P. Davis to the Secretary of State, March 24, 1926, 832.00/565 USDS; Gilberto Freyre, *Manifesto regionalista*, 4th ed. (Recife, 1967), pp. 30–36.

6. Manuel Bandeira, *A Brief History of Brazilian Literature* (New York, 1964), p. 147.

7. Josué de Castro, *Death in the Northeast* (New York, 1969), p. 125; Freyre, *op. cit.*, pp. 67, 73; Wilson Martins, *op. cit.*, pp. 110–116; Luiz Delgado, *Gestos e vozes de Pernambuco* (Recife, 1970), pp. 321–326.

8. Hélio Silva, *1926*, p. 82; Távora, III, *op. cit.*, pp. 92–93; Gama, *op. cit.*, p. 108; U.S. Consul in Recife (Davis) to the Secretary of State, February 20, 1926, USDS, 832.00/561.

9. Moreira Lima, *op. cit.*, p. 347; João Alberto to Miguel Costa, January 26, 1926, in Moreira Lima, *op. cit.*, p. 591; João Alberto, Requisição, January 7, 1925, in Hygínio Cunha, *op. cit.*, pp. 169–170. Siqueira Campos sometimes paid out money to prisoners who had been mistreated by his soldiers. Tabajara de Oliveira, *op. cit.*, p. 166. For jagunço views of João Alberto and Siqueira, see *O Sertão* (Lencois, Bahia), March 4, 11, 18, 1928, in Walfrido Moraes, *Jagunços e heróes* (Rio de Janeiro, 1963), pp. 182–183.

10. Euclydes da Cunha, *Os sertões (Campanha de Canudos)*, 16 ed. (Rio de Janeiro, 1942), pp. 114–117.

11. *Ibid.*, p. 117.

12. *Ibid.*, pp. 121–125.

13. João Alberto, *op. cit.*, p. 144; Moreira Lima, *op. cit.*, p. 182.

14. Emydio Miranda to Prestes, January 25, 1926, in Moreira Lima, *op. cit.*, p. 610; Moreira Lima, *op. cit.*, pp. 240–241, 275; João Alberto to Miguel Costa, January 26, 1926, in Moreira Lima, *op. cit.*, pp. 591–592; João Alberto, *op. cit.*, pp. 135–136; Waldemar Lima to Miguel Costa, January 24, 1926, in Moreira Lima, *op. cit.*, p. 590. For the Feitosas see Billy Jaynes Chandler, *The Feitosas and the Sertão dos Inhamuns* (Gainesville, Florida, 1972).

15. Moreira Lima, *op. cit.*, pp. 240–243, 247; Landucci, *op. cit.*, pp. 112–113.

16. Raimundo Nonato, *Os revoltosos em São Miguel (1926)* (Rio de Janeiro, 1966), pp. 42, 62–63, 66–79, 84–86, 125–127; Moreira Lima, *op. cit.*, pp. 247–250; Miguel Costa to Prestes, February 3, 1926, in Moreira Lima, *op. cit.*, pp. 610–611.

17. Nonato, *op. cit.*, pp. 79–80, 89–114, 127–131; Landucci, *op. cit.*, p. 113; Moreira Lima, *op. cit.*, p. 250; *Diário do Congresso Nacional*, May 28, 1926, pp. 343–344; Dias Ferreira, *op. cit.*, pp. 177–179.

18. João Alberto, *op. cit.*, p. 137; Moreira Lima, *op. cit.*, pp. 250–251, 260; Manoel Otaviano, *Os mártires de Piancó: Campanha Carlos Prestes* (João Pessoa, 1954), p. 130; *A União* (João Pessoa), February 6, 10, 1926. The conspirators in Paraíba city were caught with a "Manifesto," which apparently received little, if any, distribution. U.S. Consul in Recife (Davis) to the Secretary of State, February 10, 1926, USDS, 832.00/559.

19. Manoel Otaviano, *op. cit.*, pp. 29, 47–77.

20. *Ibid.*, pp. 78–97.

21. *Ibid.*, pp. 110–112, 115.

22. *Ibid.*, pp. 109–111; Dias Ferreira, *op. cit.*, p. 179; Moreira Lima, *op. cit.*, p. 255; *Cf. Diário do Congresso Nacional*, July 20, 1926, p. 1435.

23. Moreira Lima, *op. cit.*, pp. 255–258; Dias Ferreira, *op. cit.*, pp. 179–180; Manoel Otaviano, *op. cit.*, pp. 112, 115–116, 121. Landucci (*op. cit.*, p. 114), writing twenty years after an event he did not witness, says that white flags were flying over Piancó when Cordeiro's men entered the town.

24. Manoel Otaviano, *op. cit.*, pp. 117–123, 139–140; Moreira Lima, *op. cit.*, pp. 257–258; *Diário do Congresso Nacional*, July 20, 1926, p. 1435; Dias Ferreira, *op. cit.*, pp. 180–181. *Cf.* Landucci, *op. cit.*, pp. 114–115. Moreira Lima states that Padre Aristides and his men were overpowered by rebels inside the house, which lends credence to Manoel

Otaviano's claim that they had run out of ammunition; otherwise, it is hard to imagine the revolutionaries rushing the jagunço stronghold. However, Batista Luzardo (in the *Diário do Congresso Nacional*) claims that they did just that and captured much unspent ammunition in the house. João Alberto (*op. cit.,* p. 138), who was not in Piancó that day, says that Padre Aristides, in trying to surrender, shouted "A thousand votes for [my] life!" This is disbelieved by Manoel Otaviano (a priest and political opponent of Padre Aristides) and another Paraibano writer, although they cite no eyewitnesses to support their position. Celso Mariz in Manoel Otaviano, *op. cit.,* unpaginated preface.

25. Manoel Otaviano, *op. cit.,* pp. 121–122.

26. *Ibid.,* pp. 121–122, 128–129; Landucci, *op. cit.,* pp. 115–116; Moreira Lima, *op. cit.,* p. 258. On June 10, 1926 Batista Luzardo presented the official revolutionary account in the Brazilian Congress, claiming that the massacre at the claypit was set off when Padre Aristides infuriated Lieutenant José da Maia, who shot the priest twice in the head. There is no mention of throat cutting in this account. *Diário do Congresso Nacional,* July 20, 1926, pp. 1435–1436. This is contradicted by Durval Soares (interview, Rio de Janeiro, December 13, 1965) who says that Padre Aristides' throat was cut to save ammunition. There is no mention of Lieutenant José da Maia, supposedly a Paraibano volunteer who joined the column a few days prior to February 9, in the conscientious work of Padre Manoel Otaviano, Piancó's well-informed parish priest, which goes into exhaustive detail on the roles played by local and state personalities in the events at Piancó. Nor does Moreira Lima mention Maia. See Américo Chagas, *O chefe Horácio de Matos* (São Paulo, 1961), pp. 202, 206, for more on the rebel practice of pulling prisoners behind horses.

27. Landucci, *op. cit.,* p. 113; Moreira Lima, *op. cit.,* p. 259; *A União* (João Pessoa), February 16, 1926.

28. Tabajara de Oliveira, *op. cit.,* pp. 166–167.

29. Cícero Romão Batista to Luíz Carlos Prestes e seus companheiros de luta, February 20, 1926, in Morél, *op. cit.,* pp. 131–133; Moreira Lima, *op. cit.,* p. 244.

30. Moreira Lima, *op. cit.,* pp. 257–270; *Diário do Congresso Nacional,* July 20, 1926, p. 1436; Manoel Otaviano, *op. cit.,* pp. 126–127, 140.

31. Moreira Lima, *op. cit.,* pp. 260–270; Dias Ferreira, *op. cit.,* pp. 181–182; Landucci, *op. cit.,* pp. 117–119; João Alberto, *op. cit.,* p. 139;

Ary Salgado Freire to Miguel Costa, February 21, 1926, in Moreira Lima, *op. cit.*, p. 592.

32. João Alberto, *op. cit.*, pp. 139–140; Moreira Lima, *op. cit.*, p. 275.

33. Prestes to Miguel Costa, February 24, 1926, in Moreira Lima, *op. cit.*, pp. 593–594.

34. Landucci, *op. cit.*, pp. 119–120, 151; Moreira Lima, *op. cit.*, pp. 270–275; Prestes to Miguel Costa, February 25, 1926, in Moreira Lima, *op. cit.*, p. 613; Dias Ferreira, *op. cit.*, pp. 184–186.

35. Moreira Lima, *op. cit.*, pp. 276–282; Dias Ferreira, *op. cit.*, pp. 186–187; Landucci, *op. cit.*, pp. 125–127; João Alberto, *op. cit.*, pp. 142–144, 148.

36. João Alberto, *op. cit.*, p. 147; Moreira Lima, *op. cit.*, pp. 279–280; Dias Ferreira, *op. cit.*, pp. 187–188; Gama, *op. cit.*, p. 142.

37. Moreira Lima, *op. cit.*, pp. 282–287; Gama, *op. cit.*, p. 151; Agenor Duarte to Seraphim Joaquim da Silva, March 12, 1926, in Moreira Lima, *op. cit.*, p. 628; Landucci, *op. cit.*, pp. 123–124, 128; Dias Ferreira, *op. cit.*, p. 188. Moreira Lima records only one combat for the period March 13–26: an encounter between a wayward rebel patrol and federal and state troops (from Rio Grande do Sul and São Paulo), presumably along the railroad, sometime before March 19.

38. Interview with Arquimedes de Matos, Itacira, Bahia, June 14, 1965; Walfrido Moraes, *Jagunços e heróis: a civilização do diamante nas lavras da Bahia* (Rio de Janeiro, 1963), pp. 12–22; Theodoro Sampaio, *O Rio de S. Francisco e a Chapada Diamantina*, 2 ed. (São Paulo, 1905), pp. 139–145.

39. Moraes, *op. cit.*, pp. 38–48; Olympio Barbosa, *Horácio de Mattos: Sua vida e suas lutas* (Salvador, Bahia, 1956), pp. 3–9; Américo Chagas, *O cangaceiro Montalvão* (São Paulo, 1962), pp. 83–87.

40. Chagas, *Horácio*, pp. 21–36; Moraes, *op. cit.*, pp. 48–55.

41. Pang, *op. cit.*, pp. 164–214; Barbosa, *op. cit.*, pp. 15–65; Moraes, *op. cit.*, pp. 55–103; Chagas, *Horácio*, pp. 37–106.

42. Chagas, *Horácio*, pp. 167, 173; interview with Arquimedes de Matos, Itacira, Bahia, June 14, 1965; marginal notes by Arquimedes de Matos in a copy of Barbosa's *Horácio de Mattos;* Moraes, *op. cit.*, pp. 146–147, 164, 166.

43. Moraes, *op. cit.*, pp. 147–163; Chagas, *Horácio, pp.* 157–176; Horácio de Queiróz Mattos, *Manifesto* (Lençóis, Bahia, 1930), pp. 12–14.

44. *O Sertão* (Lençóis, Bahia), April 26, 1925, April 25, 1926; Barbosa, *op. cit.,* pp. 67–72; Moraes, *op. cit.,* pp. 163–165; Chagas, *op. cit.,* pp. 157, 176–179.

45. Moraes, *op. cit.,* pp. 121–129. Moraes presents impressive evidence from local archives to prove his points. His assessment of Horácio's objectives, not surprisingly, agrees with that of Arquimedes de Matos (interview, Itacira, Bahia, June 14, 1965).

46. Mattos, *Manifesto,* p. 14; Franklin de Queiroz to Horácio de Matos, March 24, 1926, and Batalhão Patriótico Lavras Diamantinas, Boletim no. 1, March 14, 1926, in Horácio de Matos archives, formerly in Itacira, Bahia, hereafter cited as HMA.

47. Possibly, the total number of Horacistas in this fight was only three; Manuel Querino and the two jagunços who were killed. Chagas, *Horácio,* p. 198. Moreira Lima, *op. cit.,* pp. 286–287.

48. Moreira Lima, *op. cit.,* pp. 288–294; Mattos, *Manifesto,* p. 14; João Alberto, *op. cit.,* pp. 149–150. Horácio's two relatives were probably shot after being captured with the incriminating correspondence. *O Sertão,* April 11, 1926. Moraes, *(op. cit.,* p. 170) says that their bodies were found nude with their skulls smashed. Chagas (*Horácio,* p. 201) says that they were taken to Alagadiço and shot in the public plaza.

49. Landucci, *op. cit.,* p. 129; Moreira Lima, *op. cit.,* pp. 294–306; João Alberto, *op. cit.,* pp. 150–152; Dias Ferreira, *op. cit.,* pp. 189–191.

50. João Alberto, *op. cit.,* pp. 154, 158.

Chapter ix

1. Anísio Spinola Teixeira, "O alto sertão da Bahia," *Revista do Instituto Geográfico e Histórico da Bahia,* no. 52 (1926), pp. 294–296, 303; Moreira Lima, *op. cit.,* pp. 306–310; Plano do Coronel Horácio, May 29, 1926, HMA.

2. Chagas, *Horácio,* pp. 206–208; Moreira Lima, *op. cit.,* pp. 310–318; Landucci, *op. cit.,* pp. 130–131; *O Sertão,* July 4, 1926; Plano do Coronel Horácio, May 29, 1926, and Batalhão Lavras Diamantinas, Alterações ocoridas com o 3° Sargento Dioclydes Franklin de Queiroz, December 15, 1926, HMA.

3. Moreira Lima, *op. cit.,* pp. 221, 330–345; Moraes, *op. cit.,* pp. 173, 184; Chagas, *Horácio,* pp. 208–210; *O Sertão,* July 4, 1926; Batalhão Lavras Diamantinas, Alterações, December 15, 1926, HMA.

4. Moreira Lima, *op. cit.*, pp. 349–355; Landucci, *op. cit.*, pp. 131–132, 137–141; João Alberto, *op. cit.*, pp. 155–158; Dias Ferreira, *op. cit.*, pp. 195–196; Wilson Lins, *op. cit.*, p. 95; *O Sertão*, May 30, 1926.

5. Moreira Lima, *op. cit.*, pp. 356–369, 371; Gama, *op. cit.*, pp. 162–172; Landucci, *op. cit.*, pp. 129, 133; Dias Ferreira, *op. cit.*, pp. 196–200. Moreira Lima, (*op. cit.*, p. 275) notes that the column invaded Bahia with "close to 1200 men," that fewer than 50 volunteers joined the column in Bahia (p. 346), and that the rebels "were reduced to 900 combatants, at the most" when they left the state (p. 371). Landucci (*op. cit.*, p. 129) says that they lost "close to 300 precious lives" in Bahia.

6. Moreira Lima, *op. cit.*, pp. 140–141, 356–393; Dias Ferreira, *op. cit.*, pp. 201–204; Hygínio Cunha, *op. cit.*, pp. 143–152; Horácio de Matos to Francisco Rocha, August 19, 1926, Horácio de Matos to Luiz Tavares Guerreiro, August 19 and 20, 1926, Batalhão Lavras Diamantinas, Alteracões, December 15, 1926, Scarcella Portela to Saturnino de Aguiar, July 11, 1926, HMA.

7. Franklin de Queiroz to Horácio de Matos, September 16, 1926, Antonio Moreira dos Santos to Horácio de Matos, October 2, 1926, Pedro Pinheiro to Horácio de Matos, September 30, 1926, Receipt for requisição de 3 burras pertenecente ao Senr Nicolau Tolentino, December 3, 1926, HMA; Audrin, *Entre sertanejos*, p. 260; Coutinho, *op. cit.*, p. 38; interview with Wilson Lins, Salvador, Bahia, June 17, 1965. In Bahia, Horácio had tried to restore horses cast off by the rebels to their rightful owners (Plano do Coronel Horácio, May 29, 1926, HMA); on the other hand, Horácio's troops in Goiás certainly took some property—cattle caught and butchered on the open range, for example—without giving receipts. Franklin de Queiroz, Ligação, September 8, 1926, HMA.

8. Moreira Lima, *op. cit.*, pp. 409–410; Dias Ferreira, *op. cit.*, pp. 205–207; Landucci, *op. cit.*, pp. 143–145; João Alberto, *op. cit.*, pp. 160–161; Oswaldo Cordeiro de Farias, "Siqueira Campos," in Chevalier, *op. cit.*, pp. 68–69.

9. Tabajara de Oliveira, *op. cit.*, pp. 162–163.

10. Moreira Lima, *op. cit.*, p. 182; Landucci, *op. cit.*, pp. 171–172.

11. Moraes, *op. cit.*, pp. 179–180; Coutinho, *op. cit.*, pp. 38–41; Franklin de Queiroz to Horácio de Matos, September 8, 13, and 19, 1926, HMA.

12. João de Minas, *op. cit.*, pp. 28–53. This book is patently dishonest, but some fairly accurate descriptions and a few basic facts may be

picked out of its mass of falsification. See also Moreira, Lima, *op. cit.,* pp. 412–427.

13. Moreira Lima, *op. cit.,* pp. 427–444, 449; Antonio Moraes de C. to Severino da Silveira Moraes, October 19, 1926, in Moreira Lima, *op. cit.,* p. 631; João Alberto, *op. cit.,* pp. 163–164.

14. João Alberto, *op. cit.,* pp. 165–168; Claude Lévi-Strauss, *Tristes Tropiques* (New York, 1971), pp. 192–196; Corrêa Filho, *Pedro Celestino,* pp. 219–221.

15. João Alberto, *op. cit.,* pp. 167–169.

16. Moreira Lima, *op. cit.,* pp. 449–450; João Alberto, *op. cit.,* p. 177.

17. Moreira Lima, *op. cit.,* pp. 444–445, 447–452; Siqueira Campos to Prestes, April 30, 1927, in Moreira Lima, *op. cit.,* pp. 459–460, 463.

18. Moreira Lima, *op. cit.,* pp. 466–477; Tabajara de Oliveira, *op. cit.,* pp. 69–86.

19. Siqueira to Prestes, April 30, 1927, in Moreira Lima, *op. cit.,* pp. 459–465; Moreira Lima, *op. cit.,* pp. 478–491; Coutinho, *op. cit.,* pp. 41–42; Dias Ferreira, *op. cit.,* pp. 216–229; Landucci, *op. cit.,* pp. 175–179; João Alberto, *op. cit.,* pp. 170, 173–174; Arquimedes de Matos to Horácio de Matos, November 28, 1926, Franklin de Queiroz, Instrucções, undated, Batalhão Lavras Diamantinas, Boletim no. 281, December 20, 1926, 1° Tenente Manoel Campos de Menezes, Parte de combate, December 31, 1926, Batalhão Lavras Diamantinas, Boletim no. 293, January 1, 1927, HMA.

20. Dias Ferreira, *op. cit.,* pp. 227–233; Landucci, *op. cit.,* pp. 177–179, 183–185, 210; João Alberto, *op. cit.,* pp. 174–189; Moreira Lima, *op. cit.,* pp. 474, 488–497; Coutinho, *op. cit.,* pp. 42–43; interview with Arquimedes de Matos, Itacira, Bahia, June 14, 1965.

21. Moreira Lima, *op. cit.,* pp. 497–499; Heliodoro Carmona Rodó, Miguel Costa, Luís Carlos Prestes, Atã, February 4, 1927, in Moreira Lima, *op. cit.,* pp. 498–504; Antônio de Siqueira Campos, Entrega de armamento, March 24, 1927, in Carneiro, *Siqueira,* II, p. 399; Oswaldo Cordeiro de Farias, "Siqueira Campos," in Chevalier, *op. cit.,* p. 67; Coutinho, *op. cit.,* pp. 42–43; interview with Wilson Lins, Salvador, Bahia, June 17, 1965. The rebels were allowed to keep their sidearms and Winchester rifles for hunting and protection.

Index